The Democratic Arts of Mourning

The Democratic Arts of Mourning

Political Theory and Loss

Edited by
Alexander Keller Hirsch and
David W. McIvor

LEXINGTON BOOKS
Lanham • Boulder • New York • London

Published by Lexington Books
An imprint of The Rowman & Littlefield Publishing Group, Inc.
4501 Forbes Boulevard, Suite 200, Lanham, Maryland 20706
www.rowman.com

6 Tinworth Street, London SE11 5AL

British Library Cataloguing in Publication Information Available

Library of Congress Cataloging-in-Publication Data

Names: Hirsch, Alexander Keller, editor. | McIvor, David Wallace, editor.
Title: The democratic arts of mourning : political theory and loss / edited by Alexander Keller Hirsch
and David W. McIvor.
Description: Lanham, Maryland : Lexington Books, 2019. | Includes bibliographical references and
index.
Identifiers: LCCN 2018050094 (print) | LCCN 2018061508 (ebook) | ISBN 9781498567251 (Elec-
tronic) | ISBN 9781498567244 (cloth) | ISBN 9781498567268 (pbk) Subjects: LCSH:
Collective memory--Political aspects--United States. | Memorialization--Political
aspects--United States. | Bereavement--Political aspects--United States.
Classification: LCC HM1027.U6 (ebook) | LCC HM1027.U6 D44 2019 (print) | DDC 909/.0973--
dc23
LC record available at https://lccn.loc.gov/2018050094

To J. Peter Euben, who, for a generation of students and colleagues, brought the connection between arguments and stories to life; and who, in the process, pushed us all out of complacency and comfort and toward a lively and cheerful practice in deep awareness of life's fragility.

Contents

Introduction

The Democratic Arts of Mourning

David W. McIvor and Alexander Keller Hirsch

The Democratic Arts of Mourning

"While philosophy may begin in wonder that things are the way they are . . . political theory begins with loss. Loss animates it as an enterprise and forms its problematic" (Euben, 2003, 87). If, as J. Peter Euben has argued, the practice of political theory is animated by loss, then the very enterprise can be understood in terms of a work of mourning—even as an artifact of grief. Yet mourning is an ambivalent phenomenon. As much as it reveals or reflects a loss, mourning also presumes attachment. In mourning, the world appears impoverished—"cold and empty" in the famous phrasing of Freud (1917, 247)—and yet this implies the warmth of a world that was once enchanted with meaning. Mourning links subjects to their past, but it can also sustain an impression of who they aspire to become in the future. Janus-faced, mourning therefore looks backward and forward, simultaneously. It seeks a new future in which a condition of possibility for renewal can be found, but mourning also testifies to the thrownness that occasions what was damaging in the past or what troubles us in the present.

This ambivalence can also be seen in another aspect of mourning's dual character: it is, at once, personal *and* social—private *and* political. Although mourning is often envisioned as a solitary form of reckoning, political life is inevitably intertwined with experiences of attachment, loss, and grief. The most deeply personal losses are also embedded within the social worlds from which they are made. Even Job, whose story of suffering includes a deeply personal account of mourning, finds his plaint is ultimately the token of a longing to restore a sacred and symbolic order where subjects of pain truly deserve the suffering they undergo. Over the course of his story, Job regrets the loss of his family, articles of possession, and even his own bodily integrity, but his mourning reaches its fullest expression only when he articulates a desire to reinstate a regime of meaning where sign, rule, and norm govern the borders, positions, and boundaries that make life bearable (Hirsch 2016). Job yearns, in other words, for a world where structure, predictability, and law are returned after his own horizon of meaning has collapsed (Alford 2009). Thus, his mourning, ostensibly personal, in fact reveals an aspiration for a more just world.

The story of Job, then, shows the simultaneity of the personal and the social nature of loss and, hence, of mourning. From this, we can see how the subject of mourning entails not merely the idiosyncratic pathways of personal grief but also questions of collective attachments, symbols, and memories. Mourning entails rituals and narratives that are inherently civic and public and that reflect political choices and struggles over contested ideals and visions for collective life (Stout, 2010). A bank might close, for instance, in order to honor the legacy of Martin Luther King, Jr.; or it may close to dignify the memory of Robert E. Lee. This example also demonstrates how many detachments—and many forms of mourning—are linked with systemic injustices that vary historically yet often track along asymmetrical relations of power and privilege. Not all losses are made visible, let alone honored. As such, loss, grief, and mourning—and the exposure to vulnerability to which they attest—are distinctively political phenomena.

This volume reflects upon mourning's ambivalence and brings its political nature into clearer focus, by examining the multiform ways in which mourning shows up in both contemporary politics and within contemporary political theory. Political theorists, in the first decades of the twenty-first century, have turned repeatedly toward themes of loss, grief, and mourning, reflecting a similar cultural turn toward these concerns (as Rebecca Comay puts it, we inhabit a "trauma-besotted, memory-obsessed 'wound culture'" [2011, 129]). Political theorists have articulated the themes of loss and mourning with and against political theory's traditional concerns such as authority, power, freedom, agency, and justice (Butler, 1997, 2005, 2009; Honig, 2001 and 2013; Allen, 2004; Balbus, 2005; Barker, 2008; Hirsch 2015; Luxon, 2015; McIvor, 2016; Stow, 2017). Concurrently, mourning has become a significant theme in other academic disciplines including English, cultural studies, continental philosophy, sociology, and history (Eng and Kazanjian, 2002; Moglen, 2005; Derrida, 1994, 2003; Rose, 1996; Gilroy, 2005; Crimp, 1989; LaCapra, 2001). With this volume, we take stock of how political theorists have interpreted mourning as a political thematic, and offer further reflections on how the discipline might guide understanding of the politics of loss, grief, and mourning.

In this introduction, we first situate recent scholarship on mourning by tracing its debts to previous work on the politics of tragedy. We then describe some of the defining frameworks, claims, and distinctions made by contemporary theorists of mourning, before defending the particular framework—the democratic arts of mourning—offered here. The individual chapters that follow extend and deepen these conversations, demonstrating how mourning inflects contemporary political struggles, and how political theory's vocational commitments place it in both intimate proximity and critical distance to these struggles.

Political Theory's Tragic Attunement

Political theory's recent turn to mourning has been both preceded and accompanied by influential scholarship on the politics of tragedy that explores both the institution of Athenian tragic drama, as well as notions of "the tragic" or a "tragic sensibility." The civic rituals and surviving works of Greek tragedy in particular have served as repeated provocations for political theorizing (Euben, 1990; Alford, 1992; Saxonhouse, 1995; Monoson, 2000; Markell, 2003; Ober, 2005; Connolly, 2005; 2008; 2013; Ahrensdorf; 2009; Honig, 2013; Schlosser, 2014; Johnston, 2015; McIvor, 2016; Stow 2017). Although tragedy is sometimes typified as a genre of performance that insists on catastrophic conclusions, or as an art form that maligns hubris and expresses a fatalist vision of the human condition, Athenian tragedy is, as many have pointed out, irreducible to these interpretations. The tragedies of Aeschylus, Sophocles, and Euripides offered a searching reflection on the vicissitudes of public pain and the politics of mourning. Featuring characters embroiled in ethical and political conflict and exposed to conditions and forces beyond their control, tragedy articulated a complex view of human action and responsibility. As A. C. Bradley once wrote, "That men start a course of events but can neither calculate nor control it, is a *tragic* fact" (Bradley, 1991, 15). Often, such tragic stories presented characters whose acknowledgment (*anagnorisis*) of these constitutive features of human and political life arrived too late.

Abundant evidence indicates that the tragedies were not performed solely for the sake of entertainment. Martha Nussbaum, for instance, has argued that classical tragic drama contained a civic and political function insofar as it was built upon the "acceptance of the ethical significance of uncontrolled reversals" (1992, 111). Tragedy foregrounded what Nussbaum terms the fragility of goodness by providing both reminders of human vulnerability and of the ultimate fallibility of moral and political modes of responding to ethical and political dilemmas (1986). For Nussbaum and others, Greek tragedy's educative effects can still reach contemporary audiences. By understanding the chosen and unchosen circumstances of our actions, she argues, we can better approach our own civic and ethical responsibilities. Tragedy—as both lived and textual experience—serves as a reminder that the work of justice requires acknowledging the active tension between values rather than neutralizing those tensions or pursuing their ultimate reconciliation. Likewise, Bernard Williams has argued that the spirit of tragedy informs moral philosophy in revealing the "inadequacies of one's own perceptions" by divulging a complex, multifaceted world operating well beyond one's view (1993, xvii). Further, Williams argued that the Greek tragedians demonstrated a world in which the things that matter most are not under the control of reason, but are instead the product of luck and circumstance (1981). Tragedy, in this respect, facilitates the development of moral wisdom along with the ethical virtues of temperance and prudence. The Athenian institution of tragedy did not promise reconciliation or easy choices, and it thereby chastened any political or moral project that offered the allure of safety or repose.

Greek tragedy was also a democratic institution. Many classical scholars have emphasized the symbiotic relationship between tragedy and Athenian democracy (Arrowsmith, 1963; Zeitlen, 1996; Monoson, 2000; Goldhill, 2004; Ober, 2015). For Sara Monoson, the act of witnessing tragic performances was a "vigorous civic practice" that was "closely identified with the exercise of democratic citizenship" (2000, 88). The civic import of tragedy, according to Simon Goldhill, was linked with its ability to interrogate Athenian civic and political values from *within* an institution exemplifying those values (1987). For J. Peter Euben, the festival at which the tragedies were performed—the Great Dionysia—was a civic and political institution as important to Athenian democracy as the citizen assembly or the courts. According to Euben, the tragic festival contained a "democratic pedagogy" insofar as it contributed to democratic norms of self-critique and self-scrutiny while also dramatizing cultural exclusions and social inequalities (1986, 2–3; see also Euben, 1990).

For Euben, political theory has a similar responsibility to its audience as the Greek tragedians had toward the democracy at Athens. Political theory fulfills this responsibility by "enriching the theoretical imagination" in ways that cultivate greater sensitivity toward the tragic aspects of human life and the conflicted and contested dynamics of politics. Political theory, therefore, is an enterprise with a tragic core; or, in the words of Judith Shklar, "political philosophy is tragic thought" (1975, 4). For these authors, tragedy, democracy, and political theory are entangled and densely interwoven in an active nexus.

Tragedy is often also tied to the experience of mourning (Loraux, 1998, 2002; Taxidou, 2004). Although many scholars of Greek tragedy, such as Nicole Loraux, have reflected on the ways in which it embodied a public reflection on mourning, Bonnie Honig has shown how different modes of mourning—and the contestation over them—is reflected in Attic drama. For Honig, aristocratic forms of "Homeric mourning" feature dirges that commemorate the "unique individuality of the dead, the loss to the surviving family caused by death, and the call for vengeance," (2013, 100). In particular, Homeric mourning demonstrates "extravagancy, out of control behavior, including loud wailing, tearing the hair, and lacerating one's face," (ibid., 113–101). Honig contrasts Homeric mourning, which she identifies with the elite celebration of the irreducible individual hero, with the mourning practices of Creon in Sophocles's *Antigone*, which emphasizes the substitutability of the dead. Whereas Antigone appears to speak for an aristocratic mourning culture in decline, Creon represents the democratic polis of Athens in its attempt to uphold norms of equality (within heavily proscribed limits). Tragedy embodies—for Nussbaum and Williams—enduring lessons for moral and political life; but it also reflects, *pace* Honig, ongoing social contestations within the democratic polis.

In a different key, Steven Johnston has argued that tragic genres more generally reflect an awareness of what is "tragic" about inhabiting a world that is "difficult, forbidden, uncertain, volatile, resistant, dangerous, and lethal" (2015, 12). On Johnston's reading, tragedy shows how the uncertainty and danger that accompany political communities and social action are enduring—not disposable—features. In response, Johnston counsels the cultivation of a "tragic sensibility," which is attentive to "grievance, maltreatment, suffering, and damage" without attempting to moralize or otherwise provide ultimate meaning for this suffering (ibid., 9). Rather than moralizing tragic aspects of human life, a tragic sensibility represents "cheerful yet defiant resignation" that might attenuate "the will to blame, assign responsibility, and punish" (ibid., 40). For Johnston, as for Nietzsche before him, a tragic sensibility might provide friction against a politics of *ressentiment* and guilt—the difference being that Johnston, along with Euben and Nussbaum, offers this tragic orientation in defense of democratic forms of life (Nietzsche, 1993).

Others, such as Paul Gilroy, have argued against the notion that a tragic sensibility is tantamount to resignation, by indicating that tragedy is first and foremost about locating creative ways to survive and live with the intractable quality of conflict endemic to political experience. The goal is less to find ways of becoming free from the troubling questions such conflicts evoke; rather, as Gilroy defines tragedy, the objective is "suffering made useful but not redemptive" (2010, 150). Similarly, Joshua Dienstag has argued that tragedy is inherently anti-utopian, yet for this very reason it provides a basis for projects of "self-renovation and self-fortification" in light of the difficult aspects of existence (2009, 224). Tragedy, therefore, is as much an "ethic of radical possibility" that is linked with the experience of "radical insecurity" (ibid., 201).

Whether faced with an attitude of resignation or reinvention, the "tragic" stands in for the inscrutable and recalcitrant aspects of life. George Steiner has argued that tragedy testifies to what he terms the "otherness" of the world, an otherness that is both "outside and within" human life (1962, 7). Correspondingly, the "tragic imagination," in the words of Rowan Williams, speaks to "what is utterly unresolved in human experience" (2016, 20). The subject matter of tragedy—both in its ancient and modern instantiations—is "human shipwreck of some kind," and the tragic audience, unsettled and disturbed, is thereby confronted by ethical and political imperatives without reliable aids or guidelines (ibid., 5). The "stark fictions" of the Greek tragedies—in the words of Bernard Williams—reveal "the horrors" inherent to human life (2006, 58). Such stark reminders provide a check against moralistic attempts to "make the world safe for well-disposed people" (ibid., 59). Tragedy may not defeat morality or concepts of political agency, but it erects insuperable obstacles to consolation and to the easy realization of our moral or political aspirations. We can learn from tragedy and possibly prepare for it—as Machiavelli counseled in *The Prince*—but we cannot overcome tragedy or still its power.

From Tragedy to Mourning

Recent work in political theory has taken seriously the idea that the discipline bears a relationship to tragic thought, yet has sought to push beyond or to use tragedy as a means of thinking how social actors might acknowledge, face down, or work through—in short, *mourn*—the difficult, terrible, or inscrutable features of their condition. If tragedy recognizes fragility, pain, and suffering, along with the lamentable inadequacy of our moral and political modes of response, then mourning can be envisioned—at least in part—as a means of working with, narrating, and transmuting experiences of tragedy or the tragic. The relationship between tragedy and mourning, as discussed above, is intimate. Rowan Williams, for instance, has argued that tragic drama is "a vehicle for collective mourning" (2016, 148). Similarly, Stanley Cavell has argued that tragedies like Shakespeare's *Hamlet* are about the "learning of mourning," or a coming to understand how to "take one's place in the world" (1987, 186). Yet recent work in political theory has moved beyond the framing of mourning *within* tragedy to examine mourning as a concept in its own right (Honig, 2001; Butler, 2004, 2009; McIvor, 2016; Stow 2010, 2017).

However, there are some objections to this turn to mourning that should be acknowledged at the outset. For some, mourning may have little to do with politics, since the former is taken to be a personal or private process whereas the latter inherently involves public decisions, institutions, and practices. Famously, the labor activist Joe Hill—facing execution after being charged (falsely) with murder—implored a friend with the phrase "don't mourn, organize!" implying a contrast if not a contradiction between mourning and politics (Rosemont, 2003, 180). For others, mourning draws our attention to responsibilities that are *social* but perhaps not *political*. Loss, grief, and mourning may be social phenomena, but it is unclear how they relate to conversations about justice, since the latter—it has been argued—requires the neutral application of fair procedures rather than the selective recognition of particular losses (Rawls, 1971).

However, from a different perspective mourning is inherent to the activity of politics and to the enterprise of political theory. According to Sheldon Wolin, for instance, the very concept of the political is haunted by loss. For Wolin, political moments are by their nature evanescent, "episodic" and "rare" (1997, 1). Whereas politics is ceaseless, the political is an occasional and hence precarious experience. As Wolin understood it, political theory's role is in part to be a chronicler of these political moments and, hence, to act as a caretaker for the "birthright" of "politicalness" (1989, 139). Political theory must, then, occasionally operate through a register of "invocation," which sensitizes its audience to the fragility of the political while simultaneously providing an opportunity for affective re-investment in these evanescent moments or the disavowed inheritance of the political (Wolin, 2000).

Democracy, Wolin argued, is also intertwined with loss. Famously, Wolin argued that democracy should be conceptualized as a "fugitive" moment—a temporary experience of solidarity or commonality that is quickly defeated by reassertions of pluralism. Even when democratic experiences lead to fundamental political and institutional transformations, democracy is often subsequently truncated or attenuated. Democratic revolutions eat their young—or at the least they deny to their progeny the same experience of the political, which becomes constrained by institutional forms or co-opted and controlled by elites. Democracy, for Wolin, thereby needs to be reconceptualized as a "mode of being conditioned by bitter experience" (1997, 23). It is from out of this bitter experience that citizens might be better able to craft rejoinders to antidemocratic tendencies and forces.

Anne Norton goes further, indicating that democracy inheres in the daily practice of existential self-shattering: "Democracy requires that we encompass the possibility (even the enactment) of our own annihilation. Democracy requires that at some moments, and in some respects always, one will cease to be" (Shapiro et al., 2004, 80). By this, Norton means that participating in democracy not only requires that we act in concert to shape power, but also at times an undoing of the self—seen as the very locus of sovereign agency. Democracy for Norton involves surrender to the flux of self-abeyance, to "the prospect of one's own annihilation, of aphasia, of nonbeing," and the practice of democracy can thereby be seen as the ultimate "practice of loss" (Connolly and Botwinick, 2001, 166).

Similarly, for Danielle Allen the politics of loss and the corresponding need for a politics of mourning are endemic to democracy (2004). Because

the burdens of collective decision-making will always be unevenly distributed, the matter of how those burdens or losses are to be acknowledged and
honored is an omnipresent political question. As Allen describes, there are
multiform ways that democratic societies can fall short of the civic obligation
of mourning, such as through the identification of scapegoats who will repeatedly bear the burdens of loss. Race, gender, and class have served as
convenient sources of scapegoating in the American political tradition, fore-
stalling the work of mourning that might bring the political economy of loss
into clearer focus. Yet Allen's work is oriented toward frameworks—such as
the "politics of friendship"—and particular practices by which democratic
communities might acknowledge and repair the damages associated with
sacrifice, disrespect, and disregard. From the perspectives of Wolin, Norton,
and Allen, then, politics is conditioned by loss and mourning, and political
theorists carry a responsibility to recognize and clarify this condition.

The most influential voice within recent social and political theorizing on
the subject of mourning in recent years, however, is undoubtedly that of
Judith Butler (1997, 2004, 2009). Butler has conceptualized mourning in
slightly different ways throughout her career (McIvor, 2012). In one mode,
Butler has viewed mourning as a work of political and social subversion or
disruption. In her reading of *Antigone*, for instance, Butler interprets the
infamous protagonist's laments as inherently subversive. They speak to, on
Butler's reading, the inherent limits of the law, of representation, and of the
subject itself. Laws, like subjects, are dependent on "repetition" or perpetual
"reiteration or rearticulation" (1997, 99). Antigone's mourning draws attention to this performative dependency, which troubles cultural forces of prohibition and makes space for "incoherent" subjects to speak for socially prohibited forms of desire.

In her later work Butler shifts slightly her approach to mourning from
subversion toward acknowledgment. In particular, Butler focuses on how the
politics of loss and grief might permit greater recognition of "precarious
lives" (2005). For Butler, political communities are perpetually engaged in a
struggle to determine whose lives and losses are "grievable." For Butler,
however, this political struggle over who and what can be mourning is
layered over an ontological condition of vulnerability—a fundamental non-
sovereignty in which our bodies are always exposed to and dependent upon
others. In recognizing universal precariousness, we are better prepared to
address political and social conditions of "precarity"—the asymmetrical exposure of particular bodies to harm. For Butler, there is a politics to acknowledging both ontological vulnerability and social precarity, insofar as doing so
might make space for more humane forms of life. In envisioning what these
forms of life might look like, Butler argues that loss—and perpetual mourning—might become the basis for solidarity within communities—"a place
where belonging takes place in and through a common sense of loss (which

does not mean that all losses are the same). Loss becomes condition and necessity for a certain sense of community, where community does not overcome the loss, where community *cannot* overcome the loss without losing the very sense of itself as community" (Eng and Kazanjian, 2003, 468). Communities, like subjects, are inscribed by loss and absence, yet mourning over these losses provides an orientation for both ethics and politics.

As the above discussion makes clear, mourning has been operationalized within political theory in different ways and for different purposes. Wolin argues that political theory is charged with a work of mourning or invocation over the birthright of the political and the fragile or fugitive nature of democracy. Norton and Allen link the capacity to mourn to democracy's (and the subject's) ability to confront its fallibility and its absences. For Butler, relatedly, the politics of mourning reflect ongoing struggles over which lives are "grievable" and over whether or not social and ontological situations of vulnerability can be recognized. Mourning—it has been argued—is the basis for the work of political theorizing and for the political work of building communities of solidarity.

However, there are more layers to this story and additional frameworks for interpreting the politics of loss. Mourning, for instance, is often contrasted with melancholia, as a different relationship to loss and hence an alternative trajectory for politics. Freud (1917) famously argues that mourning is a transitional process that begins with the ego wanting to die along with the lost object. The process ends, as Henry Staten observes, with the ego being "persuaded by the sum of the narcissistic satisfactions it derives from being alive to sever its attachment to the object that has been abolished" (2001, 255). Withdrawing libidinal investment in the lost object over time, the mourner is eventually prepared to attach to new love objects. Mourning, for Freud, contrasts sharply with melancholia, which he likens to mourning without end, an infinite sorrow characterized by the subject's inability to enchant new objects with desire. Melancholia thus can be understood as sustained and pathological fidelity to what was lost, and results from the "inability to resolve grief and ambivalence precipitated by the loss" (Eng and Kazanjian, 2003, 3). By contrast, in Freud's sense, mourning's subjects move on, eventually, and are not bedeviled by such an impasse. Melancholia is viewed as a kind of failed mourning; mourning represents a successful "working through" of loss whereas melancholia is a repetitious "acting out" of the loss (LaCapra, 1999).

Analogically, Wendy Brown has described the inability to move beyond or "work through" failed political projects as a form of "wounded identity" and "left-wing melancholy" (Brown, 1995 and 2003). Brown follows in the tradition of Walter Benjamin, who in 1931 warned against the tendency of certain members of the left to aestheticize defeat through "know-all irony" rather than getting on with the material work of politics (Benjamin, 1974).

Defying both Brown and Benjamin, however, Enzo Traverso has argued that melancholia is a seemingly inescapable affect in a world bereft of utopian political visions (Traverso, 2016). Others have gone further, finding within melancholia a valuable framework for approaching the unforgettable or open wounds within political communities. The "acting out" of repetitive and compulsive melancholia is claimed as a generative form of defiance rather than being seen as an unproductive cousin to mourning or "working through." Instead, edicts to release the lost object are seen to collude with hierarchies of power and privilege and a logic of displacement at the core of late modern capitalism (Eng 2000; Kazanjian and Nichanian, 2003). David Eng and David Kazanjian argue that melancholic attachment enables "the past [to] remain steadfastly alive . . . bringing its ghosts and specters, its flaring and fleeting images, into the present" (2003, 4). On their reading, affective legacies of loss, insofar as they can maintain a "melancholic defer-ral of closure," become sites for resistance and even creative transformation. Melancholia "preserves the lost object in the domain of the psyche" (ibid., 88). By this it "leaves history open for continual re-negotiation. . .a space from which the voice of prophecy might be heard" (ibid., 88).

Theoretical struggles over concepts such as melancholia—and the fre-quent references to Freud—demonstrate how psychoanalysis has influenced the turn toward mourning in political theory and elsewhere. For many, psychoanalytic theorists are essential interlocutors for the work of conceptu-alizing the politics of mourning (Gilroy, 2004; Butler, 2005, 2009; Balbus, 2005; McIvor, 2016). Psychoanalysis, in the words of Joel Kovel, "widens the semantic range" and sensitizes political and social theory to the intercon-nections between the psyche and the political (1994, 7). Psychological de-fenses and dramas seem to repeatedly manifest in social and political scenes, implying that the latter cannot be fully understood without attention to the former. Beyond Freud, political theorists have turned to other figures in the psychoanalytic tradition to conceptualize the work of mourning or the power of melancholia, including Melanie Klein (McIvor, 2016), D. W. Winnicott (Honig, 2001); and Jacques Lacan (Zizek, 2000; Eng and Han, 2000).

Yet as Nancy Luxon has argued, the turn toward psychoanalysis in politi-cal theory carries some risks, including the risk that politically necessary affects such as anger or aggression might be viewed as pathological (2015). Luxon herself interprets appeals to mourning in political theory as the at-tempt to either "elevate certain tragedies to heightened political status" or to "legitimize a claim to a past of some kind" (ibid., 1). Mourning is, corre-spondingly, seen as offering theoretical and political "salves"—either an "opportunity to develop a more critical relation to the past" or to organize politics around "critical ambivalence" and "resistance" (ibid., 2). Although Luxon warns against the ways in which discourses of mourning traverse the "uneasy hinge" between personal and political scenes, she argues that political communities face urgent questions around "what it might mean to organize a space around a shared vulnerability and agency," and she laments the paucity of public spaces and practices in and through which this political work might take place.

More recent analyses of the politics of mourning have turned to these urgent practical and political questions. David McIvor has argued that mourning represents a process whereby individuals and communities acknowledge the ambivalence and complexity of their political traditions and institutions (McIvor, 2016). Seen in this light, mourning is not a private process but a public, intersubjective means of working through social traumas and everyday forms of disrespect or misrecognition. Civic and political institutions and practices, such as truth and reconciliation commissions and social movements can be productively interpreted as instantiations of the "democratic work of mourning" (ibid., xii; Rankine, 2015). Similarly, Alexander Keller Hirsch has argued that public memorials represent material instantiations of the work of mourning. As Hirsch argues, "memorials often attempt to make the parallactic shift of mourning possible by converting loss into an object. By rendering it into a thing—a stone tablet, perhaps, or a commemorative statue—such memorials symbolize the desire for the past to truly become past" (Hirsch, 2018, 7). For Simon Stow, certain traditions of public mourning—for instance those associated with the African American funerary tradition—offer productively critical, tragic, and democratic forms of grief work, even if Stow simultaneously notes how public mourning is often shadowed by politically pernicious forms of nostalgia or romantic identification (2010). Stow has argued that public mourning—despite its dangers—can be the "source of critical-theoretical reflection, democratic pedagogy, and political innovation" (2017, 26)

Of course, even these claims about mourning and politics are contested within political theory. Bonnie Honig, for instance, has warned against the ways a framework of mourning can neutralize political action because it seems to contain an *anti*-political will or intention (2013). Mourning represents a politics of "mortalism" or the idea that, since all mortals perish, death can become the basis for political solidarity. Yet mortalism, on Honig's reading, offers a pre-political solution to dilemmas that can only be addressed through messy and contingent—and always agonistic—struggles. Mourning, therefore, can be a mode of political engagement that conceals its politics, resting instead on pre-political claims about the moral authority of victimhood or post-political visions of mortal humanism.

The themes of loss and mourning, then, open onto varied and contested terrains, reflecting ongoing conversations about how democratic societies and citizens deal with sacrifice, death, disability, and absences forced and unforced—or, conversely, how societies *refuse* to engage these questions through denial, disavowal, or scapegoating. Viewed from this light, the politics of mourning appear in a dizzying variety of locations and through a wide variety of practices. Eulogies, public memorials, official apologies, courtroom trials, public protests, transitional justice hearings, and even quotidian struggles for agency or a political birthright are evidence of the proliferation of sites for reckoning with loss and its aftereffects, and they underscore the urgency of bringing the insights of political theory to bear on these questions and concerns.

The Democratic Arts of Mourning begins from these starting points—the proliferation of the politics of mourning and political theory's increasing attention to those politics. The chapters that follow take measure of the current discourses on mourning in political theory, and explore how the language and practices of mourning relate to some of the pressing challenges and emergent possibilities facing democratic societies and citizens in the first decades of the twenty-first century. The term "democratic arts" reflects our assumption—following Wolin and others—that democracy is a praxis of mourning (Hirsch, 2011). "Democratic arts" also refers to the possibility that citizens can craft creative collective rejoinders to experiences of loss, such as when residents in Greensboro, North Carolina, organized a truth and reconciliation commission charged with examining the "Greensboro Massacre" of 1979 (McIvor, 2016). Similarly, the Black Lives Matter social movement was created in a moment of grief following the death of Trayvon Martin and the legal exoneration of his killer in 2013 (Rankine, 2015; see also chapters 7 and 8 below). Citizens and communities can identify and practice a variety of democratic arts of mourning and, by acting in the face of these bitter experiences, momentarily reclaim and inhabit their birthright as political beings. As Hirsch has argued, democratic societies need to reconceive reconciliation with past loss less in terms of the messianic tradition of healing through time, and more in terms of an agonistic tradition that emphasizes the unfulfilled, evanescent, and episodic quality of all political action (Hirsch, 2011).

The Latin root for "art" is also the root for the English words artifice and artifact. Artifacts of loss—memorials and monuments, for instance—reflect the ongoing contestation at the heart of the politics of mourning. They represent the perpetual struggle to identify and honor losses worth mourning. For this reason they deserve our careful attention and scrutiny. Yet social movements can also embody the democratic arts of mourning. Like memorials they are also the product of political labor and a form of public artifice. They participate, as do the artifacts of civic mourning, in the continual work of democracy. By reflecting on the artifacts, practices, rituals, and narratives of public mourning, political theory can become better attuned to the pathologies and possibilities of democracy, and by tuning into the possibilities of democracy political theorists are perpetually drawn into conversations and contestations about loss, grief, and mourning. The chapters that follow embody this doubled work of reflection and attunement.

The Volume's Structure

The individual chapters below are grouped into five thematic areas that, together, help to unpack the democratic arts of mourning. The first chapter, by C. Fred Alford, pairs with the themes of the Introduction and reflects further on the relationship between politics and mourning by sounding a few discordant notes to the song crafted above. Alford explores the object relations school of psychoanalysis to show why groups or collectivities *cannot* mourn. For the psychoanalyst Hanna Segal, the ability to confront and mourn loss is essential for cultivating the creative spark that sustains life, yet Alford argues that, while this is difficult for individuals, it is (nearly) impossible for collectivities. Instead of experiencing guilt or mourning, groups deflect feelings of loss by scapegoating convenient enemies. Political leaders further repel the work of public mourning by obfuscating or lying about the past or their role in producing tragic mistakes. In the face of this mendacity, the best we can do, Alford argues, is to "call out" the lies of political leaders and to locate artful forms of mourning and political practice "on a small scale."

Chapters 2 and 3 represent the second theme: artifacts or symbols of mourning and remembrance. In chapter 2, Steven Johnston builds on his earlier work on violence, tragedy, and democratic politics with a discussion of the politics of memorialization in the context of proposals for a "War on Terror" Veterans Memorial on the National Mall in Washington, D.C. Johnston argues that such a memorial might "constitute an occasion to reinvent and reimagine American democracy's memorial life," and, in so doing, improve Americans' capacities or appetites for facing uncomfortable truths of empire and sacrifice. Johnston compares his proposal with the example of the Vietnam Memorial, and discusses new public rituals that might embody some of the spirit of the Great Dionysia—the Athenian festival at which the tragedies of Aeschylus and Sophocles were first performed.

In chapter 3, Heather Pool examines the linkages between symbolism, sovereignty, and racial dominance by exploring in detail the context and the aftermath of the 2015 mass murder committed at the Emanuel African Methodist Episcopal Church in Charleston, South Carolina. Pool explores the politics—both explicit and unstated—involved in the removal of the Confederate Battle Flag from the grounds of the South Carolina State House in the aftermath of the shooting. Tracing the evolution of the symbolism of the Confederate Battle Flag from the Civil War until present day, Pool argues that its removal reflected a "performance of neutral sovereignty" by a state ostensibly committed to moving beyond a history of racial dominance. However, Pool argues that the institutional legacy of white dominance was left untouched and unexamined by the act of removing the Confederate flag. In this respect, the quick removal of a fraught symbol was a "symbolic removal" that emphasized political pageantry over public debate and examination.

Pool suggestively argues that the (barely) repressed symbols and substance of white dominance in South Carolina quickly found an outlet in the campaign (and now presidency) of Donald Trump.

Chapters 4 and 5 examine the subject (and subjects) of taboo. In her chapter, "Mourning Denied: The Tabooed Subject," Claudia Leeb explores the relationship between taboos and the work of mourning. Leeb affirms the value and necessity of mourning as both a theoretical and practical concept for political life, but argues that social taboos function as fundamental obstacles to the productive work of mourning. In developing her argument, Leeb engages with the work of Theodor Adorno, Sigmund Freud, and Giorgio Agamben to show how taboos enforce social amnesia over historical crimes and enduring injustices. Reading Sophocles' *Antigone* through the lens of taboo and refused grief, Leeb then turns to the specific case of refused grief in Austria over the genocide against the Roma and Sinti populations. Leeb traces the long and haunting history of taboos surrounding the Roma and Sinti peoples in Austria, and reflects on the absence of public discourse or memorials over the fate of these populations under the Austrian Anschluss with Germany during the period of National Socialism. For Leeb, efforts to raise consciousness about these crimes can erode the power of taboos and, as such, might permit forms of social mourning and enable broader practices of political responsibility and solidarity.

In chapter 5 Osman Balkan explores the tabooed body of Tamerlan Tsarnaev, who was responsible, along with his brother Dzhokhar Tsarnaev, for the bombing of the Boston Marathon in April, 2013. After his death in the ensuing manhunt, Tamerlan Tsarnaev's body was subject to intense political contestation. Protesters and counter-protesters emerged in response to plans for the body's burial, and public pressure ultimately forced the expulsion of Tsarnaev's body from the Commonwealth of Massachusetts. After much deliberation, his body was interred at a Muslim cemetery in Doswell, Virginia, a small town approximately twenty-five miles north of the state's capital, Richmond. As news about his whereabouts spread, another round of protests erupted, this time involving baffled Virginians who were distressed about the fact that the "Boston Bomber" had been surreptitiously buried in their state. Balkan examines the question of why the disposal of Tamerlan Tsarnaev's remains was so politically fraught. In the process, Balkan shows how dead bodies serve as perennial sites of political conflict "because the treatment of the dead, including where and how dead bodies are buried, is an important means through which political actors express, enact, and contest the boundaries of national, political and moral communities."

Chapters 6 through 8 take up the theme of the protest politics of grief and grievance. In "Reparations, Refusals, and Grief: Idle No More and the Unlearning of Colonial Rule," Vicki Hsueh examines the hunger strike of Chief Theresa Spence of Attawapiskat Nation in 2012–2013, and the concurrent

Idle No More social movement that originated in response to Canadian legislative abuses of indigenous treaty rights. Both Spence's hunger strike and the emergent protests of Idle No More quickly became targets of insult and derision, and Hsueh argues that such dismissals illuminate a crucial aspect of modern reparations discourse. For Hsueh, even expanded discourses of reparations that move beyond a strictly juridical approach to include other political or affective forms are haunted by colonial logics of expropriation and exclusion. Colonial logics render indigenous forms of suffering and loss difficult to acknowledge and hence impossible to grieve. By connecting reparations discourses to the work of sustained and "viscerally compelling" protests, Hsueh argues for a notion of "reparative refusal" encapsulated by the affective body politics of the Idle No More movement. For Hsueh, the democratic arts of mourning require the "mindful engagement of bodies."

Chapters 7 and 8 each examine the nascent social movement Black Lives Matter. In "Burning Rage: Disenfranchised Mourning and the Political Possibilities of Anger," Shirin Deylami explores the connection between mourning and the supposedly "unruly" emotions of anger or outrage. Beginning with a description of the protests in Ferguson, Missouri, following the death of Michael Brown, Deylami roots her exploration of the affective politics of mourning in the burgeoning social movement Black Lives Matter. Deylami argues that political theorists have not adequately understood the political potential of outrage. Through a reading of the work of Frantz Fanon, Deylami shows how anger and outrage can illuminate specific structures of disenfranchisement, allowing space for political movements that can challenge conditions of precarity and articulate demands for redress. In this context, Deylami interprets the political work of outrage following the death of Michael Brown, showing how this grief and anger, filtered through the practices of an emergent social movement, formed the basis for a systemic analysis of racism and a larger critique of policing practices.

David Temin, in chapter 8, focuses on how Black Lives Matter activists have emphasized the language of state violence to draw attention to systemic practices of injustice ranging from police abuse, criminal sentencing patterns, and social disinvestment in Black communities. To examine the politics of grief, grievance, and mourning in this context of systemic abuses and injustices, Temin turns to a reading of the late work and activism of Martin Luther King, Jr. By examining the transitions in King's activism—away from notions of loss and redemption toward a more critical and interrogative mode— Temin's analysis offers a somewhat more skeptical perspective on the value of mourning as an interpretive framework for examining politics in the post–Civil Rights era.

The final three chapters examine themes of sound, silence, and survival in the context of public mourning. In chapter 9, "Music, Mourning, and Democratic Resilience: Bruce Springsteen's *The Rising*," Simon Stow turns to discussions of the politics of popular music in order to identify examples of democratic public mourning. In resistance to the idea that public mourning is potentially antidemocratic—because it often serves to delegitimize ongoing political contestation—Stow identifies forms of mourning that might serve "as a resource for engendering democratic resilience." In particular Stow examines the music of Bruce Springsteen and specifically his 2002 album *The Rising*—written in the immediate aftermath of September 11th. Stow argues that Springsteen's musical methodology of blending "celebration and critique of America" represents a particular ethic in response to death that "generates critical reflection, democratic engagement, and a rejection of revenge." By modeling vulnerability and reflectiveness in the face of loss, Springsteen's album served as a democratically generative counterpoint to the certainty and single-mindedness that typified much of political discourse in the years following 9/11. Stow's chapter also meditates on larger issues such as the role that popular music can play in democracies during moments of intensified public grieving.

In "Speaking Silence: Holding and the Democratic Arts of Mourning," Joel Schlosser explores the democratic arts of mourning through a tension between what he sees as a developmental promise of working through and the difficult challenge of "holding the unspeakable." Schlosser reflects on the differences between loss and catastrophe by thoughtfully weaving together Greek tragedy, psychoanalysis, and political theory. Whereas losses might be more readily identified and mourned by those who remain, catastrophe represents the possibility of the "end of language . . . meaning . . . and relationships." Schlosser explores this tension through a reading of Euripides's *Trojan Women*. For Schlosser, Greek tragedy functioned as a space of holding for "unintelligible suffering," which stands in contrast to, and in productive tension with, the developmental logics often associated with practices of working through or mourning. The performance of *Trojan Women* held a space for the unintelligible through its use of rhythm, metaphor, and song. For Schlosser, the performed silence prefigures a different kind of agency than that offered by the impulses of working through. This form of agency, he argues, is germane to experiences of catastrophe and to crises of intelligibility.

Finally, the book concludes with an interview with Bonnie Honig. Honig's writings over the past several decades have included a number of influential reflections on the politics of loss and mourning. In this interview, Honig returns to those themes and reflects upon the limitations of lamentation as a framework for political theory and political action, while also emphasizing the importance that mourning might play in democratic resilience and survival.

Each of the chapters below touches upon the overriding questions of this book: what forms do the politics of mourning take? What forms, if any, are overruled, prohibited, or sublimated, and why? How might citizens or social movements galvanize the democratic arts of mourning in response to felt losses, systemic injustices, or social traumas? What role can political theory or political theorists play within these conversations and contestations? Finally, whose losses will animate politics and the enterprise of political theory in the years to come, and how will political theorists acknowledge and take up the challenging inheritances of those losses? The democratic arts of mourning are rooted in democracy's absences, failures, and losses, but they also limn the highest democratic aspirations. In dark and increasingly undemocratic times, they offer an ambivalent orientation toward both damage and repair that might sustain political aspirations through the work of attending to loss. Under tragic circumstances, the past may be unforgettable and the present may seem irreparable; yet for these very reasons the democratic arts of mourning are more imperative than ever.

WORKS CITED

Ahrensdorf, P. 2009. *Greek Tragedy and Political Philosophy: Rationalism and Religion in Sophocles' Theban Plays*. Cambridge, UK: Cambridge University Press.

Alford, C. Fred. 1992. *The Psychoanalytic Theory of Greek Tragedy*. New Haven, CT: Yale University Press.

———. 2009. *After the Holocaust: The Book of Job, Primo Levi, and the Path to Affliction*. Cambridge, UK: Cambridge University Press.

———. 2013. *Trauma and Forgiveness: Consequences and Communities*. Cambridge: Cambridge University Press.

Allen, Danielle. 2004. *Talking to Strangers: Anxieties of Citizenship since* Brown v. Board of Education. Chicago: University of Chicago Press.

Arrowsmith, William. 1963. "A Greek Theater of Ideas." *Arion*. Vol. 2, No. 3, pp. 32–56.

Balbus, Isaac. 2005. *Mourning and Modernity: Essays in the Psychoanalysis of Contemporary Society*. New York: Other Press.

Barker, Derek. 2008. *Tragedy and Citizenship: Conflict, Reconciliation, and Democracy from Haemon to Hegel*. Albany, NY: SUNY Press.

Benjamin, Walter. 1974. *Screen*. Vol. 15, No. 2 (July), pp. 28–32.

Bradley, A. C. 1991. *Shakespearean Tragedy*. New York: Penguin.

Brown, Wendy. 1995. *States of Injury: Power and Freedom in Late Modernity*. Princeton, NJ: Princeton University Press.

———. 2003. "Resisting Left Melancholia," in Eng and Kazanjian, eds., *Loss: The Politics of Mourning*. Berkeley, CA: University of California Press.

Butler, Judith. 1997. *The Psychic Life of Power*. Stanford: Stanford University Press.

———. 2003. "Afterword," in Eng and Kazanjian, eds., *Loss: The Politics of Mourning*. Berkeley, CA: University of California Press.

———. 2004. *Precarious Life: The Powers of Mourning and Violence*. London: Verso.

———. 2009. *Frames of War: When is Life Grievable?* London: Verso.

Cavell, Stanley. 1987. *Disowning of Knowledge: In Seven Plays of Shakespeare*. Cambridge, UK: Cambridge University Press.

Comay, Rebecca. 2011. *Mourning Sickness: Hegel and the French Revolution*. Palo Alto, CA: Stanford University Press.

Connolly, William. 2005. *Pluralism*. Durham, NC: Duke University Press.

———. 2008. *Capitalism and Christianity, American Style*. Durham, NC: Duke University Press.

Introduction

———. 2013. *The Fragility of Things*. Durham, NC: Duke University Press.

Crimp, Douglas. 1989. "Mourning and Militancy," *October* 51, pp. 3–18.

Derrida, Jacques. 1994. *Specters of Marx*, trans. Peggy Kamuf. London: Routledge.

———. 2003. *The Work of Mourning*. Chicago: University of Chicago Press.

Dienstag, Joshua Foa. 2009. *Pessimism: Philosophy, Ethic and Spirit*. Princeton, NJ: Princeton University Press.

Eng, David. 2000. "Melancholia in the Late 20th Century." *Signs*. Vol. 25, No. 4, pp. 1275–1281.

Eng, David, and Shinhee Han. 2000. "A Dialogue on Racial Melancholia," *Psychoanalytic Dialogues*. Vol. 10, No. 4, pp. 667–700.

Eng, David, and David Kazanjian eds. 2003. *Loss: The Politics of Mourning*. Berkeley, CA: University of California Press.

Euben, J. Peter. *1986. Greek Tragedy and Political Theory*. Berkeley: University of California Press, 1986).

———. 1990. *The Tragedy of Political Theory: The Road Not Taken*. Princeton, NJ: Princeton University Press.

———. 2003. *Platonic Noise*. Princeton, NJ: Princeton University Press.

Felski, Rita, ed. 2008. *Rethinking Tragedy*. Baltimore: Johns Hopkins University Press.

Frank, Jill. 2005. *A Democracy of Distinction: Aristotle and the Work of Politics*. Chicago: University of Chicago Press.

Freud, Sigmund.1917. "Mourning and Melancholia." *The Standard Edition of the Complete Psychological Works of Sigmund Freud, Volume XIV (1914–1916): On the History of the Psycho-Analytic Movement, Papers on Metapsychology and Other Works*, 237–258.

Gilroy, Paul. 2005. *Postcolonial Melancholia*. New York: Columbia University Press.

———. 2010. *Darker than Blue: On the Moral Economics of Black Atlantic Culture*. Cambridge, MA: Belknap Harvard Press.

Goldhill, Simon. 1987. *Reading Greek Tragedy*. Cambridge, UK: Cambridge University Press.

———. 2004. *Love, Sex, and Tragedy: How the Ancient World Shapes Our Lives*. Chicago: University of Chicago Press.

Hirsch, Alexander Keller. ed. 2013. *Theorizing Post-Conflict Reconciliation: Agonism, Restitution, and Repair*. London: Routledge.

———. 2015. "Hope, Without Guarantees: Mourning, Natality, and the Will to Chance in Book XXIV of the Iliad," *Theory and Event* 18, no. 1.

———. 2016. "Walking off the Edge of the World: Sacrifice, Chance, and Dazzling Dissolution in the Book of Job and Ursula K. LeGuin's 'The One Who Walk Away from Omelas,'" *Humanities* 5.

Honig, Bonnie. 2001. *Democracy and the Foreigner*. Princeton: Princeton University Press.

———. 2013. *Antigone Interrupted*. London: Cambridge University Press.

Horowitz, Gregg. 2002. *Sustaining Loss: Art and Mournful Life*. Stanford, CA: Stanford University Press.

Johnston, Steven. 2015. *American Dionysia: Violence, Tragedy, and Democratic Politics*. Cambridge, UK: Cambridge University Press.

Kazanjian, David, and Marc Nichanian. 2003. "Between Genocide and Catastrophe." *Loss: The Politics of Mourning*. Berkeley, CA: University of California Press.

Kovel, Joel. 1994. *White Racism: A Psychohistory*. New York: Columbia University Press.

LaCapra, Dominick. 2001. *Writing History, Writing Trauma*. Baltimore: The Johns Hopkins University Press.

Loraux, Nicole. 1998. *Mothers in Mourning*. Ithaca, NY: Cornell University Press.

———. 2002. *The Mourning Voice, An Essay on Greek Tragedy*. Ithaca, NY: Cornell University Press.

Luxon, Nancy. 2015. "Beyond Mourning and Melancholia: Nostalgia, Anger, and the Challenges of Political Action." *Contemporary Political Theory*, Vol. 15, No. 2, pp. 139–159.

Markel, Patchen. 2003. *Bound by Recognition*. New York: Princeton University Press.

McIvor, David. 2012. "Bringing Ourselves to Grief: Judith Butler and the Politics of Mourning." *Political Theory* 20 (10): 1–28.

————. 2016. *Mourning in America: Race and the Politics of Loss.* Ithaca, NY: Cornell University Press.

Moglen, Seth. 2007. *Mourning Modernity: Literary Modernism and the Injuries of American Capitalism.* Stanford, CA: Stanford University Press.

Monoson, S. Sara. 2000. *Plato's Democratic Entanglements: Athenian Politics and the Practice of Philosophy.* Princeton, NJ: Princeton University Press.

Nietzsche, Friedrich. 1993. *The Birth of Tragedy.* New York: Penguin Classics.

Norton, Anne. 2001. "Evening Land," in *Democracy and Vision: Sheldon Wolin and the Vicissitudes of the Political,* edited by William Connolly and Aryeh Botwinick. Princeton, NJ: Princeton University Press.

Nussbaum, Martha. 1986. *The Fragility of Goodness: Luck and Ethics in Greek Tragedy.* Cambridge, UK: Cambridge University Press.

————. 1992. "Tragedy and Self-Sufficiency: Plato and Aristotle on Fear and Pity." *Essays on Aristotle's Poetics,* edited by Amelie Oksenberg Rorty. Princeton, NJ: Princeton University Press.

————. 2016. *Anger and Forgiveness: Resentment, Generosity, Justice.* Oxford: Oxford University Press.

Ober, Josiah. 2005. *Athenian Legacies: Essays on the Politics of Going on Together.* Princeton, NJ: Princeton University Press.

————. 2015. *The Rise and Fall of Classical Greece.* Princeton, NJ: Princeton University Press.

Rankine, Claudia. 2015. "The Condition of Black Life Is One of Mourning," *New York Times,* June 22.

Rawls, John. 1971. *A Theory of Justice.* Cambridge, MA: Harvard University Press.

Rose, Gillian. 1996. *Mourning Becomes the Law: Philosophy and Representation.* Cambridge: Cambridge University Press.

Rosemont, Franklin. 2003. *Joe Hill: The IWW and the Making of a Revolutionary Working-class Culture.* Chicago: Charles H. Kerr.

Saxonhouse, Arlene. 1995. *Fear of Diversity: The Birth of Political Science in Ancient Greek Thought.* Chicago: University of Chicago Press.

Schlosser, Joel. 2014. *What Would Socrates Do? Self-Examination, Civic Engagement, and the Politics of Philosophy.* Cambridge, UK: Cambridge University Press.

Scott, David. 2013. *Omens of Adversity: Tragedy, Time, Memory, Justice.* Durham, NC: Duke University Press.

Shklar, Judith. 1975. "Hannah Arendt's Triumph." *The New Republic.* December 27.

Staten, Henry. 2001. *Eros in Mourning: From Homer to Lacan.* Baltimore: Johns Hopkins University Press.

Steiner, George. 1961. *The Death of Tragedy.* New York: Knopf.

Stow, Simon. 2010. "Agonistic Homegoing: Frederick Douglass, Joseph Lowery, and the Democratic Value of African American Public Mourning," *American Political Science Review,* Vol. 104, No. 4, pp. 681–697.

————. 2017. *American Mourning: Tragedy, Democracy Resilience.* Cambridge, UK: Cambridge University Press.

Stout, Jeffrey. 2010. *Blessed are the Organized: Grassroots Democracy in America.* Princeton, NJ: Princeton University Press.

Tarnopolsky, Christina. 2014. *Prudes, Perverts, and Tyrants: Plato's Gorgias and the Politics of Shame.* Princeton, NJ: Princeton University Press.

Taxidou, Olga. 2004. *Tragedy, Mourning, and Modernity.* Edinburgh: Edinburgh University Press.

Traverso, Enzo. 2016. *Left-wing Melancholia: Marxism, History, and Memory.* New York: Columbia University Press.

Villa, Dana. 2001. *Socratic Citizenship.* Princeton, NJ: Princetone University Press.

Williams, Bernard. 1981. *Moral Luck.* Cambridge: Cambridge University Press.

————. 1993. *Shame and Necessity.* Berkeley, CA: University of California Press.

————. 2006. *Philosophy as a Humanistic Discipline.* Princeton, NJ: University Press.

Williams, Rowan. 2016. *The Tragic Imagination.* Oxford: Oxford University Press.

Wolin, Sheldon. 1989. *The Presence of the Past: Essays on the State and the Constitution.* Baltimore: Johns Hopkins University Press.

————. 1997. "Fugitive Democracy," *Democracy and Difference: Contesting the Boundaries of the Political,* edited by Seyla Benhabib. Princeton: Princeton University Press.

————. 2000. "Political Theory: From Vocation to Invocation" *Vocations of Political Theory.* Jason Frank and John Tambornino, editors. Minneapolis: University of Minnesota Press, pp. 3–21.

Zeitlen, Froma. 1996. *Playing the Other: Gender and Society in Classical Greek Literature.* Chicago: Chicago University Press.

Zizek, Slavoj. 2000. "Melancholy and the Act," *Critical Inquiry.* Vol. 26, No. 4.

Chapter One

Groups Can Hardly Mourn

C. Fred Alford

At the site of the destroyed twin towers in New York City, in the lobby of an insurance company building near Ground Zero, a mural was displayed throughout most of 2002. It consisted of a series of self-portraits done by thousands of children, many of whom lost a parent or relative in the 9/11 attacks, others who had lost parents in wars around the world. An extract from one of Hanna Segal's first psychoanalytic papers was placed beside the mural, serving as its motto.

> It is when the world within us is destroyed, when it is dead and loveless, when our loved ones are in fragments, and we ourselves in helpless despair—it is then that we must re-create our world anew, re-assemble the pieces, infuse life into dead fragments, re-create life. (Segal 1952, 199)

Marygrace Berberian, an art therapist and social worker who came up with the idea for the project, in which eventually 3,100 children's self-portraits of grief were combined, says "Children were recreating life in their art. . . . Creativity allows for describing, building and reconfiguring an injured object so that mourning can begin" (Berberian 2003, 33).

Segal insists on the unconditional necessity of acknowledging loss and mourning if the creative impulse is to exist. Conversely, it seems as if Berberian recognizes that it is creativity, rebuilding an injured object, that allows mourning to begin. The process works both ways. "It is only when the loss has been acknowledged and the mourning experienced that re-creation can take place" in the work of art, including the art of life (Segal 1952, 199).

What is so difficult, indeed almost impossible, is for groups to recognize mistakes, and for groups to mourn their losses. What is difficult in individuals is almost impossible in groups. And yet it is necessary if groups are not to

1

remain stuck in the paranoid-schizoid position, as Melanie Klein puts it. Segal was Klein's most loyal and influential student.

Segal (1997) writes about the need for an enemy after the end of the cold war, the triumphalism that followed, and the inability of groups, especially nations, to deal with the guilt over wasting so many lives and so much money that could be spent otherwise. Instead of guilt, paranoid-schizoid defenses, and with these defenses another war, came to the fore.

> Those who do not remember their history are bound to repeat it, but facing the reality of history exposes us to what is most unbearable. This is particularly difficult in groups, where the task is one of admitting that we made a mistake of vast proportions and have to take responsibility for the consequences. But unless we do that, our manic and schizoid defenses will make us blind to these realities and lead us to further dangers. (Segal 1997, 167)

What should individuals do in the face of the moral, emotional, and intellectual intransigence of groups? First they should "expose lies." Education, the second stage, involves explaining the psychological motivations behind the lies (Quinodoz 2008, 153). Not everyone wants to lie; they are unaware of and unable to use the truth.

It's worth thinking about what these lies might consist of. Consider the truth: that the United States made a terrible mistake in Iraq and Afghanistan, costing thousands of American lives, ruining tens of thousands more, costing trillions of dollars, out of our fear and disorientation after 9/11. Some leaders did it for political gain, some out of fear, some out of conviction. All were wrong, as were those people who followed and supported them.

FROM FREUD TO SEGAL

In *Mourning and Melancholia* (1917, 24–50), Freud argues that melancholy is a revolt against loss. Instead of slowly abandoning its attachment to the loved and lost object, the ego identifies with the lost object. This is what Freud means when he says that "the shadow of the object fell upon the ego." (249)

In melancholia, love is withdrawn from the object, but instead of being invested in another object (person, country, ideal), as usually happens after a period of mourning, the ego identifies with the lost object. The ego is judged by another part of the ego as though it were the object, and dealt with harshly. In other words, in melancholia part of the ego becomes the lost object, and another part of the ego berates the ego for *being* the lost object. Melancholy is an expression of self-reproach.

Freud changed his mind in *The Ego and the Id* (1923). In this later work, the ego's identification with its lost object becomes "the sole condition under which the id can give up its objects . . . it makes it possible to suppose that the character of the ego is a precipitate of abandoned object-cathexes and that it contains the history of those object choices." (29)

In this account, the ego is composed of its losses. Loss is how we grow up. In some ways Freud comes surprisingly close to the story told by Klein and Segal. For both women, mourning cannot take place unless and until the lost object is internalized. We never let go of anyone or anything we have loved and lost. Instead, we take the lost one inside, where it becomes part of us for the rest of our lives. In a sense, melancholy is part of self-development, as loss involves not only the physical loss of the other, but the losses entailed in growing up and moving on, leaving parents and other loved ones behind. Judith Butler (1997, 132–150) makes a similar argument.

Klein and Segal differ from Freud in their account of how we come to terms with our losses: by giving loss a creative form, restoring life to a shattered and deadened psyche. The creation need not be a self-representation, as were most of the paintings of the children of 9/11. The creation can be far away from the original subject and object. The point is that creation is the way we give form to a shattered psyche, restoring life to dead life, including our own. The way out from under the shadow of mourning is through creative acts. They need not be artistic in the conventional sense. A renewed psychic investment in children or grandchildren may also be creative.

The transformation of shattering loss into creative form is the transformation of the paranoid-schizoid position into the depressive position, as Klein (1975a, 1975b) calls these two states of mind. In the paranoid-schizoid position, the self is shattered and under attack. Pain and loss are attributed to hostile external forces. The depressive position is the resolution of the paranoid-schizoid position, in which loss is transformed by creative acts of reparation, making both self and world whole again, at least for a little while. The resolution is always temporary, vulnerable to further losses. We spend our lives moving between these two positions. If we are fortunate we spend most of our time in the depressive position, which is not the same as being depressed.

Groups and nations appear to be able to collectively mourn, insofar as they carry out rituals of group mourning, which are numerous and generally unremarkable. But group rituals that look like mourning are generally about group affirmation, strengthening the ties that bind the group. Mock mourning it might be called, after Melanie Klein's (1975c) concept of mock or manic reparation—that is, reparation that is grandiose, imagining that all losses can be readily repaired, or they didn't really happen. Much public ritual has this quality. Not only is the affect different, but the rhetoric reveals it. Language that reflects a desire to impose loss on another group is not really about mourning. This language may range from calls for military retaliation to the usual patriotic sloganeering. If we are the best, then everybody else is worse.

One might argue that successful mourning is about making something new, whereas melancholia is about becoming the lost object. The statement is succinct, but from a Kleinian perspective the problem is more complex and morally problematic. In the children's 9/11 mural, the children mostly represented themselves and lost loved ones. For Klein and Segal, it seems to make no difference what is repaired. Creative activity may have nothing to do with what is lost. For example, Klein writes about colonists' "ruthless cruelty against native populations." And how might the colonists and their descendants make reparation? By "repopulating the country with people of their own nationality" (Klein 1964, 104–105). One might argue that Klein wrote in less politically and morally aware times, but the problem is really deeper than that. Reparation is about creativity, not morality. And how might they be connected? This is the task of reparative leaders, who are unfortunately rare.

A reparative leader is a man or woman who is able to share his or her reparative imagination, as I will call it, with their group. Nelson Mandela and Desmond Tutu are exemplary. The truth and reconciliation commissions they fostered appear to have done little to encourage reconciliation or forgiveness, but that was not really their point, even if this was not generally realized at the time (De La Rey and Owens 1998; Hayner 2001). Truth and reconciliation commissions created a place and space in which the truth could be told. Truth telling is the first and most important step in reparation, for it says that if the truth can be told, then it can be borne. It is the fear that the truth is unbearable that makes the harm ungrievable. It is the fear that the truth is unbearable that leads leaders and followers to make mock reparation, which is always born of the fear that real reparation is impossible, the group too weak, the damage too vast.

It is unfortunate that leaders combining a reparative imagination with moral vision are so rare. Their appearance at just the right historical moment is even rarer. As I will argue later, the individual remains the center of value, but groups threaten—any group threatens—this value by submerging the individual voice. This is another reason why reparative leaders are so important, liberating the individual to mourn. Though we don't usually think about it this way, mourning is an act of self-assertion, one that must come from within.

LOSS, MOURNING, AND POWER

Many losses that are deemed public reflect the power of some to inflict loss on others. Whether this mourning is recognized publicly is also a matter of power. The transfer of power in South Africa was exactly that: the recognition by whites, in the face of black power and world condemnation, that they lacked the power to hold on. Some also lacked the will.

Judith Butler, a feminist philosopher, states that "some people think that grief is privatizing, that it returns us to a solitary situation and is, in that sense, depoliticizing." Butler disagrees, arguing that grief "furnishes a sense of political community of a complex order . . . bringing to the fore the relational ties that have implications for theorizing fundamental dependency and ethical responsibility" (2004, 22–23).

In reality, much of political and social life is about denying this dependency, and when it cannot be denied seeking to impose it on others. In other words, politics is not just about my group securing power at your expense. Politics is about imposing my group's weakness, dependency, and loss (for human weakness, dependency, and loss are universal) on your group. To put it simply, politics isn't ontology. Politics is frequently driven by a desire to deny reality, in this case our mortal givenness, and that of those we love. In the short run, politics is about getting some people to live short miserable lives so that others may live longer more pleasant ones. In the long run, of course, we are all dead, but politics is rarely about the long run.

In private relationships, both family and social, dependency and responsibility are sometimes rewarding for she who needs and he who gives. Relationships are enriched, lives bettered for both parties in times of grief and need. This is rarely the case in politics. Or if it is, then those who argue the case should provide a few examples, for counter-examples can be found in the newspaper every day.

To be sure, Butler politicizes grief in her analysis of ungrievable lives. An ungrievable life, says Butler is already in some sense illegitimate, and at least in that sense unreal. Illegitimate and unreal, such a life is "ungrievable." An ungrievable life, Butler (2004, 34–35) continues, "is not quite a life; it does not qualify as a life and is not worth a note. It is already the unburied, if not the unburiable." The problem with Butler's analysis is not that she is wrong about ungrievable lives. The problem is that many grievable lives should not have to be grieved in the first place. Death has come before its time in the interests of the power of others. Butler is at once overly and insufficiently subtle.

From Pericles' Funeral Oration, in which the fallen are praised for living up to the values of Athens, to the mourning rituals honoring the dead bodies returned from Iraq and Afghanistan, the attitude is one of honoring the soldier, not the individual (Thucydides, 2.43). Honoring the grievable lives of anonymous, interchangeable persons is better than dishonoring them, but one should not make too much of these formalities either. A grievable life, even an honored life, is not necessarily a valued life. It is simply a life that fits a known and accepted social category. That this social category may at the same time come with the barely visible subtitle, such as "disposable life" should not come as any great comfort. A grievable life may be a life squandered by others, even if its burial is an honorable one. This story is over twenty-five hundred years old. It is not for nothing that the old men of Argos wondered about the cost in human pain and loss of the ten-year Trojan War, and that Aeschylus would have his audience wonder too (Aeschylus, *Agamemnon*, lines 680–762). Not just about an already mythical war, but war.

Freud held the conflict between Eros and the *Todestrieb* (death drive) to be the great threat to civilization, the source of civilization's discontent (Freud, 1930). Perhaps these are only the supporting characters, with grief and mourning the real menace to civilization. Not simply because of the sadness they express, and the risk of melancholy they incur, but because feelings of grief and mourning are so unbearable that we are always trying to put them off onto others, inflicting feelings of grief and loss on others, almost as if grief and loss were a zero-sum game: the more for you, the less for me. It doesn't work that way, of course, but people seem to act as if it does. Or at least this would seem to be the psycho-logic involved, as well as a fairly reliable perspective from which to view history, from the Iraq War to the Trojan War.

As Bonnie Honig (2009) argues about Sophocles' *Antigone*, it is not Antigone who is out of control in defying her uncle Creon and privately burying her brother Polyneices. Antigone knows what she is doing, representing an order higher than the state, one rooted in the earthliest of places, the grieving family. Speaking to her sister, Antigone says

> Listen, Ismene:
> Creon buried our brother Eteocles
> With military honors, gave him a soldier's funeral,
> And it was right that he should; but Polyneices,
> Who fought as bravely and died as miserably.
> They say that Creon has sworn
> No one shall bury him, no one mourn for him
> But his body must lie in the fields, a sweet treasure
> For carrion birds to find as they search for food.
> That is what they say, and our good Creon is coming here
> To announce it publicly; and the penalty—
> Stoning to death in the public square
> There it is,
> And now you can prove what you are:
> A true sister, or a traitor to your family. (lines 21–40)

It is Creon, representative of the state, who throughout the play is on the edge of losing control, his fury destabilizing to both family and state, costing the life of his wife and his son, both of whom commit suicide out of rage against Creon and the losses he has inflicted on them. Creon is himself broken by the end of the play. Eteocles becomes a mere symbol of state power. It is Polyneices whom we remember because it is he who is buried privately, and with love, by his sister.

BETWEEN PRIVACY AND POLITICS

Butler's hope, shared with Steven White (2009), is that loss and mourning may unite us as citizens, revealing our shared vulnerability. My argument is that loss and mourning are so emotionally powerful that they threaten to overwhelm political order. Thus, they are almost always denied. When recognized, memorials are less about shared grief and sadness than they are rituals of group affirmation.

Fortunately, there is a place between private and public. Some call it the social (Arendt), others call it civil society (Putnam, Habermas).[1] It is where democratic mourning takes place if it is to take place at all.

The AIDS Memorial Quilt was first displayed in Washington, D.C., in October 1987 with 1,920 panels. It has grown to more than 48,000 panels in recent years, each panel representing a life lost to AIDS. (http://www.aidsquilt.org/). When last displayed in Washington, D.C. it covered the entire National Mall. As Peter Hawkins (1993, 757) put it, the quilt was

> a brilliant strategy for bringing AIDS not only to public attention but into the mainstream of American myth, for turning what was perceived to be a "gay disease" into a shared national tragedy.

Ungrievable lives, it turns out, are not victims of AIDS (though it took a while), as Butler argues, but soldiers who are interchangeable. Unlike Arlington National Cemetery, with its identical white tombstones, each panel in the quilt is different, reflecting the unique identity of the victim. Stitched together in large panels, the victims are remembered as individuals in that most traditional of American handicrafts, the homemade quilt. To be sure, there are ceremonies honoring the death of fallen American soldiers. Their bodies are treated with respect, but it is worth remembering that even the term "fallen" is a euphemism. From the legendary Trojan War until today, bodies do not simply topple over. They are pierced, hacked, and blown to pieces (Freeden, 2011).

As Mohr (1992, 107) argues, the focus on the individual life, and death, reflects the central claim of liberalism: that it is the individual, not groups, classes, soldiers, or citizens, that is the locus of human value. Though the AIDS Memorial Quilt of necessity often implies the sexual orientation of the victim, that is not its focus. Nor is it the focus of the documentary about it, *Common Threads: Stories from the Quilt*. That it is the death of individuals that matters is reinforced by the reading of the names of the dead, a feature of almost every display of the quilt. It is a feature of the 9/11 memorial in New York City as well on each anniversary of the attacks.

Ironically, even more than life, it is death that reminds us that there is no substitute for liberalism, the political philosophy that makes the individual the unique repository of value. Not the isolated individual, for in the quilt their lives and deaths are stitched together, but the individual in a community of others. Perhaps that is what the stitching represents. In recalling a life from the perspective of death, we remember that only the individual (not the isolated individual, but the individual) matters. I do not believe that burial practices of the military reflect the values of liberalism.

Perhaps the military cannot memorialize unique individuals and remain a cohesive unit. Perhaps it cannot be liberal. But military memorial services should change our perspective on what constitutes a grievable life, and where this grieving best takes place: in society, somewhere between the state and the individual. Nations don't mourn the loss of individuals; they reaffirm the unity of the state as Creon would do, burying one brother but not the other. Not just the individual, but individuality, is sacrificed for the state. This is not the case with the AIDS Memorial Quilt, where individuals' stories are told in symbol, such as a crocheted chef's hat or bicycle, and inscriptions from loved ones.

After reading a list of names, including her son's, Suzi Mandell walks through the display of the quilt, which seems to occupy half of the Washington Mall, and reminds us,

> Too many people . . . too many people . . . too much love gone . . . too much tragedy. I took David's story . . . and multiply that by the number of panels and it was all so horrendous. Every one of those persons that is represented by a panel is a person who was loved by somebody and that loss, the tremendous loss . . . and I kept thinking of the possibilities for David, what he could have been, what his promise was, and how cut short it was, and again multiply that by the number of panels. (*Common Threads*, quoted in Yep, 2007, 293; Mandell's commentary can be viewed in the video)

This raises the difficult struggle with militancy. Every assertion of militancy in a ceremony of loss is a denial of mourning. There is a place for militancy, and some truth to Michael Musto's warning that there should be a sticker on the quilt that reads "Don't feel that by crying over this, you've really done something for AIDS" (quoted in Sturken 1997, 213). Nevertheless, mourning is not the place for militancy, and they should be separated in ceremony as they should be separated in life, lest our mourning be but a paranoid-schizoid display of anger, fear, and revenge. About national grief, Butler asks

Is there something to be gained from grieving, from tarrying with grief, from remaining exposed to its unbearability and not endeavoring to seek a resolution for grief from violence? Is there something to be gained in the political domain by maintaining grief as part of the framework within we think our international ties? If we stay with the sense of loss, are we left feeling only passive and powerless, as some might fear? Or are we, rather, returned to a sense of human vulnerability, to our collective responsibility for the physical lives of one another. (Butler 2004, 30)

Tarrying with grief is a quality of the depressive position. Difficult for individuals, it seems almost impossible for nations.

AN ENCOUNTER WITH THE DAUGHTERS OF ANTIGONE

In an essay whose subtitle is "An Encounter with Antigone's Daughters," Jean Bethke Elshtain (1996) writes about the mothers of the Plaza de Mayo, who marched silently in a plaza across from the presidential palace. The mothers were protesting the disappearances of mostly young people during Argentina's dirty war. Beginning in 1976, and continuing for eight years, more than 30,000 were "disappeared," including children. A number of children were born in captivity, and "adopted" by military families. Estimates of these children number 400–500, many the result of rape. Most mothers stopped marching in 2006, as political conditions improved, and amnesty for offenders was revoked. Some continue to march today

Writing about the mothers, Elshtain (1996, 140) says that authoritarian regimes, especially those built on terror, always attempt to silence the "horizontal voice," the right to address others in similar situations. Not necessarily those whose children have been abducted, but others who lived in constant fear of persecution. I believe that the "horizontal voice" is the only true voice of public mourning. Any other voice, a vertical voice from above, will use the loss of life, whether at its own hands or an external enemy, to legitimate itself, its policies, its right to exist and rule.

Of all the things this chain of mothers accomplished, says Elshtain, the most important was to use the language of international human rights, "in its specifically liberal understanding," as a protection of the individual from the state (1996, 144). This is why the naming of the *desaparecidos* was so important.

Here mourning became political and it worked. The reason it worked is because the public mourning was performed by private citizens in resistance to government. Mourning was not co-opted by government and used as a call for mastery of events. Instead, it was performed by women stepping out of their traditional apolitical roles. And what did the mourners call for? Above all a list of the names of the disappeared, and the abolition of the category of

NN, no name, on grave markers. To name the disappeared is the first and most important political act.

The mothers of the Plaza de Mayo performed a political act; the children who made the murals commemorating the victims of 9/11 did not. But both involved creative symbolism. For the mothers it was the wearing a picture of the disappeared on a string or ribbon around their necks, their silence, and the regularity of their appearance every week wearing white shawls with the name and dates of the disappeared embroidered on them.

Women, Families, and the Bureaucratic State

In an article published over a decade earlier, "Antigone's Daughters," Elshtain (1982) writes not about the mothers of the Plaza de Mayo, but about American feminists. Using Antigone's resistance to Creon's refusal to bury her brother, Elshtain argues that little will be gained if women's struggle results in their right to join men in Max Weber's (1958) iron cage of rationalization, sharing the icy polar night he found there. For women to enter men's world on men's term is to abandon an identity built on the concrete, the particular, and the body, as opposed to the abstract individualism of men (1982, 51). For Antigone, the primordial morality of family precedes and overrides the values of the state (53). The true daughters of Antigone "continue to locate themselves in the arena of the social world where human life is nurtured and protected," and where death is still an occasion for reverence (56).

> For contemporary Americans, "private" conjures up images of narrow exclusivity. The world of Antigone is, however, a *social* location that speaks of, and to, identities that are unique to a particular family, on the one hand; but on another level, it taps a deeply buried human identity for we are first and foremost not political or economic man, but family men and women. (Elshtain 1982, 56)

Not politics and economics, but psychoanalysis, is the proper study of how boys and girls, men and women, come to terms with family, including its extended presence in our lives long after we leave home and start families of our own. We never outgrow our families, we never think in strictly economic or political terms. Our primordial categories are the ones we employ to comes to terms with family life, the paranoid schizoid and the depressive positions. The first reflects our rage at and fear of those who care for us. The second reflects our remorse and hope. These categories may be applied to public life, but they originate in private, and are best expressed in the social realm, as Antigone does.

The expropriation of mourning by the state is almost always enacted from the paranoid-schizoid position, in which grief is expressed as revenge. By

September 21, 2001, less than three weeks after the attack, President Bush (2001) said we have finished grieving, and it was time for resolute action to take the place of grief. Less eloquent than Pericles, Bush's argument was much the same as the Athenian's funeral oration. Pericles praises the dead, and even more Athens. The funeral oration is not about grieving the dead but celebrating the greatness of Athens. Pericles closes by reminding women who are young enough that they have a duty to bear more children, the better to repopulate the state and its army of all male citizens (Thucydides, 2.44).

WHAT ARE WE TO DO?

Calling attention to the lies of politicians, who would make the waste of life a heroic virtue, is the most important thing individuals can do. Leaders almost inevitably seek to turn grief and mourning into a justification of mastery. They should be called out.

Creative acts of mourning, even on a small scale, are also worthwhile. Sharing loss with others, while preventing its co-optation by local politicians, is important. How to mourn while leaving room for protest is also important. Black Lives Matter is interesting in this regard. More about anger than mourning, it represents a new form of protest, one less centralized, based less on the church and charismatic leaders, and more on local groups (Harris 2015). This may be the future of protest. Whether it will leave room for mourning remains to be seen. Perhaps the best it can do is to call out the willingness of "the authorities" to waste black lives. If that's as close to mourning as it gets, then at least it is a beginning, for it tells the truth.

NOTE

1. Arendt is often seen as disparaging the social. She does not. She criticizes its colonization of the public and private. Within its place, the social is necessary and valuable. See *The Attack of the Blob: Hannah Arendt's Concept of the Social*, by Hanna Pitkin (1998).

REFERENCES

Aeschylus. 1953. Agamemnon. In *Oresteia*. Translated by Richmond Lattimore. Chicago: University of Chicago Press.

Berberian, Marygrace. 2003. Communal Rebuilding After Destruction: The World Trade Center Children's Mural Project. *Psychoanalytic Social Work* 10: 27–41.

Bush, George. 2001. A Nation Challenged: President Bush's Address on Terrorism Before a Joint Meeting of Congress. *New York Times*, September 21, B:4.

Butler, Judith. 1997. *The Psychic Life of Power*. Stanford, CA: Stanford University Press.

———. 2004. *Precarious Life: The Powers of Mourning and Violence*. New York: Verso.

De La Rey, Cheryl, and Ingrid Owens. 1998. Perceptions of Psychosocial Healing and the Truth and Reconciliation Commission in South Africa. *Peace and Conflict: Journal of Peace Psychology* 4: 257–270.

Elshtain, Jean Bethke. 1982. Antigone's Daughters, *Democracy* 2 (2): 46–59.

———. 1996. The Mothers of the Disappeared: An Encounter with Antigone's Daughters. In *Finding a New Feminism*, edited by Pamela Grande Jensen, 129–148. Lanham, MD: Rowman & Littlefield.

Epstein, Robert, and Jeffrey Friedman. 2004. *Common Threads: Stories from the Quilt.* New York: New Yorker Video.

Freeden, Michael. 2011. The Politics of Ceremony: The Wootton Bassett Phenomenon. *Journal of Political Ideologies* 16 (1): 1–10.

Freud, Sigmund. 1917. *Mourning and Melancholia.* The Standard Edition of the Complete Psychological Works of Sigmund Freud, edited by James Strachey, 14: 237–258. London: Hogarth Press, 1956–1974 (24 volumes).

———. 1923. *The Ego and the Id.* The Standard Edition of the Complete Psychological Works of Sigmund Freud, 19: 3–86.

———. 1930. *Civilization and its Discontents.* The Standard Edition of the Complete Psychological Works of Sigmund Freud, 21: 59–148.

Harris, Frederick C. 2015. The Next Civil Rights Movement? *Dissent* (Summer). https://www.dissentmagazine.org/article/black-lives-matter-new-civil-rights-movement-fredrick-harris.

Hawkins, Peter S. 1993. Naming Names: The Art of Memory and the NAMES Project AIDS Quilt. *Critical Inquiry* 19: 752–779.

Hayner, Priscilla. 2001. *Unspeakable Truths: Confronting State Terror and Atrocity.* New York: Routledge.

Honig, Bonnie. 2009. Antigone's Laments, Creon's Grief: Mourning, Membership, and the Politics of Exception. *Political Theory* 37 (1): 3–43.

Klein, Melanie. 1964. *Love, Hate and Reparation*, edited by Klein and Joan Riviere. New York: W. W. Norton.

———. 1975a. Love, Guilt and Reparation. In *Love, Guilt and Reparation and Other Works, 1921–1945*, 306–343. New York: The Free Press. [original 1937]

———. 1975b. Notes on Some Schizoid Mechanisms. In *Envy and Gratitude and Other Works, 1946–1963*, 1–24. New York: The Free Press. [original 1946]

———. 1975c. Mourning and its Relation to Manic-Depressive States. In *Love, Guilt and Reparation and Other Works, 1921–1945*, 344–369. New York: The Free Press. [original 1940]

Mohr, Richard D. 1992. *Gay Ideas: Outing and Other Controversies.* Boston: Beacon Press.

Pitkin, Hanna Fenichel. 1998. *The Attack of the Blob: Hannah Arendt's Concept of the Social.* Chicago: University of Chicago Press.

Quinodoz, Jean-Michel. 2008. *Listening to Hanna Segal.* Translated by D. Alcorn. London: Routledge.

Segal, Hanna. 1952. A Psycho-Analytical Approach to Aesthetics. *International Journal of Psycho-Analysis* 33: 196–207.

———. 1997. From Hiroshima to the Gulf War and After: Socio-Political Expressions of Ambivalence. In *Psychoanalysis, Literature and War*, 157–168. London: Routledge.

Sophocles. 2005. *Antigone.* Translated by J. E. Thomas. Clayton, DE: Prestwick House.

Sturken, Marita. 1997. *Tangled Memories: The Vietnam War, the AIDS Epidemic, and the Politics of Remembering.* Berkeley: University of California Press.

Thucydides. 1954. *History of the Peloponnesian War.* Translated by Rex Warner. New York: Penguin.

Weber, Max. 1958. *The Protestant Ethic and the Spirit of Capitalism.* Translated by Talcott Parsons. New York: Charles Scribner's Sons, 1958.

White, Stephen. 2009. *The Ethos of a Late-Modern Citizen.* Cambridge, Harvard University Press.

Yep, Gust A. 2007. The Politics of Loss and its Remains. In *Common Threads: Stories from the Quilt. Rhetoric and Public Affairs* 10 (4): 681–699.

Chapter Two

Must We Always Mourn?
A War on Terror Veterans Memorial

Steven Johnston

The Mall in Washington, D.C., so the story goes, is unduly crowded.[1] Its western edge has experienced a veritable explosion of memorial building in the last thirty-five to forty years: the Vietnam Veterans Memorial in 1982; the Memorial to the 56 Signers of the Declaration of Independence in 1984; the Vietnam Women's Memorial in 1993; the Korean War Veterans Memorial in 1995; the Franklin Delano Roosevelt Memorial in 1997; the World War II Memorial in 2004; the Martin Luther King Memorial in 2011. The Washington Monument and Lincoln Memorial still dominate the landscape, but they no longer lack for commemorative company. As a result, proposals for new architecture in the monumental core are likely to encounter considerable skepticism and resistance. Despite—perhaps because of—this flurry of memorial construction marking major events and saluting prominent figures of the twentieth century, the Mall does not manifest an intelligible aesthetic sensibility or style. It betrays no singular purpose or intent. Rather, the most sacred symbolic ground in the country seems a rather confused—and confusing—place. To acknowledge, to celebrate, to honor, to salute, to idolize—these are the elementary civic ambitions at work on the Mall. This kind of accommodation to reflexive patriotism, however, cannot handle the Mall's complex subject matters. Given that most of its public architecture is dedicated to commemorating war, death, and violent loss, especially but not exclusively on a mass scale, American democracy, it might be said, does not know what or how to mourn, let alone how to do it well.

Nevertheless, Jan Scruggs, the driving force behind the Vietnam Veterans Memorial, issued a call for a national War on Terror Veterans Memorial on November 11 (Veterans Day), 2016, fifteen years and two months after the

13

September 11 attacks. His proposal could be considered an instance of what Bonnie Honig considers "part of the necessary ongoing work of democratic citizenship: to join together to build public things, maintain them, and (re)secure them as the truly *public* things . . . of democratic life" (2017, 11). Unlike the Vietnam Veterans Memorial wall designed by Maya Lin, which focuses on soldiers alone, Scruggs's memorial would commemorate *both* the war for which it was named and the veterans who fought in it. Scruggs's naming suggests, if inadvertently, that the War on Terror does not involve the terrible ambiguity that characterized the Vietnam War. The War on Terror entails its own dilemmas and difficulties, of course, but they have not ruptured the nation as did Vietnam. For one thing, this particular war, we are to believe, was forced on America, which sees itself as an innocent victim in a worldwide Manichaean struggle of good versus evil (whatever it was in Vietnam, the country was not an innocent victim). This difference alone improves the prospects that the memorial Scruggs (as well as the Global War on Terror Memorial Foundation) recommends might actually materialize.

Scruggs imagines the memorial as a site of "mourning, remembrance and healing," laudable goals that do more than honor the dead. War's casualties do not stop when the conflict comes to an end. They continue to mount. Quietly. Invisibly. Societies must find ways to deal with the multiple traumas that war produces. The erection of public monuments and memorials is one method by which societies try to negotiate them, which may involve denial and deflection as well as engagement, as Paul Fussell has argued (1975). How else can a polity face war's unrivaled horror? The monstrous and abominable must be converted into something noble and heroic. Memory always involves necessary forgetting. Focus on the service of those who fight wars. Honor the sacrifice, ignore the reasons behind it or the form it took. This approach can make a memorial a site of healing, as Scruggs argues the Vietnam Veterans Memorial wall has been for not just those who fought (in) the war but also for American democracy.[2]

Scruggs's military-centric project might not seem as urgent as (some) other demands for national recognition of death and loss. The Black Lives Matter social justice movement has been driven by the murders of young black men (Trayvon Martin, Michael Brown, Eric Garner, and Tamir Rice, to name just four) at the hands of police and their acolytes. Its activism, at its best, awakens the country to the structural racial violence that bedevils American democracy.[3] This critical awakening, it seems to me, might also enhance the visibility of other forms and targets of routine violence. Besides blacks (and people of color generally), who else might be systematically endangered because of their precarious position in America's social and political order of things? Scruggs, however unwittingly, identifies another at-risk category of young people that ordinarily eludes, even defies, categorization as victims of state violence. In fact, those in it would most likely reject the very idea that they could be victims of any kind, for they help constitute the warrior class in the United States. Yet American servicemen and women, the country's children, are routinely put in harm's way and sacrificed, often illegally and for illegitimate purposes, by the state and nation.[4] This is not meant to equate the two groups or the violence from which they suffer, but violence may be more widespread in American life than even many of its sharpest critics appreciate. Scruggs's patriotic call for a new war memorial, then, constitutes an occasion to reinvent and reanimate American democracy's commemorative life, which tends to the unthinking and the celebratory, even and especially in its mourning practices (Stow, 2007; Johnston, 2015).

What, then, might it mean to create a memorial to the war on terror and its veterans? Scruggs complains that while the events and victims of September 11, 2001, have been memorialized in New York City, Arlington, Virginia, and western Pennsylvania, American soldiers serving their country in the War on Terror have been denied fitting recognition. What, in this context, does recognition entail? Does service in any war deserve recognition? America has suffered serious casualties in this war, but does death (and thus loss) alone merit public tribute? If democracy stands for the repudiation of violence and thus war, how might this inform a memorial design? Even if the United States is the aggrieved party in this conflict, what happens when the victim of injustice commits injustice in the course of what it claims is a defensive war? If America mourns through the memorialization process, what prevents this from becoming a narcissistic exercise in self-pity? How does the United States not constitute itself as an innocent victim, lending cultural support for acts of righteous vengeance? Since America salutes veterans for their willingness to serve to protect the nation's way of life, including freedom, how do the values of that way of life fit into memorial design? Arguably no memorial should be about just veterans since veterans do not serve themselves. As they would be the first to acknowledge, they serve us. Any memorial, accordingly, must be about more than just them.

Memorial Exemplarity

In *The New York Times* op-ed piece in which Scruggs delivered his call for a new memorial, he briefly recounted his life story. He served and was seriously wounded in Vietnam. This led him, ultimately, to advocate for a tribute that might make some sense of it—and not just to veterans. He writes, "In 1981, we were fortunate enough to have Maya Lin propose her moving, if controversial, wall. . . . I hope we will find the next Ms. Lin to design the [new] memorial" (2016). It might appear that Scruggs recites his biography to establish his credentials to speak authoritatively on the issue. After all, who better than a wounded warrior and Vietnam Veterans Memorial founder to advise the country on the possibility of a new memorial? Scruggs's rehearsal of his résumé, however, is more complicated. The invocation of Lin is a subtle move. Many memorials have been designed and built on the Mall since 1982 when the (first) Vietnam Memorial opened. Scruggs did not invoke Friedrich St. Florian, who designed the World War II Memorial. Nor did he reference Cooper-Lecky, the architectural firm that managed the Korean War Veterans Memorial. The former is a triumphal colossus that embodies and worships American power in an architectural style favored and perfected by Albert Speer and the Nazi state. The latter is a mawkish, self-pitying tableau in search of a reason for being. Each site functions, by default, as a place of (nominal) remembrance, but neither aspires to something greater, something worthy of democracy itself.[5] Thus neither shows democracy as self-reflective, pondering through architectural form the inevitable ambiguities—including loss—of what it marks and honors. This lack is problematic insofar as war raises the question of democracy's troubled relationship to violence.

This is not to say that the Vietnam Veterans Memorial wall is without flaws. It, too, contains its patriotic aspects, which is one reason the Memorial Plaque was added decades later to ensure that all who served and died in Vietnam as a result of their service were honored. Only those who were killed in conventional fashion on the battlefield are eligible to have their names inscribed on the wall. This Pentagon-imposed restriction angered families who lost loved ones who were effectively killed by their military service but did not die from combat wounds. If Agent Orange killed you, or you took your own life thanks to Post-Traumatic Stress Disorder (PTSD), your name is not allowed on the wall. This was not the memorial's only failing. While Maya Lin was not responsible for the idea of listing the names of the dead and missing, her design did not address the effect of the war on Vietnam or the Vietnamese people. It was an American-centric design. That the wall was carved into the earth and made of black granite may have suggested the extraordinary levels of violence the United States inflicted on a foreign country, but this feature also highlighted the formal absence of the principal victims of what is properly called the American War.

Nevertheless, the Vietnam Veterans Memorial wall, insofar as it is considered an architectural benchmark, sets very definite limits on the form a public structure might take. As critics and opponents of Lin's scheme noted when it was first proposed, it differs greatly from its revered neighbors. The Washington and Lincoln impress by virtue of their verticality. They command the terrain not just in their immediate vicinity but as far as the eye can see on the Mall. The Vietnam wall, on the other hand, was meant to be suddenly discovered, as if stumbled upon by accident. Rather than protruding toward the sky, it was folded into the earth. It does minimal violence to its surroundings, to the nature, as it were, that houses it. There is no celebration at this site. National pride is not its purpose. Expression of power is absent (which is one reason Frederick Hart's *The Three Soldiers* hovers next to the wall; it was the political price demanded by reactionaries that had to be paid for the wall to go forward).

Though incorporated into its surroundings, Lin's Vietnam Memorial also signals the violence of the war. It can be read as a scar, an open wound. Conservative critics have denounced it as a black gash of shame. In this, they are not wrong. It was and is a black gash of shame and that should be considered one of its greatest features. It points to a nation that is not afraid but actually possesses the strength and integrity to acknowledge, if abstractly, wrongs that it has committed. Carl Schurz, an anti-imperialist senator from Wisconsin, famously declared, "My country right or wrong." Most invocations of this classic patriotic sentiment leave out the remainder of what Schurz said: "If right, to be kept right; and if wrong, to be set right." The Vietnam Veterans Memorial wall enacts, if imperfectly, Schurz's corrective principle. For Schurz this is what makes America a great republic, namely, that it can acknowledge wrong and correct it. Maya Lin's wall does what it can to "set right" America through sublime public architecture. In its refusal to posture, to call attention to itself through grand protrusion, it also declines to celebrate war. Collective violence is always to be lamented. War may (or may not) be necessary, but it is always an evil. The awesome death and destruction it entails cannot be denied. Among other things, it rains terror down on the country's newest generation of citizens: the young always fight wars. Nations thereby sacrifice those for whom sacrifices should be made— their children. This is but one of war's irredeemable perversions.[6]

Maya Lin's wall lists 58,307 names.[7] As Scruggs remarks, the wall is "society's acknowledgement of their service," but insofar as the memorial mimics aspects of burial and interment, it also questions the reasons for these costly deaths. They died serving their country, but that's the most that can be said of their sacrifice. They did not die for anything transcendent. Scruggs's call for recognition of service members following the September 11, 2001, attacks does not address the question of the War on Terror's necessity or rightness. Is it possible another generation is dying for nothing? Note the passive voice Scruggs deploys to discuss its service: "Yet there is precious little that recognizes their sacrifice" (2016). Are they making a sacrifice? Or are they being sacrificed? Or both? Scruggs's formulation does not make it clear.

Scruggs admits that he has no idea what kind of design would be appropriate for his proposed memorial. "Picturing it is hard because the conflict is so complex. Is it one war, or many? How do you commemorate a war that was never declared, that is being fought on multiple fronts with multiple enemies, that has no clear end? It is a war unlike any we have ever seen, ranging from conventional battlefields to the streets of Paris and New York" (2016). If the Vietnam Veterans Memorial wall serves as a guide, however, it is possible to say what the memorial won't be or won't look like. Presumably it would not be a celebration, which means a certain kind of modesty is called for—unlike the supersized World War II Memorial or even the Korean War Veteran Memorial with its larger-than-life-sized soldiers. For one thing, the war is not over and there is always the possibility that the United States could lose it, as it did in Vietnam. In fact, there are those who would argue that the United States has already lost the war insofar as it has fatally compromised its fundamental constitutional values and commitments in the name of national security. For another thing, the way in which this war is being fought is problematic, as in Vietnam. The War on Terror may be synonymous with the attacks of September 11, 2001, and the mass loss of innocent life, but it has also become synonymous with Abu Ghraib and Guantanamo, and thus the systematic torture of defenseless human beings, many of whom had nothing to do with the planes or the subsequent wars. What's more, since the war has been conducted, in part, at a distance by military and intelligence officials tasked with eliminating the leadership of terrorist organizations, it has been a drone war. In retaliation for the mass murder of 3,000 people, the United States has become very much like the enemy it fights, killing untold innocent civilians as it strikes targets on its most wanted hit list, which includes American citizens. How does a memorial acknowledge this kind of complexity? Is it any wonder that Scruggs has no idea what the memorial might look like? If this is to be a place of mourning, how do we mourn for those we sacrificed to make ourselves feel safe? Invoking John Schaar, how do we mourn the loss of what may be the most precious thing of all, namely, the promises we Americans made (and make) to each other to live by a certain set of principles and commitments, not just for ourselves but for the world as well? Since we are not connected by blood ties or religion, our values bring and keep us together. If we lose them, especially if we destroy them ourselves, we have lost everything (Schaar, 1981).

To keep these promises and commitments alive, polities remember and pay tribute to those whose sacrifices made them possible. This becomes especially important after the founding generation has passed from the scene. They knew from firsthand experience what enabled republican self-rule and bore the scars and disabilities that reminded others. Later generations cannot see these living examples walk among them, which is one reason why the dead are brought to life. A polity cannot have too many ceremonies, rituals, and monuments and memorials that reanimate the great accomplishments and unforgettable deeds that brought it into being and facilitate its preservation. Thus Scruggs's suggestion for a War on Terror Veterans Memorial finds a secure home in and support from patriotic thought.

Scruggs may not be able to envision a memorial, but what does he want? He wants recognition. For whom? Of what? Rather than focus on the country as a whole as he did with Vietnam, for this war Scruggs focuses narrowly on the soldiers fighting it. While the *events* of September 11 have been recognized (and properly so), "America's troops have been left out" (2016). Scruggs thus speaks for them but to us. He reminds us of what he takes to be "our" obligations, so far unmet. He thus seeks to correct a social injustice. He wants three kinds of recognition: for service, sacrifice, and commitment. He wants those in uniform during the war to be honored for their tours of duty. He wants those who have suffered as a result of their service ("nearly 7,000 have died and 52,000 have been wounded in Afghanistan and Iraq alone, and the numbers continue to grow") to be honored for making what is routinely called the ultimate sacrifice (ibid.). He wants the patriotism of American soldiers recognized, for these "service members [are not] thrill seekers, out to find adventure" (ibid.). They are committed people who love their country and are ready to defend it when given the order.

What with the grave injustice done to the American military, Scruggs's op-ed, not surprisingly, barely conceals the ressentiment driving it. He splits the polity in two. There is a small segment of the citizenry that serves and sacrifices for the greater good at incalculable cost to themselves and their families, and there is the vast majority of the population that doesn't even notice, let alone appreciate, the heroic work being done on their behalf. "[T]he country, for all its talk about veterans, has largely ignored them. America is at the shopping mall while the Army is at war, it is said" (ibid.). It is not (just) said. Scruggs says it. He is giving voice, which he concedes in the very next paragraph, to a sentiment shared in the military, namely, that a divide exists between those who fight wars and those who remain safely on the sidelines. This division, moreover, tends to be noticed predominantly by those doing the fighting. Returning troops should be welcomed home with celebrations and honors, not effectively ignored. Insofar as the American people are indifferent and ungrateful, soldiers are not only spurned but humiliated. They believe themselves to be doing something good and virtuous. When this self-assessment is not confirmed by those whose judgment ultimately matters most, namely the people, how can soldiers feel anything other than foolish? They wonder: why do we bother to serve in the first place? What we do is not appreciated, let alone valued. The lack of even minimal reciprocity stings.

Scruggs, then, seeks to educate the American people as citizens. We do not understand our civic obligations when it comes to our fellow citizens who are also soldiers—soldiers who serve the country and us. They seek recognition and we must recognize them. According to Scruggs, we are in their debt. We owe them. Not only have we not paid this debt. Most of us are unaware of our indebtedness. There is some dim awareness, but this translates into "discounts at the mall" and "priority seating on planes." Scruggs says "these are nice," but he damns with faint praise (ibid.). More importantly, Scruggs's call to establish a national memorial is not an opportunity for the country to pay its debt, as he would have us believe. It's the occasion for Scruggs to impose a debt on the American people. He cannot admit this, of course, for debts cannot ordinarily be unilaterally imposed by one party in a relationship. Nor can it be said that we automatically incur debt when others are ordered to fight (allegedly on our behalf). That he has to resort to debt imposition, however, no doubt reflects and exacerbates the ressentiment already in play.

Scruggs's call also offers insight into the nature of mourning at public memorials devoted to wars. There is grieving of loss. There is also giving vent to grievance—not just about the lack of recognition for suffering and loss, but also about the nature of the suffering and its impotence. It doesn't move people, except perhaps in the abstract. Scruggs begins his call by telling us that fifteen years ago he "heard the explosion and saw smoke billowing from the Pentagon. This was the beginning of a war, I thought. Maybe most of us did. It was, and after all this time, after thousands of service members have been killed and tens of thousands wounded, there is still no end in sight" (ibid.). But Scruggs does not know what kind of war it is or whether it is even one war. "The conflict is so complex." This prevents Scruggs from reducing the war to George Bush's melodramatic terms of good and evil (Anker, 2014). It also means that the two sources of resentment this war elicits sustain each other. Scruggs's account presumes that the human condition denies any transcendental purpose or meaning to the death and suffering that the soldiers experience. The complexity of the war they fight reveals this hard truth. This kind of revelation leads to existential resentment. Scruggs's account also understands that the structure of the American political system means that the death and suffering borne by soldiers accrues to the benefit of others without requiring a similar burden from them. The Pentagon in particular prefers this arrangement. It opposes nothing as much as a draft, which would equalize civic obligations. This one-way relationship doubles the resentment (Connolly, 1993, 171).

Yet Scruggs knows that he can't claim that the military is being exploited simply because the burdens of national security are carried by a few while its benefits are universally distributed. After all, military service is voluntary. No one is compelled to perform it. What's more, those serving are compensated for their efforts. It's a contractual relationship. Those who serve know the terms of employment when they sign up—and still they sign, and sign again.

Ironically, for all the power the military channels on the battlefield, Scruggs effectively enfeebles it in domestic cultural politics. The American citizenry fail to care sufficiently for and about its soldiers at home, which can lead to problems both foreseen and unforeseen. As Nietzsche reminds us, the impotent have been some of the greatest haters in the world (1956, 167). Rather than leave veterans no other option than to turn their rage and resentment inward, which could easily lead to depression, addiction, or suicide, Scruggs would give them a public memorial. At the same time, if the Vietnam Veterans Memorial is the example, a democratic or agonistic politics would be disallowed at the new site. Only patriotic politics will be permitted—in the name of unity. The War on Terror has not been politically disruptive and destabilizing, but even if it were it would be a mistake to forbid contestation on its grounds. It is not enough for visitors, especially citizens, to file by in quiet, respectful fashion at public memorials. Traditional mourning practices, that is, annual ceremonies and rituals honoring the dead for killing and dying for their country, already fix a conservative meaning on such sites by reducing them to a lowest common denominator—mere service.

Scruggs, accordingly, moves swiftly to a new theme, thereby doubling down on the ressentiment. Not only are those in uniform not appreciated, they are subjected to stereotypes that do them a great disservice. Having referenced the dead, wounded, disfigured, and disabled, Scruggs slanders the American people. Scruggs imagines that "we imagine [veterans] all as broken and battered. As with the Vietnam veteran, there is no proto-typical post-9/11 veteran. Most are doing well in civilian life. . . . Other stereotypes circulate: Especially today, when serving in the military is a choice, many civilians see service members as thrill seekers, out to find adventure" (2016). This means that the memorial, in some alchemical magic, serves a new purpose: it "would do much to counter these sorts of misguided impressions, and remind Americans—now and in the future—that all veterans, whatever their health and financial situation, deserve profound respect" (ibid.). The last part of the sentence brings us back to the demand for recognition (in the form of respect), but Scruggs's injunction raises a new question.

Do *all* veterans deserve profound respect (or any respect)? The war on terror has taken many ugly turns. Do the enlisted men and women who tortured prisoners at Abu Ghraib deserve respect? What about their superior officers? What about the soldiers on the battlefield? Did they all conduct themselves honorably? Does the Iraq conquest not have any William Calleys? One of the many reasons the United States should not engage in foreign occupation and nation-building through war is that waging the war inevitably puts soldiers in a position where they will kill innocent people. The conduct of war itself makes this inevitable, as Scruggs knows from his Vietnam experience, where My Lai was not the exception but more the rule. Do the soldiers who slaughtered civilians, even in self-defense, deserve profound respect? That the question can be asked suggests, pace Scruggs, that "the need for such a site is" not "obvious" (ibid.). Narrowing the focus, does not building a memorial to all veterans do a disservice to those who did serve honorably? Does not respecting all veterans unjustly equate and homogenize them?

Moreover, Scruggs includes veterans in both the Afghanistan and Iraq conflicts (among other engagements) as worthy of memorialization. These two military operations cannot be collapsed. In Afghanistan, the United States claimed to be protecting itself in the aftermath of the September 11, 2001, attacks when the Taliban government protected those responsible for it. In Iraq, the Bush administration knowingly used the fictional threat of weapons of mass destruction to illegally invade another sovereign nation. The one was arguably a necessary act of self-defense; the other was an imperial undertaking that violated the foundations of international law. The one was arguably legitimate; the other was downright criminal. Citizens answering the call to defend their country when it's under attack is admirable. Citizens willingly implicated in the invasion of another country under false pretenses is deplorable. This is not defending your country. It is placing it in even greater danger. Accordingly, what about those (thousands of) veterans who refused to serve in Iraq, many of whom deserted? Their refusal to fight an illegal war can be considered a republican act of resistance, a patriotic act. Why shouldn't they be saluted for defending our way of life (at great risk and cost to themselves)? (Ehrenreich, 2008).

Scruggs's insistence on respect raises an even larger question which touches on the very rationale of a memorial. Do any veterans deserve respect? If so, what is the argument for it? The United States employs a mercenary military force. It consists of guns for hire, and when this official force isn't sufficient for an assigned task, the state turns to private contractors (often ex-military) as a supplement. These adventurers dress in civilian clothes, but absent a state-issued uniform, what is the difference between the two forces, morally speaking? Consider what these forces do. They made it possible for the United States to conduct the illegal, immoral war (Iraq) Scruggs would recognize in the first place. Is this not an example of the danger of standing armies (paid, voluntary professional forces) rather than citizen militias? Did not the mercenary nature of the American military, at least in part, make possible a war that should not have been initiated and thus should not need memorialization? Aren't soldiers to blame, in some sense, for their own (gratuitous) deaths?

A Memorial Proposal

For public memorials to contribute to a democracy, they need to do more than exist as sites of normalization. To mention one possibility, developed below, they could incorporate the spirit of the black funeral tradition in which it is not enough to lament the dead and mark their passing. A challenge must be issued to the living. Can they carry on the legacy (or correct it, if need be) of the deceased? (Stow, 2010).[8] They could also embrace the ethos of the counter-monument tradition, in which the very reason for being of a memorial is both affirmed and questioned-cum-subverted in its architectural design (Young, 1993).[9]

Scruggs's admission that he has no idea what his proposed memorial might look like is understandable. For one thing, as mentioned above, the war on terror is a multi-front conflict with no end in sight. For another, what successes, if any, can these wars claim? Is the United States (and the West) any safer today than it was before September 11, 2001? Or have the dangers merely been displaced? What social and political price has been paid to wage these wars? What's more, the kind of service veterans have provided differs according to their specific branch and assignment: which war, which country, which mission? Are frontline soldiers and military interrogators nowhere near a battlefield to be treated identically? What about drone stick operators? They kill for country, but they risk nothing. They cannot die in action. What about those convicted of crimes? What about private military contractors? Are they to be considered veterans? The wars would be impossible without them.

Regardless, Scruggs would no doubt insist that soldiers serve not themselves but their country. Americans are told that the war on terror is not just about security and freedom but a way of life, which is rooted in the Constitution. Here things get commemoratively tricky. The Constitution in whose name soldiers fight—and often die—has not fared well since September 11, 2001. The very real danger is that the United States is destroying the way of life it is determined to defend in the course of protecting it, thereby implicating the soldiers Scruggs is determined to honor. Many who express this kind of concern argue that self-destruction is the real goal of the terrorists, who know that the United States cannot be defeated in battle or through periodic attacks. As it happens they share Abraham Lincoln's belief that if the United States is ever destroyed it can only happen by its own hands. What, then, might a memorial to the war on terror look like, especially if the terrorists have already enjoyed notable success in their ambition to provoke the United States into self-annihilation? Why not devote memorial efforts to that which is foundational, the Constitution, rather than merely instrumental, the military?

Imagine a reproduction of the Constitution consisting of the four original pages plus a fifth page for the first ten amendments. Each is roughly ten feet tall and three feet wide and would be composed of a resilient but flexible material to withstand and bend to various weather conditions.[10] The material would be colored to resemble the original parchment on which the documents were written. Take these documents and "tear" them to shreds. The shredded documents would then be tossed, so to speak, in the air in an area covering roughly 300 square feet and "reconnected" through invisible wire with noticeable gaps in the reconnections.[11] Not all of the scattered pieces would be adjacent to their original textual neighbors. The document as a whole must lose its organizational scheme. Some sections of the Constitution would be kept relatively intact—such as Article II, Section 2, on the president's power as commander-in-chief. Other sections of the document, such as the first, fourth, fifth, and sixth amendments of the Bill of Rights, would be torn a second or third time to correspond to the ways in which life, liberty and due process have been denigrated. These fragments might be splattered with red to indicate the sacrifices borne on their behalf and the victims killed in their name.

It would be inapt if the American Constitution were the sole focus of the memorial. Inclusion of fragments from the United Nations Charter, including Chapter 1, Article 2, which establishes "the sovereign equality" of states and prohibits "the threat or use of force against the territorial integrity or political independence of any state," and the United Nations Convention against Torture, which prohibits torture under any and all circumstances, would reflect both the damage done to American values (the rule of law and respect for human rights) and the international dimensions of political violence, including state violence. Terrorism is not just an American concern or problem, and the United States is not a party with clean hands. It is fully implicated in conduct and practices it abhors and officially disavows—and has been for a long time. Insofar as the Mall conceives of itself as not just a national but an international space, it invites this broader approach to memorialization.

To place the memorial in historical and political context, mock reproductions of newspaper headlines would be circulated around the political shards, including proper nouns referencing the World Trade Center and Abu Ghraib, the Pentagon and Bagram Air Base, Shanksville, Pennsylvania and Guantanamo Bay, the U.N. Charter and Iraq. Visitors would confront a Constitution in pieces floating above them, circling about one another. The semi-chaotic arrangement suggests that while the Constitution (and the way of life it represents) has suffered tremendous harm, whether the damage is permanent remains an open question. In the aerial collage the Constitution is still identifiable. It perdures. The key questions are whether it can be reassembled or will it be blown further apart never to reconnect? The answers are as uncertain as the consequences of the wars being waged to guarantee it.

The temporal dimension of Scruggs's proposal distinguishes this memorial from each of its would-be neighbors on the Mall. The War on Terror Memorial would be contemporaneous with the war itself, thereby allowing for, even encouraging mourning (and/or something else) as an ongoing practice informed by multiple affects. Some people would visit the site to grieve for a lost loved one. Others might visit the site to pay their respects for those who served and lost their lives on behalf of the country. These would be quiet, respectful sojourns. Some might go to the memorial because the so-called war on terror constitutes a recurring affront to the democratic values of the country and they object to their fellow citizens being sacrificed for them and to the wrongs committed in their name. They would mourn for the country they see disappearing before their very eyes. [12]

In the last case a single visit might not suffice. It might occur to democratic citizens to establish a perpetual vigil at the site to call attention to what is happening—often invisibly. Vigils, in turn, can provide a foundation for additional actions—rallies, demonstrations, protests, and outcries. This kind of gathering, then, could foster a self-perpetuating critical presence that results in pressure or leverage on state authorities. [13] The memorial site in this third incarnation invites politics. It welcomes opposition, contestation, disruption, and struggle. It posits the vital nature of civic space, something the United States desperately needs.

Regardless of what one thinks of democratic peace theory, it can't be denied that America has been at war, at home and abroad, during most of its existence—including every year of the twenty-first century. The memorial could bring into the open what the American state prefers to keep from public scrutiny, namely, the pursuit of foreign, military and national security policies unhindered by constitutional limits to its power—or by an activist citizenry committed to those limits. A War on Terror Veterans Memorial, done right, could make American democracy's identity a question. The orchestration of war, which has been relegated to the margins of political life, in part because the military is divorced from the rest of the body politic, might receive the attention it warrants. If such a transformation took place (a long shot, to be sure), the state might find itself held accountable where it previously enjoyed license. Memorialization, then, might engender democratization. The point here is not to predict but to experiment. Why not make it a requirement of a memorial's design that it potentially possess this kind of capability? Why not make civic space robust rather than inert? Why not dispose citizens to engage a memorial rather than passively consume it? Why not encourage citizens to become political agents rather than spectators? Why not make mourning count for something other than itself?

To appreciate the potential of such a memorial, imagine the installation of Maya Lin's wall in the late 1960s or early 1970s with the Vietnam War at its apex. The Pentagon (already) had a serious public relations problem given the media attention devoted to the daily repatriation of soldiers in body bags. With the wall it would have found itself compelled to inscribe new names on it on an almost daily basis—not just in front of family and loved ones, not just in front of angry citizens, but in front of the nation and the world. The possibility of confrontation, not just contestation, would be folded into this solemn ritual. No doubt staunch war supporters would also attend. As for organized anti-war activity, Lin's overall design, with the open green space fronting it, would have offered a dramatic setting for activism, especially by groups such as Vietnam Veterans Against the War. The black granite backdrop possesses the aesthetic gravity to enhance severalfold their already considerable moral, political, and patriotic authority to address the war. These vets escaped immortality on the wall, but thousands of their friends and comrades were not so lucky. It would be virtually impossible to ignore or silence these veteran survivors. The national media would be present to record every minute of it. This too would play out in American living rooms. The daily recording of death demands justification. Some might argue that this kind of politicization does a disservice to those killed for the country. Does it? Not necessarily.

The Black Funeral Tradition

In American political life, memorials and politics ordinarily do not mix.[14] National monumental architecture is supposed to bring people together in shared identity and common purpose. The division, rancor, and conflict that attend political struggle have no place in it. Politics can take a rest when it comes to public memorials—to honor those who have sacrificed for the greater good. As the signposts at (some of) the entry points to the Mall in Washington, D.C., announce: this is where "America and the world come to reflect, honor, and celebrate." They do not come to argue, debate, and dispute.

The same kind of (ostensibly) respectful stance is generally taken toward funerals. Long-standing rules of decorum regulate what can and cannot be said (and done) at these solemn rituals for the dead. The tumult that accompanies political expression is considered impermissible. As Simon Stow argues, the traditional approach, however widespread and whatever its merits, betrays a basic ignorance of the black funeral tradition (2010, 681, 689). This tradition can serve as a model for the kind of politics that can and must be a part of public war memorialization in America (or in any democracy for that matter).

Stow's compelling analysis of Coretta Scott King's 2006 memorial service in Georgia demonstrates the funeral's potential democratic productivity. Mrs. King was not only Martin Luther King's widow. She was a civil rights champion herself. Just four days after his murder, she protested with striking Memphis sanitation workers as they marched and demonstrated. Stow writes: "it was . . . only fitting . . . that her funeral service was very much in the civil rights tradition: part celebration, part jeremiad" (ibid., 690). A star-studded capacity crowd of 15,000 participated in the event at a Baptist mega-church, including various civil rights stalwarts, the current president, every former president except Gerald Ford, and various elected national officials.

Reverend Joseph Lowery stole the show, so to speak, and proved that funerals can contain moments of joy and laugher—even at their most serious. While gratified by the occasion and the many kind words offered in praise of Mrs. King, Lowery insisted these were not enough. He wanted more. She "was an advocate for peace and a warrior for justice," which is why people were there to honor and celebrate her life. Principally, he demanded to know if concrete actions would follow and match the noble words spoken. Lowery noted Mrs. King's concerns about the policies and priorities of the current U.S. government. George W. Bush had billions for war, but what about the poor? He noted the "lack of weapons of mass destruction over there," and cited the "weapons of misdirection right down here" (ibid., 690).

Not surprisingly, Lowery's pointed remarks drew not only considerable media attention but extensive criticism that crossed political and racial lines. It was said he did not conduct himself appropriately given the circumstances—especially toward President Bush. In response Lowery was not only unyielding but doubled down on his ethic. His critics lacked both the authority and the experience (which he possessed in abundance) to tell him how to conduct a black funeral, and if George W. Bush couldn't handle this kind of civic challenge, he should have stayed at home (ibid., 691). Lowery's attempt to recover and revive the black funeral tradition demonstrated the potential it carries within it to reanimate American democratic practices. The fact that it generated such controversy in its aftermath provided additional proof. It meant that the discussion of Mrs. King's legacy that started at her funeral would continue, even if it was mixed in with the Lowery controversy, long after it was over. Her life was creative and constructive. Her death was, too.

Still, a funeral followed by a burial is, generally speaking, a one-shot affair. While anniversaries of deaths are often marked, they do not tend to involve new commemorative activities. With memorials, however, recurrent acknowledgment is more of a built-in possibility. In addition to the inaugural rites that accompany a monument's unveiling, annual ceremonies can also be conducted at the site to keep it visible and vibrant. It's not just that orators at such yearly occasions will offer differing accounts of a memorial's meaning and purpose (which would provide one source of tension). A memorial's meaning and purpose undergo communicative change as the world around it mutates. Thus a memorial that is designed to celebrate the manly virtues of war in one era might come to reflect anti-war sentiments in a later age. [15] Not only is nothing necessarily fixed when it comes to memorials. Nothing can or should be fixed, especially if it's set in stone. Still, there is no reason to leave this to historical accident. Ambiguity can be folded into monumental design, both in the work of art itself and in the space surrounding it, which means the two combined can serve as an arena for interpretive exploration and contestation. Rather than express a lowest common denominator around which people can unite despite their differences, monuments and memorials in a democracy can aspire to something more, namely, an artistic and political vision that enables and encourages a polity to recognize singular figures and phenomena but also to consider and reconsider itself in the wake of discrete events and happenings (a war, the death of a leader, a traumatic incident, etc.). Celebration is not enough. Mourning is not enough. Critique is not enough. Reverend Lowery demonstrated that all three can be combined. And more. As Stow notes, "offering a eulogy in ragged verse," and assuming, at times, "a semicomic persona," Lowery turned the august funeral intermittently joyous, too. It need not be a strictly solemn affair where people do nothing but grieve. They can also take great pleasure in the life and life's work of a beloved and respected leader and deploy them in a bit of critical mischief. One can leave a funeral heartbroken. One can also leave it energized.

A New Memorial

Scruggs's admiration for Maya Lin's Vietnam design allows us to consider the difficulties and complexities attending recognition. If the new memorial he proposes is to be a democratically meaningful site of remembrance and mourning, it must involve more than an appreciation of and respect for loss. The Vietnam wall is famous as a site that induces multiple forms of reflection in its visitors. It also triggers profound emotions. The War on Terror Veterans Memorial, insofar as Lin is the guide, would have to induce visitors to reflect on the nature of the war being remembered—not just how it (allegedly) started, but how it has been conducted. Though many believe it is a war that must be fought (or at least a struggle that must be contested), what kind of price has it exacted (to date)? Is the war worth the price being paid for it? Can any war be worth the price incurred? How might a memorial design facilitate this line of critical thinking and affect? In Scruggs's hope for the next Maya Lin, there is also lodged a call for a memorial that will not just recognize and remember but disturb and disrupt.

Scruggs's ressentiment on behalf of the latest generation of American warriors is also expressed in his demand for equal memorial treatment: "there is precious little that recognizes their sacrifice. Discounts at the mall, priority seating on planes—these are nice, but they hardly amount to the sort of commemoration we have bestowed on veterans of previous wars. What we need is a national memorial" (2016). Scruggs's assessment is right, of course, but he also misleads. The Mall's western end had remained relatively unchanged for decades before the Vietnam Veterans Memorial arrived in 1982. The Washington, Lincoln, and Jefferson had the wide open green spaces pretty much to themselves. It was the extraordinary success of Maya Lin's wall that led to the development of subsequent memorials—not only the Korean and World War II structures but also three more Vietnam memorials. The World War II generation, for one, preferred that if any kind of tribute were to be offered, it take the form of living memorials: schools, hospitals, parks, gardens, stadiums. These vets did not necessarily want a national memorial until they were told they *also* deserved and therefore should want one. In short, if Vietnam was recognized not just on the Mall but also located in such close proximity to Lincoln, then America's other twentieth-century wars had to be officially recognized, especially World War II. Vietnam needed to be put in its (proper) place.

This abridged memorial genealogy reminds us that collective rituals of mourning, remembrance, and healing are political practices. They do not somehow flow naturally from the rhythms of history. They are the product of desires expressed and decisions made in social and political life. They are artifices. The lack of memorials to World War II and Korea on the Mall was not a problem sufficient to result in remedial action until the Vietnam generation acquired its own commemorative site. The Korean, as a result, is more a response to and rebuke of the Vietnam Veterans Memorial wall than it is a tribute to those who fought in the war.[16] In fact, the Korean Memorial's trite and silly maxim, "freedom is not free," points directly across the Lincoln reflecting pool at Maya Lin's panels, which some conservative critics dubbed "the wailing wall" given the outpouring of emotion the site generates in visitors, especially veterans and their families.

What, then, does it mean to mourn at such a site? Is it the sheer fact of lost life coupled with the crippling casualties of survivors? This seems unlikely since the consequences of service cannot help but foster reflection on the reasons for that service. If citizens sacrifice, they sacrifice for something, not just because they were ordered to do so. There has to be a reason, but if that reason loses its legitimacy, mourning can take on different aspects. It can morph into bemoaning. And then the distance between discontent and dissent (and more) is short. Regarding Vietnam, the soldiers who fought and died there, who suffered permanent injury there, did not sacrifice for American national security or freedom—despite what they were told or assumed. Neither was at stake. The war was a gratuitous exercise in imperial violence that did little more than consume those caught up in it. American soldiers died for a lie. They died, that is, for nothing. It is one thing for a country to recognize and honor the cost that some pay for the rest to flourish. It is another thing for a country to recognize that it sent its young people into battle—to kill and be killed—for no legitimate purpose whatsoever. The design of the Vietnam Veterans Memorial wall allows, perhaps encourages, this kind of accounting. The black granite gives it a funereal look and feel that, say, the Field of Stars, which salutes Second World War dead at the World War II Memorial, lacks. The Vietnam Veterans Memorial wall calls the war (and thus itself) into question. This suggests a kind of mourning that understands the permanency of some wounds, and that full healing may not be possible, even desirable, especially if it contributes (in even a minor way) to a dangerous kind of forgetting—in the case of Vietnam that the war should not have been fought and that atonement (to the Vietnamese in particular) is virtually impossible (which is not to say that restitution efforts should not be made). The ambition is not to induce a paralyzing melancholia, but to foster a kind of modesty (especially about the exercise of power) tinged with sobriety given the harm and loss that the conduct of politics entails. To remember this war in a politically productive way is to keep the pain of it alive, to "affirm" its gratuity. The Vietnam Veterans Memorial wall's ambiguity enables this kind of affectivity. It raises questions that refuse answers. It levels accusations that defy response. It threatens to make mourning, ideally a transient process, permanent.

For a democracy that is also imperial, this could prove invaluable. The Vietnam Veterans Memorial wall could serve as a mournful warning to American democracy about international adventurism and malfeasance and its potential to backfire and destroy a republican way of life. This would also make it dangerous—to those who cannot face such hard truths. Vietnam War commemoration also attracts reactionary elements in America, from conservatives who want to keep fighting the war through other means until the United States somehow magically prevails to veterans and their supporters angry at (allegedly) being disrespected, scapegoated, and ignored during and after the war.[17] Both constituencies embody the will to punish hated enemies that had the effrontery not only to resist American political and military power but defeat them. This will to punish has also taken concrete memorial form. The ominous black and white POW/MIA flag flies over Frederick Hart's *The Three Soldiers*, keeping alive the specious claim that there are lingering injustices from the war for which the governments of Vietnam and the United States bear responsibility—the former for perpetrating them, the latter for doing little or nothing about them.

The flag is thoroughly piratical. In a white circle set against a black background, it features the bowed head of a prisoner, an armed guard in a watchtower with barbed wire hovering over him, and the mantra "you are not forgotten" underneath. The flag suggests that there are Americans still in Vietnam, whether held captive by the Vietnamese or whose remains have yet to be repatriated. The claim that American servicemen were left behind in Vietnamese prison camps has always been false, as was the insinuation that some of the unaccounted for might also be in captivity. The fact that not all American remains were located and returned is part and parcel of any war. It is arguable at best that it should be a foreign policy priority to locate, retrieve, and identify them (Franklin, 1993; Hawley, 2005). For decades, it kept the war alive and allowed the United States government to punish the Vietnamese for not providing sufficient assistance in this Holy Grail. But it did allow America to convert itself into a victim in a war in which it was the (foreign) aggressor and deflect attention from the barbaric character of the war it waged.

Insofar as the Vietnam complex is a site of mourning, it is a site of perpetual mourning with no end in sight. This, as the Greeks knew, can also be dangerous (Honig, 2013). It keeps ancient wounds fresh, feeds the will to revenge, and prevents the continuation or resumption of life. If it can't foster American modesty, as suggested above, perhaps the Vietnam Veterans Memorial has outlived its reason for being. After all, insofar as one of its purposes was to help prevent the United States from making the mistake of fighting illegitimate wars that the country was not prepared to support to their conclusion, thereby sparing the country not just political turmoil but pointless loss of life, it has failed (Scruggs and Swerdlow, 1985). For some this would not constitute a failure. Conservatives keep insisting that the so-called Vietnam Syndrome, that is, a reluctance to wield American firepower abroad for fear that it might go terribly awry, must be overcome. Scruggs's Vietnam memorial ambition may have been problematic from the get-go: "I began thinking about what the war had meant to us, as a country, and how to commemorate it" (2016). The Vietnam War did not mean any one thing to America. Its meanings would always be the subject of contestation, and any Vietnam memorial would inevitably become a participant in that contestation. This is why there are four Vietnam memorials, with a long-planned fifth (a museum) only recently canceled. This contested fate awaits any War on Terror Veterans Memorial. This is why it's best to invite memorial submissions that reflect the politics of this war from the start. The Vietnam Veterans Memorial Fund merely stumbled into it with Maya Lin's wall. That politics is banned from the Vietnam complex no doubt contributes to its limited effect. It has not enjoyed the kind of reinvention that the Lincoln Memorial has enjoyed thanks to the Civil Rights Movement.

A Confederate Rescue

Vietnam is not the only flashpoint for ressentiment in American politics. Recent controversy and disturbance in New Orleans over the removal of three monuments to Confederate leaders and one monument to white racial violence during Reconstruction offers a distinct opportunity to explore the national contest over symbolic political architecture in public space. From 1884 to 1915, a span of three decades, the city erected monuments to Robert E. Lee; renegades of the Crescent City White League; Jefferson Davis; and P. G. T. Beauregard. Lee commanded Southern forces during the Civil War; Crescent City white supremacists attacked and deposed biracial Republican city and state governments; Davis was president of the so-called Confederate States of America; Beauregard directed the first military action of the war of Southern aggression against the United States (Robertson, 2017).

For the South the Civil War may have formally concluded with Lee's surrender, but it never accepted defeat. It's not just that Southerners convinced themselves that the North had prevailed only because of superior manpower and firepower. It's that the South was prepared to wage war by other means to restore as much of the old order as possible. With the collapse of Reconstruction in 1877, this ambition became more than a manifestation of a loser's resentment at a world that rejected its parasitic way of life.[18] Restoration gave the ancient régime the chance to settle scores and celebrate itself—and its alleged heroes. Thus an arrogant, unrepentant perpetrator converted itself into a self-righteous victim determined (and entitled) to flaunt its superior virtues and put its opponents in their place through violence at once physical, political, and symbolic.

New Orleans's regressive tributes to white race warriors subvert and degrade everything the United States claims it values. Mayor Mitch Landrieu's initiative to remove them from public squares was long overdue. That the workers assigned the actual labor of removal had to outfit themselves "in flak jackets, helmets and scarves to conceal their identities because of concerns about their safety" as "police officers watched from a nearby hotel" is nothing less than a democratic embarrassment (Mele, 2017). The South's racial aristocracy was indefensible and those who fought on its behalf were traitors, as Lincoln, for one, understood about Lee. There is nothing noble about fighting for a putrid cause. The monuments that were purged were testaments to murder, domination, violence, terror, and death.

The removal of these monuments is not terribly interesting—except as a political and psychological phenomenon involving those who remain nostalgic for absolute white power and privilege and resentful about its irreversible loss. One interesting question New Orleans does raise is why polities, democracies in particular, insist on thinking of monuments and memorials as permanent markers in the civic symbolic landscape. Why aren't they decommissioned on a regular basis? In other words, why doesn't the United States regularly scrutinize all of its public architecture and reevaluate their contributions to democratic political culture? Why don't we dispense with the pretense of eternity that monuments and memorials, once built, automatically enjoy?

The South is not the only object of suspicion. If not for the dignified reserve of Maya Lin's wall coupled with the insipidness of Frederick Hart's *The Three Soldiers*, the Vietnam Veterans Memorial might have become a shrine for those who refused to accept American defeat in the war and aspired to compensate themselves with an imaginary revenge on their enemies. This angry disposition was evident not just in the early 1980s in the immediate aftermath of the war. It remains in circulation to this day, for a vocal minority continues to insist that the war was both necessary and winnable. This claim is not relegated to the margins of society where it is heard only by a handful of true believers. It routinely finds its way into mainstream political discourse, too, and fuels the familiar charge that students, "professors and intellectuals" possess "visceral contempt . . . not just for the war, but for its veterans" (Moyar, 2017).

The New York Times has been running a series entitled Vietnam '67. Mark Moyar's contribution of May 17, 2017, gives voice to American resentment over the war. He presents himself as a heroic thinker who challenges unwarranted and dangerous orthodoxies about the war—first and foremost that it did not need to be fought. Thus Moyar portrays Ho Chi Minh "as a doctrinaire Communist who, like his Soviet and Chinese allies, adhered to the Marxist-Leninist view that Communists of all nations should collaborate in spreading world revolution" (ibid.).[19] Ho was no mere nationalist but a critical part of a global conspiracy that would impose communism where it was not welcome, as in "South" Vietnam. American intervention, defeat notwithstanding, actually prevented the infamous dominoes from falling by giving other Southeast Asian states "time . . . to shore up their defenses." If not for military and political miscalculations and cowardice by successive administrations, the United States could have prevailed. Militarily, America should have invaded and occupied Laos to prevent munitions from flowing south. Politically, the Johnson Administration should have initiated a public relations campaign to explain the need for the war to the American public to maintain patriotic support for it, especially starting in 1967. The United States converted inevitable victory into gratuitous defeat. As a result, according to Moyar, the wrong lessons were learned from the war, and the country is still paying a price for it: "superficial historical understanding and excessive reliance on academic theorizing [are] yielding bad advice—advice that could get men and women killed, they could even lose wars"—in "Afghanistan, Iraq and other conflict zones" (ibid.).

This op-ed piece is worth noting because Moyar offers an American version of the notorious stab-in-the-back myth perfected by Hitler regarding Germany and World War I. For Moyar the difficulty with his thesis is not just that the Cold War ended decades ago with the collapse of the Soviet Union not long after American withdrawal from Vietnam, challenging the nature of the threat communism (supposedly) posed and rendering any would-be American victory moot. The difficulty is that American escalation of the war would have resulted not in less but more death and destruction, especially for Vietnam. How many more Vietnamese would have had to die to fulfill Moyar's redemptive fantasy? To say that the United States could have won the war is to deprive the notion of winning of any recognizable meaning. Moyar would save Vietnam by destroying it, all to protect a rump state created by the United States in the first place. The real point here, though, is not to argue for an alternative historical outcome but to restore the luster of American exceptionalism and punish those who have tarnished it. A Vietnam War Memorial (rather than a Vietnam Veterans Memorial) could have served as an ideal symbolic home and meeting ground for this kind of sensibility, a site to mourn the loss of American power and prestige and to call to account those responsible for it given their betrayals. This is no doubt one reason there was such outrage over the selection of Maya Lin's sublime design. It did not readily lend itself to participation in reactionary politics. Thus, contrary to the suggestion I made above, one reason to keep Lin's wall rather than risk a replacement would be to prevent a new kind of memorial—a more sophisticated spiritual successor to Frederick Hart's *The Three Soldiers*— from contributing to this kind of politics. Otherwise the ugly revanchism of Rolling Thunder, Inc., which is now nothing more than a yearly vindictive fascist rant over Memorial Day, might become standard practice.

Confederate monuments, of course, should never have been built in the first place. The claim that these memorials reflect Southern heritage rather than Southern hate fail or refuse to admit that Southern heritage is all about racial hierarchy, violence, domination, and privilege.[20] This does not mean that they should be the only focus of a memorial second look. The United States built its fair share of Civil War monuments. There's no reason they should be exempt from scrutiny. In Washington, D.C., alone, one could start with a number of statues of Northern generals, some of whom did not merit monumentalization in the first place. There are traffic circles or islands featuring Generals Thomas, Scott, Sheridan, and McClellan. Ignoring the justifications for their original placement, what need is there for these monuments to continue? Not only are they difficult to access. No one has any reason to visit or inquire about them. Military figures on horseback contribute nothing to democratic political architecture. McClellan in particular is an inexplicable choice for timelessness. An ineffective, passive general who missed a chance to pursue Lee and deal him a crushing blow after the latter's failed invasion of Maryland in 1862, Lincoln ultimately dismissed him because he could not produce a Northern victory. In 1864 McClellan ran for president against Lincoln as a war Democrat with a party platform, which he rejected, that called for an immediate end to the war and a peace settlement with the South. He did not favor the abolition of slavery, and he would have seen the Union restored with this vile institution intact. Though not a traitor like Davis, Lee, or Beauregard, McClellan is not worthy of a statue (it is located just north of Dupont Circle on Connecticut Avenue, Washington D.C.'s main boulevard).

More importantly, the resentment riddling Southern public political architecture indicates that America's entire architectural arsenal should be examined for destructive affective traces needlessly scarring the body politic. New Orleans might be distinctive, but it is hardly unique. The South enjoys no monopoly on bile and bitterness. It's just more brazen about expressing them. Again, let's return to the country's most sacred civic destination, the Mall in Washington, D.C.

The Vietnam Veterans Memorial complex includes Frederick Hart's *The Three Soldiers*, a projection of American innocence and virtue lost because of a disloyal American citizenry that not only failed to support a distant war but eventually did whatever it could to oppose and undermine it—tantamount to aiding and abetting the enemy. *The Three Soldiers* represents America at its best, not the inscription of dead names on Maya Lin's wall, a guilt-ridden expression of mourning where pride and patriotism should be paramount. America has nothing for which it needs to apologize, let alone feel shame. *The Three Soldiers* rebukes the black (wailing) wall. Thus the Vietnam War endures at home in civic space thanks to this piece of memorial architecture.

The Korean War Veterans Memorial, which followed Hart's Vietnam sculpture some ten years later, escalates the level of ressentiment on the Mall introduced by Hart. A rebuke to Maya Lin's wall ("freedom is not free"), the Korean depicts nineteen weary, supersized soldiers on patrol in harsh terrain, mimicking the Korean landscape. A nearby plaque points visitors in a certain affective direction when it speaks of their selfless sacrifice: they "answered the call to defend a country they never knew and a people they never met." While Vietnam still haunts American memory and politics, Korea remains the war the country forgot, an unacceptable sign of disrespect. The Korean War Veterans Memorial seeks to correct the historical record books with a self-pitying tribute, at once extolling the virtues of sacrifice and complaining bitterly about its lack of recognition. The Korean War Veterans Memorial remembers, accuses, and reproaches. This combination makes the World War II Memorial its perfect counterpart, a full-blown unapologetic celebration of America's global power around the world in the aftermath of saving it ("our flag will be recognized throughout the world as a symbol . . . of overwhelming force"). It's not just that the United States insists on congratulating itself six decades after the fact (it was dedicated in 2004). It's that the United States, in a belated rush of narcissistic blindness, seems to think that no one else was involved in the defeat of Germany and Japan or suffered at their hands.

The origins of these three memorials mirrored contemporary political circumstances. Hart's Vietnam sculpture is the oldest. Each is relatively young. Yet none of the three possesses any democratic credentials. At their peak, they effectively worked in tandem to place the United States in a perpetual state of angry mourning, lamenting this and that loss, nursing this and that grievance, tending this and that injury, always reflecting, reinforcing, and reinventing American exceptionalism. This loss is unique. That grievance is unprecedented. This injury is nonpareil. What makes this kind of comportment toward life, especially democratic life, which is riddled with contingencies and ambiguities, possible? Perpetual mourning suggests perpetual self-dissatisfaction, which makes one ugly to behold and potentially dangerous to others, as Nietzsche warned. Given the destructiveness of a politics of resentment, then, it is not too soon to think about the future of these three memorials. Rather than assume their permanence, their desirability should be questioned. Do we want to keep them? If so, what justifies it? If not, what, if anything, might replace them? Should the spaces they vacate be held in reserve for some use that cannot now be anticipated or imagined? Or should new structures, less democratically compromised, be introduced?

A Dionysian America

Whether or not they are removed, the new Constitution Memorial I propose could transfigure the Mall and the culture of passivity depressing it. Two awards ceremonies would be held annually. The date for this ritual would not be September 11 but June 21, the date New Hampshire became the ninth state to ratify the Constitution, thereby putting it into effect. Since the war on terror is also a domestic war, since it involves securing the American way of life at home, which is dependent on the Constitution, these ceremonies would recognize citizens and developments that symbolize, respectively, the greatest defense of and the greatest threat to the Constitution and the democratic political values it (imperfectly, of course) embodies.

The first rite would take its cues from the Great Dionysia in which Athens honored citizens who made outstanding contributions to the city. The greatest defender shall receive a parchment copy of the Constitution (intact) and lead a parade from the memorial site (let's say Constitution Gardens) to the White House. The procession would then veer through downtown (Penn Quarter) where growing numbers of people live in Washington, and conclude at the Capitol and Supreme Court, stopping at these respective locations to drink a toast to constitutional government and democratic freedom, in particular the freedom from excessive state power. This would be a strictly BYOB (bring your own beverage) affair. Any laws against public drinking or intoxication would be suspended for the day. Citizens in attendance will also be provided with a scroll of the Bill of Rights which they can wave in celebration and defiance at each of these loci of power. The spirit of this ritual would ideally take its cues from the second line of the New Orleans jazz funeral tradition. The procession might (or might not) start off relatively small, but it would solicit and welcome growing numbers of marchers as it proceeded. Anyone could join this act of remembrance and joyful anger manifesting itself as fierce aspiration (Stow, 2008; Roach, 1996).

The second rite would borrow from the black funeral tradition and single out a figure (or party, group, or institution) not just for democratic censure but also to prod it toward (more) democratic conduct. Unlike Athens, which summoned its "allies" to the tragic festival and displayed their tribute on stage to the city, America would suspend its hegemonic tendencies, if for a moment, and bring a victim of constitutional depredation to the ceremony and offer them a public apology and make some kind of democratic atonement, perhaps at the suggestion of the victim.

The annual June 21 ritual would thus combine celebration and mourning: celebration of the wild, riotous, risky nature of freedom in a pluralistic democracy; mourning (and bemoaning and resisting) the antidemocratic forces and actors that feel threatened by and thus endanger democracy. Scruggs's idea for a War on Terror Veterans Memorial, recovered as a Constitution Memorial, might be democratically worthy after all, especially insofar as he can't imagine what it might look like but knows intuitively that it needs its own Maya Lin.

NOTES

1. This has been a long-running mantra vis-à-vis the Mall. See, for example, James Reston's piece, "The Monument Glut," in *The New York Times* from September 1995, the year the Korean War Veterans Memorial was dedicated: http://www.nytimes.com/1995/09/10/magazine/the-mon ument-glut.html?pagewanted=all.

2. A national commitment to healing runs an inherent risk of depoliticizing that which is inherently political. The call for healing can sound like a call for unity, for coming together in love and empathy, for patriotism. The healing at Scruggs's beloved wall, the most celebrated part of the Vietnam memorial complex, exacts a heavy price, however, from those who are formally excluded from recognition, something the site itself has tried—and failed—to address over the years. This is why there are currently four Vietnam Veterans Memorials. See Steven Johnston, *The Truth about Patriotism* (Durham: Duke University Press, 2007).

3. It also suggests that the Martin Luther King Memorial, however valuable, is insufficient. King needs the assistance of other memorial forms to document America's long history of racial violence. Lafayette Park, in desperate need of reconstruction, offers a fertile site for such forms. There is no need for the statue of Andrew Jackson (slave owner and notorious Indian killer) to remain in such a prominent location.

4. There is overlap here insofar as blacks are disproportionately represented in the military. See http://www.pewresearch.org/fact-tank/2017/04/13/6-facts-about-the-u-s-military-and-its-changing-demographics/.

5. The most recent addition to the mall is Martin Luther King, but Scruggs did not look in this direction either. It is a Stalinist composition that dehumanizes the figure it depicts.

6. This line of thought is developed in Steven Johnston, *American Dionysia: Violence, Tragedy, and Democratic Politics* (Cambridge: Cambridge University Press, 2015).

7. As of Memorial Day, 2015.

8. Simon Stow cites Emmett Till's 1955 funeral as an example of this critical, productive tradition. "Till's mother famously chose an open casket and eschewed the cosmetic work of the undertaker so that the world might see what racism had done to her son." More than a condemnation of racial violence, Till's funeral "was the spark that lit the civil rights fire." Stow, 689–690.

9. Regarding Scruggs's proposal, this tradition would require the memorial to fold into its design contrary elements. For example, these elements would speak to certain dissonant themes. What about the soldiers who served American democracy by refusing the Bush Administration's illegitimate expansion of the war on terror into Iraq? How are they to be recognized? Or, what about the prisoners at Guantanamo Bay who served American interests by making the country feel more secure as they were locked up and tortured? How does America pay its debt to them?

10. The exact proportions would have to be worked out.

11. I am indebted to Tim Portlock's Desert Rain for this idea: https://www.artsy.net/artwork/tim-portlock-desert-rain.

12. As Bonnie Honig argues, "public things press us into relations with others. They are sites of attachment and meaning that occasion the inaugurations, conflicts, and contestations that underwrite everyday citizenship and democratic sovereignties." Honig, *Public Things*, 7.

13. This would distinguish it from, say, the pitiful shack that Vietnam veterans maintain on the edge of the Lincoln Memorial, a minimalist structure that seems to be little more than an expression of ressentiment for perceived and imagined disrespect and mistreatment (especially regarding alleged POWs and MIAs).

14. The unstated exception is patriotic politics which, it is presumed, transcend the political. See Steven Johnston, *The Truth about Patriotism* (Durham: Duke University Press, 2007).

15. As an example, consider the Grant Memorial just west of the Capitol in Washington, D.C.

16. This line of critique is developed in Steven Johnston, *The Truth about Patriotism* (Durham: Duke University Press, 2007).

17. Rolling Thunder, Inc., which assaults Washington, D.C. with its motorcycle spectacle the Sunday before Memorial Day to express its impotent rage, is one example. Its so-called Freedom Ride or Ride to the Wall is not just a lost cause. It is a nihilistic fantasy of empowerment.

18. This was one way in which Lincoln understood slavery, expressed in the Second Inaugural and elsewhere.

19. Moyar references his "misfortunes with academia," the result of "the collective hostility [that] coalesced wherever [he] applied for an academic faculty position." He claims, of course that he "bring[s] this up not to gain admittance to the nation's ever-expanding victim class." Ibid.

20. Gary Shapiro makes the argument that Confederate monuments and memorial should be retained but contextualized. He opposes what he calls "mere erasure." This refers to "the iconoclasts who want to simply tear things down or transport them to a sculpture park." Shapiro insists that this would amount to "a form of historical denial." Instead, he argues that "much could be added: plaques concerning the war itself, disputes over slavery," etc. What's more, there is always "open space for new sculptures of those who resisted slavery, the Confederacy, the institution of Jim Crow. Representative or anonymous victims of white supremacy could be remembered." Remarkably, Shapiro does not consider, though his own logic suggests it, removal coupled with the supplementation he recommends, where plaques could discuss what has been removed and why. This approach would not suffer from the problem of "mere erasure." Shapiro, too, it seems, assumes that monuments and memorials are to be eternal. Gary Shapiro, "The Meaning of Our Confederate 'Monuments,'" THE STONE, *The New York Times*, May 15, 2017.

WORKS CITED

Anker, Elisabeth S. (2014). *Orgies of Feeling: Melodrama and the Politics of Freedom*. Durham: Duke University Press.

Connolly, William E. (1993). *Political Theory and Modernity*. Ithaca: Cornell University Press.

Ehrenreich, Ben (2008). "War Dodgers," *The New York Times*, March 23.

Franklin, H. Bruce (1993). *M.I.A. or Mythmaking in America*. New Brunswick: Rutgers University Press.

Fussell, Paul (1975). *The Great War and Modern Memory*. Oxford: Oxford University Press.

Hawley, Thomas (2005). *The Remains of War: Bodies, Politics, and the Search for American Soldiers Unaccounted for in Southeast Asia*. Durham: Duke University Press.

Honig, Bonnie (2013). *Antigone, Interrupted*. Cambridge: Cambridge University Press.

———. (2017). *Public Things: Democracy in Disrepair*. New York: Fordham University Press.

Johnston, Steven (2007). *The Truth about Patriotism*. Durham: Duke University Press.

———. (2015). *American Dionysia: Violence, Tragedy, and Democratic Politics*. Cambridge: Cambridge University Press.

Mele, Christopher (2017). "New Orleans Begins Removing Confederate Monuments, Under Police Guard." *The New York Times*. April 2.

Moyar, Mark (2017). "Was Vietnam Winnable?" *The New York Times*. May 19.

Nietzsche, Friedrich (1956). *The Birth of Tragedy and The Genealogy of Morals*, tr. Francis Golffing. New York: Anchor Books.

Roach, Joseph (1996). *Cities of the Dead: Circum-Atlantic Performance* (New York: Columbia University Press.

Robertson, Campbell (2017). "From Lofty Perch, New Orleans Monument to Confederacy Comes Down," *The New York Times*, May 19.

Schaar, John H. (1981). "The Case for Patriotism," in *Legitimacy in the Modern State*. New Brunswick: Transaction Books.

Scruggs, Jan C., and Joel L. Swerdlow (1985). *To Heal a Nation: The Vietnam Veterans Memorial*. New York: HarperCollins.

Scruggs, Jan C. (2016). "American Needs a War on Terror Veterans Memorial," *The New York Times*, November 11.

Shapiro, Gary (2017). "The Meaning of Our Confederate 'Monuments,'" THE STONE, *The New York Times*, May 15.

Stow, Simon (2007). "Pericles at Gettysburg and Ground Zero: Tragedy, Patriotism, and Public Mourning," *American Political Science Review*, 101:2, May, 195–208.

———. (2008). "Do You Know What it Means to Miss New Orleans? George Bush, the Jazz Funeral, and the Politics of Memory," *Theory and Event*, 11:1 2007.

———. (2010). "Agonistic Homegoing: Frederick Douglass, Joseph Lowery, and the Democratic Value of African American Public Mourning," *American Political Science Review*, 104: 4, November, 681–697.

Young, James E. (1993). *The Texture of Meaning: Holocaust Memorials and Meaning*. New Haven: Yale University Press.

Chapter Three

Removing the Confederate Flag in South Carolina in the Wake of Charleston

Sovereignty, Symbolism, and
White Domination in a "Colorblind" State

Heather Pool

Why did it take only twenty-three days for the state of South Carolina to remove the Confederate Battle Flag (CBF) from the grounds of the state-house after Dylann Roof, white, murdered nine black parishioners at a prayer meeting in Charleston, South Carolina, in 2015?[1] The flag had been flying at the state capitol since 1962, raised as a commemoration of the centennial of the Civil War, but then never lowered; the resignification of the CBF that had occurred mid-twentieth century had turned the flag from revered, almost sacred memorial/historical object to a symbol of contemporary resistance to the Black Freedom Movement. So why and how did the Charleston Massacre overcome fifty-three years of resistance to the removal of the CBF in a mere twenty-three days?

To begin formulating an answer to these questions, the first section provides an overview of the events in Charleston and the political context surrounding the events, while the second section traces the evolution of the meanings of the CBF from 1865 to date. The third section then offers a variety of ways we might interpret the events leading to the removal of the flag. I argue that the response to these questions lies where sovereignty, symbolism, and white domination intersect. First, the sovereignty of the state required reassertion in the wake of Roof's massive unleashing of violence on black persons, persons against whom the state frequently and disproportionately uses violence. Roof's arrest and prosecution, then, might be read as an effort to reassert sovereignty by reminding the state's (white) citizens that it alone has the monopoly on violence against black persons. Second, one of the significant symbols of the state's sovereignty—the CBF, which had flown over the capitol dome for thirty-eight years, then at the entrance to the capitol complex for another fifteen—is inextricably linked to white domination. Thus, to fully enact a performance of *neutral* sovereignty—the sovereignty of a "colorblind" state—South Carolina needed to remove the symbol of white domination. However, the symbolic removal did little to erase the institutional legacy of the interwoven nature of sovereignty and white domination; instead, it worked to make the strong connections between them less visible. In the last substantive section of the chapter, I suggest that we may be entering a new era of symbolism for the CBF, as the strong backlash against the removal contributed to early support for Donald Trump's presidential campaign.

CONTEXT AND EVENTS:
THE 2015 CHARLESTON MASSACRE

Emanuel African Methodist Episcopal Church in Charleston, South Carolina, is the oldest standing black church in the American South. A brief overview of its history demonstrates why. In 1816, Morris Brown, a black pastor, founded the congregation that would come to be known as "Mother Emanuel." Denmark Vesey, after purchasing his own freedom, enlisted several congregants to his 1822 slave revolt. Days after the plot was exposed, a white mob burned the church building down. The congregation rebuilt, and services were held at the current location until the state closed all black churches in 1834 in the wake of Nat Turner's failed 1831 rebellion. From 1834 to 1865, congregants worshipped without a building and in secret, because open services were illegal and certain to provoke white violence. The congregation became public again after the Civil War ended in 1865. A wooden structure was rebuilt in 1872 but destroyed by an earthquake in 1886; the current building was constructed in 1891. Since then, the church has hosted numerous black American luminaries, including Booker T. Washington, Martin Luther King, Jr., and Coretta Scott King (Chow 2015; Emanuel African Methodist Episcopal Church, n.d.). In short, Mother Emanuel is a repository of significant memory for the black community of Charleston, and its successes, defeats, resistance, and persistence in the face of violence mirror those of black America.

Dylann Roof, a young white man, entered this church on June 17, 2015. Charleston was already in the news that day, as both Hillary Clinton and Jeb Bush were campaigning for the 2016 presidential nominations; Donald

Trump had announced his candidacy the day before (Horowitz, Corasaniti, and Southall 2015). Roof arrived and joined an evening prayer service with about a dozen African American worshippers. After sitting with those gathered for about an hour, twenty-one-year-old Roof brandished a weapon, at which point a member of the congregation, Tywanza Sanders, stepped between Roof and one of Sanders's relatives, asked Roof what he was doing, and pleaded with him to put the weapon away. Roof responded by saying: "No, you've raped our women, and you are taking over the country . . . I have to do what I have to do" (Ellis, Botelho, and Payne 2015). Roof then opened fire, killing Sanders and eight others and gravely wounding four more (one of whom died). Those killed by Roof were the Rev. Clementa Pinckney, a pastor of Mother Emanuel AME and South Carolina State Senator; Cynthia Hurd, a librarian who directed the St. Andrews Regional Library; Rev. Sharonda Coleman-Singleton, a pastor at the church in addition to being a speech therapist and girls' track and field coach; Tywanza Sanders, a recent college graduate; Ethel Lance, a custodian at the church and grandmother; Susie Jackson, a member of the church; DePayne Middleton Doctor, an admissions coordinator at her alma mater, Southern Wesleyan University; Rev. Daniel Simmons, a retired pastor; and Myra Thompson, the wife of another pastor in Charleston (NPR Staff 2015). With ages ranging from twenty-six to eighty-seven, the dead represent those who lived through the Civil Rights years as well as those waiting for its promise to be realized. Roof was quickly apprehended alive, after which he confessed to the deeds of which he was accused.[2] In 2017, Roof was convicted of murder in federal court and condemned to death.

In response to the shootings, the United States and South Carolina state flags atop the South Carolina State House were lowered to half-staff by order of Governor Nikki Haley. In stark juxtaposition, the Confederate flag—located at a Confederate War Memorial on the grounds of the South Carolina State House—remained at full staff, unable to be lowered without a 2/3 majority in both houses of the legislature. Though not quite as long as Mother Emanuel's storied past, the Confederate flag in South Carolina has a long history. Long after the South's defeat and occupation by the Union Army, the Confederate flag had been re-installed atop the South Carolina State House in 1962, allegedly to commemorate the centennial of the Civil War but also in response to the surging Civil Rights Movement. At the conclusion of the centennial, however, the flag was not lowered. In May 2000, in response to an economic boycott by the NAACP, the Confederate flag was moved from the top of the statehouse to a flagpole on the grounds of the statehouse, as part of a monument to Confederate War Veterans (Firestone 2000).

On June 20, Roof's website was publicized. It included images of him trampling on the American flag while waving the Confederate flag, wearing clothing prominently displaying "88" (code for "Heil Hitler"), and a jacket with a Rhodesian flag patch on it (the website itself, now gone, was lastrhodesian.com).[3] While reporting after the murders speculated that race must have been a motivating factor, the discovery of Roof's website put speculation to rest. Roof was an explicit white supremacist whose allegiance to the ideology of white domination was stronger than his allegiance to the United States.

Prior to the massacre, South Carolina Republican Governor Nikki Haley had been a supporter of the 2000 compromise that kept the Confederate flag on the grounds of the statehouse. After the shootings, Haley swiftly changed her position. In a press conference on June 22, flanked by state lawmakers from both sides of the aisle, Haley noted that the flag was revered in South Carolina and pointed out that for "those who wish to show their respect for the flag on their private property, no one will stand in your way. But the statehouse is different." Her remarks recognized the symbolic power of the Confederate flag in the past and the present, but noted "that that flag, while an integral part of our past, does not represent the future of our great state." Haley drew attention to the fact that the governor has the power to call the legislature back into session after normal sessions end, and that "if they do not take measures to ensure this debate takes place this summer, I will use that authority for the purpose of the legislature removing the flag from the statehouse grounds" (Haley 2015). The next day, both houses of the South Carolina legislature agreed to debate the removal of the Confederate Battle Flag from statehouse grounds after the July 4 recess (Santaella 2015).

In response to the massacre, most presidential candidates fell in line with Governor Haley's position; the flag should come down. But it is worth dwelling for a moment on Donald Trump. The day after the shooting, Trump tweeted: "The tragedy in South Carolina is incomprehensible. My deepest condolences to all" (@realDonaldTrump, June 18, 2015). It is, of course, not incomprehensible that a young man in the United States would ally himself with white supremacist groups and act on their toxic ideology. Trump's response exemplifies a widespread response to mass murders by young white men; it must be madness, rather than toxic masculinity or explicit white supremacy or fundamentalist Christianity that drives them to do these things.[4] Surely, Trump deflects, inflammatory rhetoric from political candidates cannot be connected to acts such as Roof's. (For example, recall Trump's announcement of his candidacy: "When Mexico sends its people, they're not sending their best. . . . They're bringing drugs. They're bringing crime. They're rapists. And some, I assume, are good people." Trump 2015). Linking this kind of "hot" rhetoric to mass violence such as Roof's rampage, the leading Democratic contender for the nomination said:

> "Unfortunately, the public discourse is sometimes hotter and more negative than it should be," Clinton told Nevada journalist John Ralston, suggesting

such invective could "trigger people who are less than stable to do something like" the Charleston shooting. "I think decent people need to stand up against it," Clinton added. "We have to speak out against it. Like for example, a recent entry into the Republican presidential campaign said some very inflammatory things about Mexicans. Everybody should stand up and say, 'That's not acceptable.'" (Clinton 2015; Miller 2015)

Trump's response to Clinton's comments was: "Wow, it's pretty pathetic that Hillary Clinton just blamed me for the horrendous attack that took place in South Carolina. . . . This is why politicians are just no good. Our country's in trouble" (Miller 2015). A few days later, Trump agreed that the flag should be removed to a museum (Alemany 2015). His remarks to that effect were delivered late in the day on June 23, the day after Haley's announcement and last of the massive field of presidential candidates to state a position (Saenz 2015).[5] This delay—though slight in terms of actual time, glacial in terms of news coverage of the presidential nomination race—suggested either that he was apathetic about the presence of the CBF flying at a site of sovereignty or that he was reluctant to call for its removal, while his deft deflection of the nuance of Clinton's comments played well with those who believe whites to be an "endangered species" in the United States.

Before the debate over the removal of the CBF from the grounds of the South Carolina state capitol could occur in the legislature, South Carolina activist and artist Bree Newsome gained national attention when she scaled the flagpole and removed the Confederate flag on June 27. Newsome was arrested immediately upon returning to the ground. As she was led away, Newsome said, "Every day that flag stays up there is an endorsement of hate." Within an hour of Newsome's act of civil disobedience, the CBF had been returned to its former place and a pro-flag rally commenced shortly thereafter. This same week, according to Amy Goodman on *Democracy Now*, "at least six predominantly black churches across the South were destroyed or damaged by fire, at least three of them arsons" (Newsome 2015).

On June 28, the day after Bree Newsome scaled the flagpole to challenge the brazen alliance between white dominance and sovereignty, the *Daily Stormer*, "America's most popular neo-Nazi news site," endorsed Donald Trump for president. By the end of August 2015, support for Trump's campaign among self-described white supremacists was very high (Osnos 2015). At least some of this support among far-right white power groups was linked to the strong feelings about the removal of the Confederate flag in South Carolina and threats to remove it from other public places in Southern states, such as the dismantling of Confederate monuments that has since taken place in New Orleans (Ross 2017).

South Carolina's legislative bodies took up the debate about the place of the Confederate Battle Flag on July 7, 2015. The Senate—the immediate colleagues of slain Rev. Clementa Pinckney—concluded debate and voted to remove the flag by the end of the first day. The House took considerably longer (thirteen hours in all), as debate was drawn out by proposed amendments and efforts to stall a vote and became "increasingly contentious" (Berman 2015). When the vote happened, quickly and with some deft parliamentary maneuvering (including adjourning one legislative session, then convening the next within minutes so the vote could happen immediately), some were stunned and others elated. The bill, once signed by the governor, required the flag to be removed from the statehouse within twenty-four hours (Blinder and Fausset 2015). Governor Haley signed the bill in a public ceremony at 4 p.m. on Thursday, July 9. On Friday, July 10, 2015, twenty-three days after Dylann Roof's killing spree, the Confederate flag was removed from the flagpole in front of the South Carolina State House and taken to the Confederate Relic Room and Memorial Museum after being defiantly flown on the grounds of the South Carolina state capitol for fifty-three years. The Confederate flag was finally re-removed to the museum.

SOUTH CAROLINA AND THE
CONFEDERATE BATTLE FLAG

In *The Confederate Battle Flag*, John M. Coski (2005) provides an authoritative overview of the origins, uses, and symbolic meanings of what is now referred to as the Confederate flag.[6] However, the flag we most associate with the Confederacy was never the flag of the Confederate States of America (CSA); the CSA's original flag was the so-called "Stars and Bars," which looked uncomfortably like the American flag. After the flag's similarities caused confusion on the ground at the First Battle of Manassas, General Beauregard of the CSA determined that a more visually different "battle flag" should be used when armies met on the field of battle (8). Thus, the flag most often displayed as and called the Confederate Flag is in fact the Confederate *Battle* Flag. Importantly, this flag never flew over state capitols, nor did it fly over the Southern White House. It was flown by the army when it was in the field. Why is that significant? Because the Confederate States of America never existed during peace; its entire existence was war, and so it makes sense that the battle flag has come to stand in for the flag of state. And yet it seems important that the flag most associated with the Southern rebellion was the flag of battle, not of rule. I suggest it is fair to infer that the CBF, then, is a symbol of sovereignty: a symbol of the sovereign's power in the form of military force. In this section, I provide a summary of the shifting meanings of the Confederate Battle Flag from the end of the Civil War through today, then provide a brief history of the use of the flag in the State of South Carolina.

Shifting Meanings of the Confederate Battle Flag

Coski suggests that the CBF's display and meaning have shifted several times since the end of the Civil War. Based on his work, I identify three major periods of the battle flag's display: 1) memorialization, 2) reappearance, and 3) resignification.[7] As with all periodization efforts, there is no clear demarcation between the artificial categories I lay out, and the eras bleed into one another (particularly the first two). But there is a notable shift in how the flag was displayed and perceived in each of these periods.

During the *Era of Memorialization* (~1865–1910s), the primary purpose of displaying the flag was at memorial gatherings: Confederate holidays, dedications of memorials for Confederate dead, parades of veterans, and funerals of veterans. Many of the displayed flags were originals that had been taken onto the fields of battle—hidden and not handed over to the US Army—and thus were marked by their time on the battlefield: bloodstained and tattered. These were treated with sacred reverence. Heritage organizations like the United Confederate Veterans (UCV) and the Sons of Confederate Veterans (SCV) strongly policed the use of the flags and ensured that when flown, they were treated reverently (chapter 3). During this period, it was generally agreed upon that the war had been lost, and that the flag, as a symbol of a conquered sovereign state, should be furled as a symbol of sovereignty but maintained as a memorial symbol. This is not to say that Southerners gave up the ideology of white domination; they did not. One might instead characterize the shift as a recognition that the South had lost the war but was going to win the peace; the sovereign state may have been lost, but its goals were not forsaken and might be achieved via state politics rather than civil war (58–63). The Battle Flag, thus, came to stand not for a present threat to secede (again), but to honor the valor and sacrifice of Confederate soldiers. For example, at the 50th Anniversary of the Battle of Gettysburg in 1913, as Union and Confederate soldiers and their descendants honored their war dead together, the Confederate flag flew below the American one; four years later—during World War I—both flags were at the same height (73–77). The image of the two flags crossed and at equal height was a symbol of national reconciliation (65). As David Blight (2001) argues, this reconciliation came at the cost of federal support for racial equity. National support of the troops during World War I helped make put the Civil War and its deep divides into "history" instead of maintaining it as a present threat.

In the *Era of Reappearance* (1890s–1940s), the flag began to appear outside a purely memorial context. A few Southern states inserted elements of Confederate flags into their state flags (79–80). These changes coincided with the passage of Jim Crow statutes into law and the Supreme Court's decision that such statutes were within the proper jurisdiction of state's power. Much of the flag's reappearance outside the realm of memorialization can be traced to a single fraternity: Kappa Alpha. Kappa Alpha (KA), founded in 1865 at Washington College (where Robert E. Lee would soon become the school's president) was essentially a Confederate heritage organization: "Members should cherish the southern ideal of character—that of the chivalrous warrior of Christ, the Knight who loves God and country, honors and protects pure womanhood, practices courtesy and magnanimity of spirit and prefers self-respect to ill-gotten wealth" (89). The 1910s and 1920s saw the gradual expansion of KA "Dixie Dances" into very formal and very Confederate "Old South"–themed parties by the 1940s. Surprisingly, however, during the KKK's second incarnation in the 1910s, the Battle Flag was not mobilized as a symbol of white supremacy (84–85). Furthermore, in the many visual records we have of fatal violence visited on black bodies—lynching photographs—few if any of those images include the Confederate Battle Flag (86). The lack of display by the KKK and by those engaging in violence against black bodies is surprising. While the flag's appearance was moving beyond mere memorialization in this period, it remained, mostly, a historic item, though one clearly aligned with white supremacist ideology.

All that changed as the Confederate Battle Flag entered its current phase: the *Era of Resignification* (1940s–today). The real marker of resignification from memorialization to a straightforward political articulation of contemporary white resistance to federal civil rights intervention was the States Rights Party Convention in 1948 (chapter 5). Truman had made substantive efforts toward inclusion and civil rights protection for African Americans by forming a Civil Rights Commission in 1947 (whose 1948 report, *To Secure These Rights*, Truman quickly endorsed) as well as by ordering the desegregation of the military in 1948 (99). Southern states responded with massive resistance. This resistance became embodied in the Confederate Battle Flag, which, like many other strange artifacts of 1950s life, became an inexplicably huge fad that swept the country; the 1950s were prime fad years, as television went national and commercial jet travel became more available, creating a favorable climate for nationwide campaigns (110–112). Similarly, NASCAR was founded in 1949, and quickly became a site for the new "rebel" spirit (126). Coski suggests that during the "flag fad" of the 1950s, the battle flag came to stand for a more generalized rebelliousness, defined not necessarily by white supremacist commitments but as a yearning for individuality in an era of comformity. However, by the mid-1950s, while those other more individualized meanings may have accreted to the symbolic Confederate Battle Flag, it once again was being used to explicitly endorse white domination in the form of resistance to the Civil Rights Movement and federal intervention (128). This explicit reinvigoration of the flag for contemporary rather than memorial purposes was new, and its conjunction with observations of the centennial of the Civil War created a perfect storm for the Confederate flag to become a central site of contestation over the place of race in the American polity.

The Confederate Battle Flag in South Carolina

At the instigation of John D. Long, son of South Carolina's leader of his county's KKK in the 1870s and a "staunch segregationist," South Carolina's House voted to display the Confederate Battle Flag in the House chambers in 1938, followed by its display in the Senate chambers in 1956, which coincided with Long's election to both houses (82, 245). In 1962, like in many Southern states, the flag was raised over the South Carolina State House in recognition of the Civil War Centennial. In a blurring of the line between memorial purposes and Southern resistance, the resolution that led to raising the CBF made no mention of the centennial and thus left the meaning of the action vague. Coski asserts that "it was assumed widely that the centennial was the impetus for the resolution and that the flag would come down upon the commemoration's close in 1965" (245). But the flag was not removed in 1965. The state's Black Caucus took up the cause of removal in 1972, and it remained a topic of agitation and debate for the next four decades. For flag supporters, the flag "represented a proud period of the state's history, 'the only time when the state made a total commitment to anything'" (245). To its opponents, the flag could honor the valor and "commitment" of the soldiers just as well if housed in the state's Confederate Relic Room rather than on top of the statehouse.

For years, compromises were pursued and failed; the closest the opponents came to resolution was in 1994. An agreement was reached that would remove the flag from the statehouse and insert into the journals of both houses the following statement:

> Confederate flags are not racist emblems *per se*. It depends on how they are utilized. The misuse of them as emblems for racial purposes is deplored and condemned. These emblems have been misused. These are battle flags which should not be displayed for political purposes.
>
> The State is displaying the Confederate flags as symbols of our heritage. They are not flown in defiance of any government or as a statement regarding any civil rights, constitutional, or racial issues. These flags represent the valor which was displayed by the men and women of this state in another time. That heritage of honor, courage, and independence is worthy of remembering (247–248).[8]

This public statement tried to walk a fine line; arguably so fine that it vanishes into meaninglessness. To recognize that the flag symbolizes "heritage" and recognition of "valor"—while not linking these to the fight to secure a state-protected slave economy—segregates violence from state sovereignty and white domination and equates white loss during a secession attempt with black loss during peace.[9] Furthermore, the attempt to fix the meaning of a symbol is impossible, and the effort to do so—to clarify that the flag stands for heritage not hate—implies a certain anxiety that seeks resolution but does not lead to substantive action. In addition to this public statement, the flag was to be removed from atop the statehouse but still displayed at two Civil War monuments on the grounds of the capitol, now paired with a new civil rights memorial, funded by private donations but overseen by a state commission, which would fly an "appropriate flag" (possibly a Black Liberation flag, 247). But this compromise failed, and the Republican Party—many of whom were outspoken flag supporters—won a considerable victory in the 1994 state legislative elections, winning the South Carolina House for the first time since Reconstruction (248).

In January of 2000, the state NAACP, backed by the national organization, enacted a statewide boycott, calling for "the removal and relocation of the Confederate battle flag to a place of historical rather than sovereign context" (249). In May of 2000, those calling for removal and those refusing removal reached a compromise. The Confederate Battle Flag was moved from high atop the statehouse and placed on a pole at ground level by a Confederate monument and near the main entrance to the Capitol grounds; additionally, the CBF was removed from the House and Senate chambers. The state also recognized Martin Luther King, Jr.'s birthday as a state holiday (established as a federal holiday in 1983), while at the same time making Confederate Memorial Day a state holiday (250). The compromise was unsatisfying, in part because the flag was now more obvious than ever. Flag supporters gathered to protest the removal of the flag from the dome and cheered as it was raised over the memorial, some holding signs that read: "Off the dome and in your face." Coski writes:

> "Off the dome and in your face" was an appropriate metaphor for the compromise. The flag no longer flew in a place that implied sovereignty over or official approval by the people of South Carolina. Flying high over the capitol dome may have been a symbolically significant place for the flag, but it was barely visible to the naked eye. In contrast, flying alone on a pole at the main entrance to the capitol grounds (and across from the city's main commercial artery) made the flag more visible than ever. Few people entering the capitol grounds from the city could miss the flag and the implied approval of the state's Confederate past. (251)

The flag remained there until July 10, 2015, when it was finally removed and sent to the Confederate Relic Room. The question, then, is why. Why did such a massive display of white violence against black bodies finally prompt the legislators and governor of South Carolina to remove the Confederate Battle Flag from a "sovereign context" and return it to a historical one?

The debate about the place of the Confederate Battle Flag in the United States is embedded within larger debates about the nature of the state and the basis of its power. Should the state be a reflection of aspirational ideals of liberalism, defined by equality, freedom, and a neutral umpire? Or is the state to reflect only the will of a (racial) majority? Conflicts over how to understand the authorizing power of the state help make sense of the events of 2015. I argue that—given its tortured history—the Confederate Battle Flag must be read as a symbol of sovereignty that cannot be separated from white domination. The decision to remove the flag from the statehouse grounds in South Carolina, then, might be read as an avowal by legislators of the substantive conflict between white domination and liberal democratic ideals. As Locke (1980) and Schmitt (2005) both suggest, there is tension between conceptualizations of sovereignty and constitutional liberalism; in this instance, the actions of the legislators seemed to recognize that in order to uphold liberal, democratic ideals, they needed to remove a symbol that favored one group over another. This recognition by the state legislators required the flag's removal to sustain the fiction of popular, democratic sovereignty and a neutral liberal state. But the flag's quick removal without a substantive effort to combat white domination may leave those seeking racial justice with an ever-shifting enemy that is even harder to combat now that its most visible, "in your face" symbol has been removed.

In essence, debates over the display of the Confederate Battle Flag are linked to the question of who should rule and whether white domination can be separated from sovereign power. The flag itself symbolizes many things, but sovereignty—who should rule, what form that rule should take, and how far it extends—is at the heart of the debate.

WHY DID SOUTH CAROLINA REMOVE THE CONFEDERATE BATTLE FLAG SO QUICKLY?

In the following section, I offer four ways we might understand the meaning of removing the Confederate flag from the South Carolina state capitol. In reality, all are woven together. But the shootings and the prompt removal of the Confederate Battle Flag deserve sustained attention because the violence was both extraordinary and ordinary, while the response was, too. As I will suggest below, following Jenny Edkins's work in *Trauma and the Memory of Politics*, the aftermath was a blend of politics and the political. I seek here to disentangle the multiple strands of meaning that may become settled after this series of events.

Possibility One: The State Must Be
(Symbolically) Impartial/Colorblind

Roof's deeply racist manifesto explicitly noted his reasons for targeting blacks; blacks were inferior, dangerous, and threatened white domination. In every way, Roof was the apotheosis of the ideology of white supremacy, symbolically represented by the CBF flying at the entrance to the capitol building. The genteel racism of Southern "heritage" this is not; it is more akin to the genocidal racism directed toward Native Americans. The number of bodies and the explicit white supremacist justifications, when laid out before the Confederate flag, prompted the people of South Carolina to recon- sider flying the CBF in a sovereign context. Roof's manifesto, with its disre- gard for the rational liberal legal order, rendered his violence against black bodies exceptional. Against the context of his writings, his actions did not look like low-level, everyday white violence against black bodies; it looked like terrorism. [10] This perfect storm of horror served to interrupt the previous- ly encoded meanings of "heritage" that many saw in the flag.

Thus, it could well be that legislators in South Carolina came to believe that flying a symbol of white domination in a sovereign context was a direct challenge to aspirations of a colorblind state. Flying the CBF negated any pretense of a Lockean neutral umpire. In Weberian terms, the conflict be- tween the legitimating authority of custom and the legitimating authority of law was exposed to such a degree that it could not be sutured together again (Weber 2004, 34). Thus, legislators debated some thirteen hours about the meaning of the flag, and a considerable majority of them decided that the flag should now become a historical symbol rather than remain a sovereign one. It appears that legislators flirted with custom as legitimating authority, but the majority determined that a rational legal system that does not obviously favor one group was a better option.

To use Charles Mills's terms, this was a moment when the grip of the "epistemology of ignorance" was loosened, exposing the paradoxes of "ra- cial liberalism" (Mills 1997, 93; Mills, 1998, chapter 6). Mills argues that whites in the West do not question racial segregation or white domination because whites are trained to be ignorant; this leads to a state that divides those it rules into white persons who are citizens (and at least formally to be treated as equals) and nonwhite subpersons who are subjects (who are to be ruled by all whites). If this is true, then the majority of legislators supported removing the symbol of white domination and moving toward actual demo- cratic liberalism in an effort to *become* rational and act as impartial rulers should; they sought to move closer toward the aspirational ideal of a liberal state. The words of the legislators suggest that the now-exposed clash be- tween the liberal, rational value of equality and the authoritarian, traditional value of white domination—played out against a body count of nine black bodies in a church—motivated them to vote to remove the flag. Based on the celebration after the fact and various self-congratulatory speeches about a new day in South Carolina, many saw this removal of a symbol of white domination as a substantive, material move toward justice.

But while this was a step in the right direction, without being paired with actual efforts to redress past injustices, the symbolic removal is disingenuous. Removing a symbol that made clear that white supremacy and state power are comfortable mates made that connection harder to see (literally). By removing the offending symbol, the sons and daughters of the "white moderates" that Dr. King critiqued in 1963 believed they had taken an important step. And they had! Removing a racist symbol from a sovereign context *is* an important step. But it is also the very least that could be done. Imagine, for instance, that the flag removal had been accompanied by a commitment of state legislators and the governor that ensured equal funding for black and white schools across the state. Or provided more funding for job training for blacks in neighborhoods with high incarceration rates. Or instituted programs that worked to get black persons into positions of authority. The symbol of removal would then have been paired with a material commitment to racial justice. In the absence of that pairing, the removal remains symbolic; it is an aspiration to colorblindness, not racial justice.

Coski carefully notes that the meaning of the flag has shifted over time, and that context is crucial to any interpretation. I grant that, and, for the sake of argument, that many Americans who wave the Confederate flag are not (consciously) advocating a racial state. And yet to wave the CBF in any context is to advocate the symbol of a racial and racist state—a sovereign nation whose primary purpose was to protect the legal institution of chattel slavery—regardless of intention. Cheryl Harris (1993) reminds us that the legal protections of property rights can be read as legal protections for whiteness, and for states in the Confederacy, that was the main justification for secession. As Ian Haney López argues in *White by Law* (2006), whether an action is racist cannot be determined by a reduction to individual intent. Thus, advocating colorblindness essentially perpetuates white dominance. Surely, there can be no image as tone-deaf as arguing for a doctrine of colorblindness while waving a Confederate flag, and yet many Americans do precisely that.

While Coski is correct that the flag has evolved to symbolize personal independence and a "rebel spirit" more generally, I am less convinced that its meaning can be separated from a nation that engaged in armed rebellion and whose sole purpose was to maintain slavery . . . or at least it cannot be separated from its origins without a willed forgetfulness. In *Trauma and the Memory of Politics*, Jenny Edkins (2003) argues that this willed ignorance is crucial to the maintenance of mythic sovereign power. Edkins links the memorial practices of sovereign states to the memory of trauma and suggests that when designed or supported by the state itself, these memorial practices can obscure trauma and violence by glorifying sacrifice. Sovereign states usually provide memorials we feel good about rather than ones recalling the horror and violence accompanying the enactment of sovereign power. This orchestrated forgetting, according to Edkins, fosters a willingness to acquiesce to the forms of order that perpetuate sovereign power. To forget the violence of founding and the brutality of battle, we commemorate valor and heroism rather than the wounds of war; we forget how men were expended like things. Edkins writes: "Sovereign power produces and is itself produced by trauma: it provokes wars, genocides, and famines. But it works by concealing its involvement and claiming to be a provider not a destroyer of security." This is accomplished partially through rituals of memorialization and commemoration. Thus, "resistance to state narratives of commemoration . . . constitutes resistance to sovereign power" (Edkins 2003, xv).

I am not persuaded that symbolic or narrative resistance achieves material or institutional change. But I am persuaded that flying the CBF over a Confederate Memorial on the grounds of the South Carolina State House works to obscure an enormous amount of violence: the violence of slavery as well as that of the war itself.[11] As white Americans mobilize the Confederate Battle Flag as a symbol of "heritage not hate," that action resignifies and rewrites this past as one of honorable duty rather than one saturated with racial domination: a past that a rational, white, liberal subject can recover as a "good identity" and about which s/he no longer feels guilt. Nor does this rational, white, liberal subject feel any need to act to change material conditions in the present. Edkins's work helps us think through how the enactment of sovereignty symbolized by the flag is purged of its violence and thus made to appear rational and reasonable. This enables a rational, liberal, white citizen to take pride in a past that might otherwise be regarded as illiberal and irrational. Thus, to be asked *not* to fly the CBF is, for those whites who wish to do so, to suffer a symbolic loss (Hooker 2017).[12]

To be a mournable loss, though, does not mean it is a loss that is justly mourned. Freud's definition of mourning is "the reaction to the loss of a beloved person or an abstraction taking the place of a person, such as fatherland, freedom, an ideal, and so on" (Freud 2005, 203). Nothing in that widely used (though basic) definition suggests that we only mourn losses we *ought* to—we may mourn losses of privilege which we had no right to or people we misguidedly loved. In Freud's framework, the mourner eventually works through their grief and returns to reality. Once "reality-testing" has confirmed the loss of the beloved, "it demands that the libido as a whole severs its bonds with that object" (Freud 2005, 204). That many whites experience the removal of the CBF or Confederate memorials as mournable losses suggests not a desire to return to a lost nation, but a desire to reinstate white domination—the true, if unjust, mournable loss. The Confederate Battle

Flag, then, is a symbol of attachment to white domination conveniently over-laid with the slightly more acceptable language of sovereignty. Thus, the cry to protect it is a desire not for the long-lost state/sovereign power of the Confederacy, but a desire for unchallenged white domination.

Perhaps worse is that the removal of the symbol then makes the connec-tions between sovereign power and white domination even less visible than before. It is the equivalent of gaslighting—to convince someone that what is really happening is nothing but a figment of her imagination. It is easy to imagine that a state flying the Confederate flag is probably not one that prioritizes racial justice or equality. But with the symbol gone, and the proc-lamation of colorblindness and equality secured by the symbolic removal, any experience of racial injustice can be dismissed as "subjective."

Possibility Two: Sovereign Power Asserts
Its Legitimate Monopoly of the Use of Violence

The status quo for 400 years has been that black lives are vulnerable, even expendable. The existing sovereign order, allied as it is with white domina-tion, was actually upheld by Roof's action. With rare exceptions, this pattern holds from European colonization of the Americas to date. Roof's actions were *not* a disruption of the status quo—they are barely out of the ordinary in the overall scheme of the violence visited on black persons before and during slavery, Jim Crow, and the Civil Rights Movement; the contemporary mass incarceration of people of color; disproportionately early deaths from lack of health care and poverty in the black community; and police shootings of young men that has led to the rise of Black Lives Matter. At the risk of sounding hyperbolic, given the context of early twenty-first-century Ameri-ca, Roof's actions were not extraordinary. When we extend that to state violence against nonwhite persons, it becomes even less extraordinary. In 2015 alone, police in the United States killed more than 100 *unarmed* black persons, out of the 1,146 total persons killed by police (Mapping Police Violence; *The Guardian*).

What was extraordinary was not that a young white man murdered sever-al black persons, but rather that their status as innocents was immediately secured by the circumstances of their death. As Andrew Dilts (2014) points out, one of the foundational tenets of liberalism is the right to punish. But we are only to punish the guilty, so how did the circumstances ensure the inno-cence of the victims so that they were immediately understood as deserving of (white) sympathy? They were Christians, rather than Muslims or Sikhs or Hindus. They were at a prayer meeting on a weekday, typical behavior only for the most devout. They were not gathering to prepare a protest for Black Lives Matter or any other political movement; their assembly was in no way explicitly political. The prayer meeting took place at a church that holds

tremendous historical significance to black Americans (and was targeted by
Roof for this reason). The dead included a state legislator, pastors and pastor's spouses, a librarian, a recent college graduate, and a church janitor; the
range in ages helped ensure that they were not perceived to be a threat or
involved in criminal activity. One could imagine a group of a dozen young
men praying being responded to differently, perhaps even if all the other
circumstances held constant. They welcomed Roof to the meeting and he sat
with them for about an hour. All of these circumstances add up to make those
who died unimpeachably "good" victims. Essentially, then, the circumstances outweighed their blackness. If the default perception of blacks in
America is criminal, literally everything about this assembly of persons other
than their blackness challenged that default label. Innocence here is crucial to
the response by the media and the public at large, as well as by politicians in
South Carolina. Whites killing blacks is ordinary. On the other hand, blacks
being immediately portrayed as innocent is not.

Given white complacency regarding black death, the federal prosecution
of Roof for actions targeting black persons is worth further discussion. On
one hand, not that long ago, blacks in the South were murdered in broad
daylight and no one was arrested. In that sense, the arrest and prosecution of
Roof is certainly a step in the right direction. But in many ways, the legal
case that secured his conviction and eventual execution works to uphold a
legal solution to political responsibility.[13] The federal government's prosecution of Roof helps maintain what Scheingold calls the "myth of rights" and
furthers its liberal and individualist assumptions (Scheingold 2004). Thus,
the prosecution of Roof by the federal government accomplished two note-
worthy and seemingly incompatible outcomes. On the practical level, it was
a departure from everyday processes in which whites who murder blacks are
not convicted or receive lighter sentences while blacks who murder whites
are executed or receive longer sentences. The prosecution of Roof is thus
important because the taken-for-granted reality is that black lives do *not*
matter. Here we have an instance where they did. But on the ideological
level, the federal government's prosecution of Roof upholds the taken-for-
grantedness of sovereignty; that the federal government, at least, takes this
level of black death as a threat to its monopoly on the legitimate use of force.
In essence, we might read the swift prosecution of Roof as an effort to assert
that *only the sovereign* can use this much violence against black persons.
Recall that Weber's definition of a state requires a monopoly on the legitimate use of force; to assert its status as sovereign, the state must punish those
who use violence without its consent.

Possibility Three: The People as Sovereign

We might read the decision to remove the flag as an effort to uphold a story of democratic sovereignty where the people, via the legislature, are supposed to be sovereign. In this reading, legislators simply enacted the will of the people by removing the flag. A university public opinion poll in the fall of 2014 (less than a year before the shooting) found that only one third of South Carolinians wanted the flag to come down, while in the months after the shooting, that number doubled to two in three (Shain 2015; Public Policy Polling 2015; Southall 2015). In short, the decision by legislators to remove the flag fuels the belief that "the people" are the source of sovereign power. As the people's will shifted, so too did the legal system. This upholds the fiction of sovereign power bound by and to the people's will.

But recall that Schmitt (2005) identifies the liberal-constitutional story of sovereignty as a paradox; the sovereign as the people is incoherent, because "sovereign is he who decides the exception" and suspends the rules (Schmitt 2005, 5). In responding to the wishes of a majority, the state's political leadership upheld a story about sovereignty that tethers sovereign power to the people's wishes. This fiction helped ensure the perceived legitimacy of sovereign power, but a power whose might can be curbed by and toward the will of the people. As the previous possibility suggests, though, my read is that sovereign power asserted itself through a monopoly of violence rather than to protect democratic sovereignty.

Possibility Four: Subsuming the Political to Politics

Jenny Edkins, following Žižek, distinguishes between the political and politics. Politics is made up of "the routine, regular processes that take place in parliaments, elections, political parties and the institutions of government," while the political is "more lively, less dogmatic, less predictable . . . the arena of innovation and revolution, a field of sudden, unexpected and abrupt change, a point at which the status quo is challenged. It might be where what we might call "real politics" resurfaces, challenging the claims of the imposter that has taken its place" (Edkins 2003, xiii; 12). These political moments may be experienced as traumatic, as escaping the straightforwardly linear aspect of time that we assume to be true. Edkins writes:

> In the linear time of the standard political processes, which is the time asso-
> ciated with the continuance of the nation-state, events that happen are part of a
> well-known and widely accepted story. What happens fits into a pattern. We
> know almost in advance that such events have a place in the narrative. We
> know what they are. In trauma time, in contrast, we have a disruption of this
> linearity. Something happens that doesn't fit, that is unexpected—or that hap-
> pens in an unexpected way. It doesn't fit the story we already have, but de-

mands that we invent a new account, one that will produce a place for what has
happened and make it meaningful. Until this new story is produced we quite
literally do not know what has happened: we cannot say what it was, it doesn't
fit the script—we only know that "something happened." (Edkins 2003, xiv)

In moments of disruption or trauma, the meaning of the event is not clear as
it is happening or even immediately after or possibly ever. As Wolin (2004)
reminds us, the task is for the political theorist or analyst is to put the pieces
(which are always in motion) together in way that makes sense.

Using Edkins's distinction between politics and the political, the events of
June and July 2015 in South Carolina exhibit traits of politics and the political. As Edkins suggests above, when such disruptive events occur, sovereign
power seeks to contain the political by turning it into politics. This is precisely what took place in South Carolina, as the marriage between white domination and sovereign power became clear. But rather than take substantive steps
to rewrite the material conditions that led to actors like Roof taking a gun and
killing African Americans because they are black, the response was purely
symbolic. Thus, the political—a contest about who we really are, what we
want, and an effort to make collective meanings—was subsumed into the
routine politics of a legislative debate (and over a symbol, at that!), with the
outcome a law enacted within twenty-four hours.

The state of South Carolina responded to the mass shooting by having a
public and explicitly political discussion of the elephant flying in front of the
statehouse—the Confederate Battle Flag. It was not unusual for them to
debate this question; as discussed earlier, there had been several efforts to
find a compromise for the flag's removal from 1972 to 2015. What was
extraordinary is that they *did* remove it, *and* that they explicitly linked the
removal to the murders at Mother Emanuel Church. In this sense, mourning
led to action and both the mourning and the action moved in the direction of
racial justice. But the removal cost nothing in terms of the actual practices of
institutionalized white domination. As Hooker (2017) reminds us, any perceived "loss" at the removal of the flag was symbolic rather than material;
further, to equate the mourning of symbolic, long-past white losses with
actual, contemporary black death is a moral failure. They could give up a
colored bit of fabric without changing anything else. Even worse? They
could feel as though they had done something important and in the interest of
racial justice.

The effort of the state of South Carolina's political leadership to give meaning to the events in Charleston were successful in that their actions upheld a
narrative supporting a particular conception of sovereignty: that the state is
colorblind, that the sovereign holds the actual monopoly on the use of force,
and that the people are sovereign. These are mostly incompatible—the state

is empirically white supremacist, individuals kill more citizens than the sovereign does, and state power regularly thwarts the interests of the people. And yet each of them is a story that provides some level of comfort in this sense; the sovereign is keeping us out of Hobbes's state of nature.

The outbreak of meaningful debate in response to a terrible slaughter supports Edkins's claim that the political requires a retelling of the story to give events meaning. This was a moment when the political—with its danger, existential threat, and profound ambivalence—shone through. Undoubtedly, those whites seeking to remove the flag found the removal a fitting tribute to the dead at Mother Emanuel Church. But that the debate itself was contained in the statehouse and led to a symbolic response suggests that politics won out over the political: that legislating this removal killed a democratic moment. A progressive narrative of improvement in racial relations was secured; a symbol of white domination was retired to the museum; and whites could celebrate having done something to pursue racial justice. Because politics won out over the political, though, the underlying expectations did not change, nor did the institutions that daily maintain white domination as sovereign power's ally.

CONCLUSION: A NEW ERA OF EXPLICIT WHITE DOMINATION?

The aftermath of Charleston suggests that the events in Charleston—a white supremacist murdering nine African Americans in a church located in a state that flew a symbol of white domination at its capitol complex—was a political moment that was returned to the order of politics. As the debate about whether tradition or a rational legal order would best justify state practices, it might be that the people—particularly the one in three citizens who, when faced with a conflict between tradition and legality, stuck with tradition—found the entire issue confusing and unsettling, and so turned toward Weber's third form of legitimate authority: the charismatic leader. [14] Donald Trump's focus on immigration and alarms about criminals and rapists hiding in plain sight did not directly cause Dylann Roof to shoot nine worshippers at Mother Emanuel Church. But by positioning himself as the leader who would save the "real" Americans from the violence and criminals within and without—the leader who will approximate Hobbes's sovereign and free us from the tedious and tragic work of democratic politics—his policy goals aligned with the most radical wings of the American white supremacist movement and drew in many white Americans who find politics distasteful or confusing. Trump ran on a ticket fundamentally built on "white democracy" (Olson 2004).

I am not saying that the events in Charleston solely caused Trump's ascent. However, the deeply racialized language he used in his announcement (as well as the multiple examples of racism displayed throughout his public life), the context of Black Lives Matter (and white Americans' perpetual refusal to take its demands seriously), and a white supremacy movement that had recovered from its long hibernation after the Oklahoma City bombing provided a context in which some of the most antidemocratic, illiberal elements in American society could burst forth. It was a movement highly motivated by the symbol of the Confederate Battle Flag. Evan Osnos (2015), a *New Yorker* correspondent researching white supremacist movements in the summer of 2015, observed a speech delivered to the League of the South, a white supremacist organization. According to Osnos, speaker Michael Hill claimed "that the recent lowering of the Confederate flag was just the beginning. Soon, he warned, adopting the unspecified 'they,' they will come for the 'monuments, battlefields, parks, cemeteries, street names, even the dead themselves.' The crowd was on its feet, cheering him on. 'This, my friends, is cultural genocide,' he said, adding, 'Often, as history has shown, cultural genocide is merely a prelude to physical genocide.'" Later, Osnos writes that in the wake of the calls to remove the flag from the South Carolina State House grounds:

> Defenders of the flag were galvanized, and they organized more than a hundred rallies around the South, interpreting the moment, months of racial unrest in Ferguson and Baltimore, as a sign of backlash against political correctness and multiculturalism. Trump's language landed just as American hate groups were more energized than at any time in years. Griffin, the blogger for the League of the South, told me that the removal of the flag had crystallized "fears that people have about what happens when we become a minority."

This energized sector of the electorate helped Trump win at the polls in November 2016. It is worth wondering if the Confederate Battle Flag is undergoing yet another evolution of meaning: one of explicit, unashamed white domination, essentially unlinked to the heritage and historical arguments that so long provided cover for white people to fly the flag without taking responsibility for an unjust racial order.

The Confederate Battle flag symbolizes many things. One of those—inseparable from the flag itself—is white domination: what Weber might call rule by custom or tradition. The message of white dominance was symbolically eschewed by the people of South Carolina when the Confederate flag was finally sent to the Confederate Relic Room in July 2015. But was the removal too quick? Was it, too, merely symbolic? My suspicion is that the flag came down too quickly; as often happens, we were too easily drawn to the pageantry and symbolism rather than a harder but more important debate over the substance, institutionalization, and objectification of white dominance.

We can imagine another response: that South Carolina removed the flag *while simultaneously* enacting a program of affirmative action meant to repair the racial divide in the state: that it gave up arresting young black men for possession of controlled substances, committed to a substantive program of repairing subsidized housing, provided massive support to primarily black schools, and improved public transportation. In the absence of such a program, the removal of the symbol of white domination leaves the institutions of sovereign power, allied with white domination, intact while making the connections between them even harder to see. And as one symbol of a past-that-is-not-yet-past fell, another symbol rose: a white savior in an apocalyptic present that requires a *true* sovereign who can return us safely to a past that never existed—Donald Trump.

ACKNOWLEDGMENTS

My thanks to fellow panelists, discussant Andrew Valls, and audience members (particularly Simon Stow) who attended the "Diverse Legacies of Violence" panel at the 2015 American Political Science Association meeting. Additionally, I am grateful for the opportunity to have presented a version of this paper to the members of The Ohio State University's Political Theory Workshop (organized by Inés Valdez and Benjamin McKean), with particular thanks to Navid Farnia and Amy Shuster for their thoughtful comments and suggestions (to which I wish I had more successfully responded). Finally, I extend my gratitude to Jennifer Fredette, Kirstine Taylor, and Lisa Clarke, as well as the editors of this volume, Alex Hirsch and David McIvor, for helpful comments on drafts.

NOTES

1. Regarding the use of "black" and "white" as terms to describe racialized groups, I have chosen to capitalize neither. For a discussion of capitalization of these terms contemporary to the events discussed here, see Perlman 2015.

2. It is important to remember that in April 2015, only a few months before Roof's rampage, police officer Michael Slager, white, shot Walter Scott, black, in the back several times as Scott fled a traffic stop. The shooting was recorded by a bystander and released to the media. Scott died at the scene. Slager was indicted for murder, but the trial resulted in a hung jury. Slager was later charged with civil rights violations and obstruction of justice (as a result of lying in a police report about the circumstances of the shooting), and eventually pled to a lesser charge of excessive force. The difference between police treatment of Scott after a traffic stop and Roof after mass murder is telling and stark (CNN Library 2017).

Rev. Pinckney spoke on the floor of the SC Senate after Scott's death, advocating for a bill requiring body cameras for police officers as one way to reduce to police violence against black people (Pinckney 2016). Central to Pinckney's commentary was the inequality that surrounded black lives.

3. Though not the focus of the discussion here, the website was located by Twitter users and first publicized by Gawker rather than law enforcement or traditional media outlets (O'Connor 2015).

4. Butler's distinction between explanation and exoneration is helpful here (Butler 2004, 23).

5. Romney came out strongly against the flag in the June 20 Republican debate, and several other candidates followed suit after Governor Haley's call for removal on June 22. Several Republicans, though, said that the decision should be left to the state of South Carolina: Cruz, Fiorina, Huckabee, Jindal, Perry, Rubio, and Santorum. Donald Trump was the last of the presidential candidates to state a position (Saenz 2015).

6. In the following section, all references are to Coski (2005) unless otherwise noted.

7. These are my categories, derived from the meticulous research overview presented by Coski (2005). Any errors or flaws in the framework presented here are solely mine.

8. Interestingly, the leaders of the States' Rights Party tried to distance themselves from the Confederate flags, but their followers continued to wave them with zeal. Coski notes that the Confederate flag is notably absent in political campaigning by candidates, so this effort to separate the flag from "political-ness" is not entirely without precedent.

9. I will further elaborate this argument in the final section. I follow here Jenny Edkins's claim about the violence of sovereignty in *Trauma and the Memory of Politics* (Edkins 2003).

10. Terrorism by white supremacists has claimed more bodies than terrorism by any other group in the United States, so this shouldn't be a shock. As Leti Volpp (2002) and others have pointed out, when members of a minority group take similar actions, they are made to stand in for the entirety of the group they represent, while when a white person acts in this way, his actions are explained as mental illness or deviance. Thus, not all white men were rounded up after the Oklahoma City bombing, but a considerable number of Muslims/Arabs/Middle Easterners were after September 11.

11. Edkins's work pinpoints something important about how the stories that sovereign power tells obscure violence, but I am not persuaded that symbolic or narrative resistance is enough. I doubt Edkins would argue that either, but it might be implied by her focus on the symbolic rather than on institutions. I am more persuaded by Clarissa Rile Hayward's take on the relation of narrative, memory, and institutional change in *How Americans Make Race*. As Hayward (2013) explains, the "narrative identity thesis" misses too much and must be supplemented with institutional analysis; when stories become institutions, their original intent persists even when the stories about their existence change.

12. As Juliet Hooker (2017) argues, whites in the United States unjustly equate symbolic losses—relative economic losses, not being able to use derogatory terms for people of color, or not being able to fly the Confederate flag without being called racist—to actual black bodies in the streets killed by police.

13. As several recent theorists have noted, legal responsibility alone does a poor job of capturing political responsibility (Young 2001; Lavin 2008; Schiff 2014; Satkunanandan 2016; Vázquez-Arroyo 2016).

14. Weber would disagree with how I use this phrase. Weber was relatively confident that the party system would weed out tyrants because to rise any higher than a standard bureaucrat required a kind of apprenticeship that would cull the worst elements out. Weber's description of the charismatic leader is one who takes responsibility for his actions, knowing that there is no way that he can actually be responsible for their effects; it is a difficult moral position and ethical position that requires character and integrity. But Weber's recognition that people are drawn to those who portray certainty seems helpful in thinking about the attraction of so many Americans to Donald Trump.

WORKS CITED

Alemany, Jacqueline. 2015. "Donald Trump Tees Off on the Confederate Flag." CBS News, June 23, 2015. http://www.cbsnews.com/news/donald-trump-tees-off-on-the-confederate-flag/.

Berman, Mark. 2015. "South Carolina Governor Signs Bill Removing Confederate Flag from Statehouse Grounds." *Washington Post*, July 9, 2015. http://wapo.st/1J6ISfp.

Blight, David W. 2001. *Race and Reunion: The Civil War in American Memory*. Cambridge: Harvard University Press.

Blinder, Alan, and Richard Fausset. 2015. "South Carolina House Votes to Remove Confederate Flag." *New York Times*, July 9, 2015. https://nyti.ms/2jI6SUd.

Butler, Judith. 2004. *Precarious Life: The Powers of Mourning and Violence*. New York: Routledge.

Chow, Kat. 2015. "Denmark Vesey And The History Of Charleston's 'Mother Emanuel' Church." NPR News. May 16, 2015. http://www.npr.org/sections/codeswitch/2015/06/18/415465656/denmark-vesey-and-the-history-of-charleston-s-mother-emanuel-church.

Clinton, Hillary. 2015. Interview with Jon Ralston. "Hillary Clinton on 'Ralston Live,' with video and transcript." *Ralston Reports*, June 18, 2015. https://www.ralstonreports.com/blog/hillary-clinton-ralston-live-video-and-transcript .

CNN Library. n.d. "Controversial Police Encounters Fast Facts." CNN. http://www.cnn.com/2015/04/05/us/controversial-police-encounters-fast-facts/index.html.

Coski, John M. 2005. *The Confederate Battle Flag: America's Most Embattled Emblem*. Cambridge: Harvard University Press.

Dilts, Andrew. 2014. *Punishment and Inclusion: Race, Membership, and the Limits of American Liberalism*. New York: Fordham University.

Edkins, Jenny. 2003. *Trauma and the Memory of Politics*. New York: Cambridge University Press.

Ellis, Ralph, Greg Botelho, and Ed Payne. 2015. "Charleston church shooter hears victim's kin say, 'I forgive you.'" CNN, June 19, 2015. http://www.cnn.com/2015/06/19/us/charleston-church-shooting-main/.

Emanuel African Methodist Episcopalian Church. n.d. "History," on Emanuel African Methodist Episcopalian Church website. http://www.emanuelamechurch.org/pages/staff/.

Firestone, David. 2000. "South Carolina Votes to Remove Confederate Flag From Dome." *New York Times*, May 19, 2000. http://www.nytimes.com/2000/05/19/us/south-carolina-votes-to-remove-confederate-flag-from-dome.html .

Freud, Sigmund. 2005. "Mourning and Melancholia," in *On Murder, Mourning, and Melancholia*. Translated and edited by Shaun Whiteside. New York: Penguin/Modern Classics, 2005.

The Guardian. n.d. "The Counted: People Killed by the Police in the US." *The Guardian*. https://www.theguardian.com/us-news/ng-interactive/2015/jun/01/the-counted-police-killings-us-database.

Haley, Nikki. 2015. "Transcript: Gov. Nikki Haley of South Carolina on Removing the Confederate Flag." *New York Times*, June 22, 2015. https://nyti.ms/2kzuFDC.

Harris, Cheryl. 1993. "Whiteness as Property." *Harvard Law Review* 106, no. 8: 1707–791.

Hayward, Clarissa Rile. 2013. *How Americans Make Race: Stories, Institutions, Spaces*. New York: Cambridge University Press.

Hobbes, Thomas. 1994. *Leviathan*. Indianapolis: Hackett Publishing Company.

Hooker, Juliet. 2017. "Black Protest/White Grievance: On the Problem of White Political Imaginations Not Shaped by Loss." *South Atlantic Quarterly* 116, no. 3 (July): 483–504.

Horowitz, Jason, Nick Corasaniti, and Ashley Southall. 2015. "Nine Killed in Shooting at Black Church in Charleston." *New York Times*, June 17, 2015. https://nyti.ms/2jFlpzX.

Lavin, Chad. 2008. *The Politics of Responsibility*. Champaign: University of Illinois.

Locke, John. 1980. *Second Treatise of Government*. Indianapolis: Hackett Publishing Company.

López, Ian Haney. 2006. *White by Law: The Legal Construction of Race* 10th Anniversary Ed. New York: New York University Press.

Mapping Police Violence. n.d. Website. https://mappingpoliceviolence.org/unarmed/.

Miller, Jake. 2015. "Donald Trump: Hillary Clinton blamed me for Charleston shooting." *CBS News*, June 19, 2015. http://www.cbsnews.com/news/donald-trump-hillary-clinton-blamed-me-for-charleston-shooting/.

Mills, Charles. 1997. *The Racial Contract*. Ithaca: Cornell University Press.

———. 1998. *Blackness Visible: Essays on Philosophy and* Race. Ithaca: Cornell University Press.

Newsome, Bree. 2015. Interview with Amy Goodman. "'This Flag Comes Down Today': Bree Newsome Scales SC Capitol Flagpole, Takes Down Confederate Flag," *Democracy Now*, July 3, 2015, https://www.democracynow.org/2015/7/3/this_flag_comes_down_today_bree.

NPR Staff. 2015. "The Victims: 9 Were Slain At Charleston's Emanuel AME Church." NPR News, June 18, 2015. http://www.npr.org/sections/thetwo-way/2015/06/18/415539516/the-victims-9-were-slain-at-charlestons-emanuel-ame-church.

O'Connor, Brendan. 2015. "Here Is What Appears to Be Dylann Roof's Racist Manifesto." gawker.com, June 20, 2015. http://gawker.com/here-is-what-appears-to-be-dylann-roofs-racist-manifest-1712767241.

Olson, Joel. 2004. *The Abolition of White Democracy*. Minneapolis: University of Minnesota Press.

Osnos, Evan. 2015. "The Fearful and the Frustrated: Donald Trump's nationalist coalition takes shape—for now." *New Yorker*, August 31, 2015. http://www.newyorker.com/magazine/2015/08/31/the-fearful-and-the-frustrated.

Perlman, Merrill. 2015. "Black and White: Why Capitalization Matters." *Columbia Journalism Review*, June 23, 2015. https://www.cjr.org/analysis/language_corner_1.php.

Pinckney, Clementa. 2016. "Speech on Walter Scott Shooting, April 14, 2015," in *Charleston Syllabus: Readings on Race, Racism, and Racial Violence*. Edited by Chad Williams, Kidad E. Williams, and Keisha N. Blain. Athens: University of Georgia Press.

Public Policy Polling. 2015. "South Carolinians Support Removal of Flag, Want Tougher Gun Laws." September 10, 2015. http://www.publicpolicypolling.com/main/2015/09/south-carolinians-support-removal-of-flag-want-tougher-gun-laws.html.

Ross, Janell. 2017. "'They Were Not Patriots': New Orleans Removes Monument to Confederate Gen. Robert E. Lee." *Washington Post*, May 19, 2017. http://wapo.st/2q1WvuD?t.

Saenz, Arlette. 2015. "Here's Where the 2016 Candidates Stand on the Confederate Flag Issue." ABC News, June 23, 2015. http://abcnews.go.com/Politics/2016-candidates-stand-confederate-flag-issue/story?id=31947516.

Santaella, Tony. 2015. "Lawmakers Agree to Debate Confederate Flag." WTLX, June 23, 2015. http://www.wltx.com/news/lawmakers-agree-to-debate-confederate-flag/234981674.

Satkunanandan, Shalini. 2016. *Extraordinary Responsibility: Politics beyond the Moral Calculus*. New York: Cambridge University Press.

Scheingold, Stuart A. 2004. *The Politics of Rights: Lawyers, Public Policy, and Political Change*, 2nd Edition. Ann Arbor: University of Michigan Press.

Schiff, Jade Larissa. 2014. *The Burdens of Political Responsibility: Narrative and the Cultivation of Responsiveness*. New York: Cambridge University Press.

Schmitt, Carl. 2005. *Political Theology*. Chicago: University of Chicago Press.

Shain, Andrew. 2015. "Winthrop Poll: Majority in SC Back Confederate Flag's Removal." *The Herald*, September 30, 2015. http://www.heraldonline.com/news/state/south-carolina/article37020057.html.

Southall, Ashley. 2015. "Most Americans Support South Carolina's Removal of Rebel Flag, Poll Says." *New York Times*, August 5, 2015. https://nyti.ms/2uewEFj.

Trump, Donald. 2015. "Full Text: Donald Trump Announces a Presidential Bid." *Washington Post*, June 16, 2015. http://wapo.st/1HPABjR.

Vázquez-Arroyo, Antonio. 2016. *Political Responsibility: Responding to Predicaments of Power*. New York: Columbia University Press.

Volpp, Leti. 2002. "The Citizen and the Terrorist." *Immigration and Nationality Law Review* 23: 561–586.

Weber, Max. 2004. "Politics as a Vocation," in *The Vocation Lectures*. Edited by David Owen and Tracy B. Strong. Translated by Rodney Livingston. Indianapolis: Hackett Publishing Company.

Wolin, Sheldon. 2004. *Politics and Vision: Continuity and Innovation in Western Political Thought*, Expanded Edition. Princeton: Princeton University Press.

Young, Iris Marion. 2001. *Responsibility for Justice*. Oxford: Oxford University Press.

Chapter Four

Mourning Denied

The Tabooed Subject

By Claudia Leeb

Recent discussions in political theory regarding the concept of mourning have been rather controversial.[1] On the one hand we have thinkers, such as Bonnie Honig (2013), who suggest that there is a radical divide between mourning and politics, and on the other side there are those, like Judith Butler (2006), who foreground the political possibilities of mourning. In between, we find thinkers, such as David McIvor (2016) and Giunia Gatta (2015), who argue that mourning can in some instances and in stages become the impetus for political agency.

In this chapter, I argue that the work of mourning of and by those in (post)-crime generations[2] for the victims of past crimes is the precondition to a) take responsibility for such crimes, b) show solidarity with the victims of crimes (such as the support of victims' claims for reparations), and c) make sure that the crimes of the past are not repeated. As the psychoanalytic and the early Frankfurt school critical theorists Alexander and Margarete Mitscherlich put it: "history does not repeat itself, and yet it often incorporates a repetition compulsion whose grip can be broken only when historical events bring about a change in the level of consciousness" (1975: 50).

Only if people engage in the painful work of mourning for the victims of past crimes can this change in the level of consciousness be brought about. If mourning as a theoretical and practical concept is dismissed, then people are in danger to repeat the horrors of the past. The core aim of this chapter is to get a better understanding of those factors that hinder individuals and collectives to accomplish the work of mourning. It shows that making past crimes a taboo topic interferes with the work of mourning, which is why political and social theorists must pay close attention to the connection between taboo and

65

failures to mourn. I bring the Mitscherlichs in conversation with Theodor W. Adorno, Sigmund Freud, and Georgio Agamben, to defend my argument. The chapter is composed of four sections, including the introduction.

The second section, "Working Through the Past: Taboo and Mourning," first establishes the definition of "working through the past" and then brings the concepts of taboo and mourning in conversation to learn more about the barriers to mourning that hinder a successful working through the past. The third section, "Tabooed Antigone: Mourning Denied," further establishes the connection between the taboo and denied mourning, by showing how Antigone's status as the tabooed subject effected that mourning was denied to her. The fourth and last section, "Taboo and Mourning in Austria's Genocide on Roma and Sinti," explains the taboos Austrian politicians erected around Austria's support and contributions to the Nazi crimes, and the status of Roma and Sinti as tabooed "Gypsies," as core reasons why Austrians have failed to mourn the annihilation of that part of their population, and why there is continuing violence upon them in contemporary Austria.[3]

Working Through the Past: Taboo and Mourning

The German early Frankfurt School critical theorist Theodor W. Adorno distinguishes, in relation to the crimes perpetuated by the National Socialist regime, "working through the past" (*Aufarbeitung der Vergangenheit*) from "mastering of the past" (*Vergangenheitsbewältigung*) (2010, 183). Whereas mastering the past implies the intention "to close the books on the past and, if possible even remove it from memory" (Adorno 2010, 183), working through the past implies an enlightenment about what has happened "that must work against forgetfulness" (Adorno 2010, 223). Such working through the past implies the strength to comprehend the incomprehensible (Adorno 2010, 223). It also implies the strength to confront unconscious individual and collective guilt, instead of resorting to defensive mechanisms that aim at keeping such guilt and the uncomfortable feelings connected to it repressed (Adorno 2010).

I agree with Adorno that people need to aim for a working through the past, instead of a mastering of the past. In my book *The Politics of Repressed Guilt: The Tragedy of Austrian Silence*, I expose the defensive mechanisms that Austrians use to not confront their guilt pertaining to the Nazi era with the attempt to forget what had happened (Leeb 2018).[4] In this chapter I go a step beyond this book and argue that working through the past, besides confronting guilt feelings, also requires that people engage in the painful work of individual and collective mourning for the losses of the victims.

As Alexander and Margarete Mitscherlich, in relation to the crimes of the National Socialist regime, point out: "the murder of millions of people cannot be mastered" but must be "worked through" (1975: 1–5). Such a working through also implies a "working through the losses," which is accomplished in the work of mourning (Mitscherlichs, 1975: xvi–xvii). However, here it is important to note that confronting unconscious guilt and the work of mourning are intimately connected tasks, insofar as the former can only be accomplished if one engages in the work of mourning (and vice versa).

As such "without a working-through of guilt, however belated, there could be no work of mourning" (Mitscherlichs, 1975: 50). The use of defensive mechanisms to fend off unconscious guilt (such as projecting or displacing one's guilt onto the victims, and reversing roles and turning into a victim oneself) are also effective in that they hinder an engagement with the painful work of mourning, which underlines another aspect of the connection between confronting guilt and the work of mourning.

However, to get a better understanding of the barriers to a successful working through one's past, one must take a closer look at the functioning of taboos in (post)-crime generations and their connection to and effects upon mourning. Adorno mentions briefly the effects of official taboos that hinder a working through the past in "The Meaning of Working Through the Past" (Adorno 2010), and the Mitscherlichs devote a section in one of their later chapters in their *The Inability to Mourn* where they also briefly mention that the taboos postwar elites erected stand in the service of forgetting the millions of murders of the National Socialist era (1995: 99). However, Adorno and the Mitscherlichs do not establish a link between taboos and the failure to mourn in more depth, which I attempt in the remainder of this section, by also bringing Sigmund Freud's *Totem and Taboo* (1989) into the discussion.

There are four interconnected themes that connect the taboo to a failure to mourn.[5]

First, when someone or something is taboo it means that one is prohibited to approach the tabooed subject or object, including discussing why it is taboo, which implies that the taboo is "expressed in prohibitions and restrictions" (Freud 1989: 24). Taboo restrictions differ from moral restrictions, because they do not provide a system that explains in general terms why certain restrictions must be observed. Taboo prohibitions "have no grounds and are of unknown origin," and they impose themselves on us on their own account (Freud 1989: 24–25). Taboos are not only effective at one historical moment, as they can travel from one generation to the next. Taboos "often survive with unbroken strength through long periods of history" (Mitscherlichs, 1975: 107). However, the desire to violate the taboo remains in the unconscious.[6] As such, "the basis of taboo is a prohibited action, for performing which a strong inclination exists in the unconscious" (Freud 1989: 41). Furthermore, most people are unconscious of the effects taboos have upon them.

One of the central aspects of taboos is that they can also lead to "a loss of memory—an amnesia—the motives for the prohibition (which is conscious) remain unknown" (Freud 1989: 39). Insofar as tabooed topics are not to be discussed, then historical subjects that have become taboo are likely to fade from one's memory. Here we can establish an important (dis-)connection to the work of mourning. Mourning, according to Freud, is an activity, where one tends to be "preoccupied with the dead (wo/)man, to dwell upon (her/)his memory and to preserve it as long as possible" (1989: 72). Insofar as a taboo is likely to lead to a loss of memory or a forgetting from one generation to the next, and mourning aims at preserving the memory of the dead as long as possible, the taboo is directed against the work of mourning or becomes a barrier to mourning. In other words, if there is no memory of the crimes perpetuated by the collectivity, because the taboo has obscured that memory, then members of the collectivity cannot engage in the work of mourning. This first element that connects the taboo to mourning is interconnected with the second element.

Second, the taboo, besides the objective prohibition "thou shalt not" touch, also implies an "inhibition of thought" (Mitscherlichs, 1975: 91). Insofar as the taboo inhibits our critical thinking, one of its side effects is that it keeps people's "state of knowledge at a low level" (Mitscherlichs, 1975: 91). As an example, Austrian political elites established a taboo in regards to the Austrian contributions to and support of the millions of people murdered by the National Socialist regime. The taboo declared an area of memory as untouchable (Austria as a perpetrator nation), which told (or commanded) people that they must not touch the tabooed memory, and that they must not ask any further questions. However, there is also collusion with the taboo— the broader population was only too ready to accept the taboo offered by elites, because the taboo spreads "a subjective sense of security against the consequences of the past" (Mitscherlichs, 1975: 99), and gave Austrians (over generations) the feeling that there is a part of Austria's history they do not need to feel guilty and responsible for.

Here we find another important (dis-)connection to mourning. Insofar as the work of mourning can be accomplished only "when one knows what one has to sever oneself from" (Mitscherlichs, 1975: 66), and the taboo is erected to keep us from gaining such knowledge, the taboo is in an effective barrier to the work of mourning. To come back to the example above, even if there is a memory about the millions of victims of the Nazi regime, but I have no knowledge regarding the specific details about how the collectivity I associate myself with contributed to such crimes, because a taboo inhibits gaining such knowledge, I cannot engage in the work of mourning. However, even if there is a memory of past crimes and I have knowledge of them, this does not mean that I necessarily engage in the work of mourning, which leads me to the next (dis-)connection between taboo and mourning.

Third, to engage in the work of mourning, I need to have sympathy for the lives that have been lost (Mitscherlichs, 1975: 42). This requires not just knowledge of the losses, but also a feeling of care or concern for those lives. Taboos forestall any sympathy with the victims, because violation of the taboo makes the offender herself taboo (Freud 1989: 29). This is so, because the principal prohibition of the taboo is the taboo against touching. The prohibition not only applies to immediate physical contact, but extends to anything that directs one's thoughts to the forbidden object (Freud 1989: 35). The reason for the prohibition to touch or "come in contact with" the taboo is its contagious nature, which implies the danger to become "infected" with the taboo. As Freud puts it, "anyone who violates a taboo by coming into contact with something that is taboo becomes taboo (herself/) himself and that then no one may come into contact with (her/)him" (Freud 1989: 35–36).

Insofar as one can only engage in the work of mourning if one has sympathy with those who died, as mourning is a process of emotional detachment, this requires there to have been some emotional attachment in the first place. Here the taboo, which threatens that one can become tabooed and with that a shunned subject oneself, is an effective barrier to the work of mourning. In other words, people can only engage in the work of mourning if they have sympathy for, and thus some emotional attachment to, with the victims of crimes. As the Mitscherlichs point out, that "the same lack of empathy still appears today in relation to the wounded feelings of those whom Germany oppressed, supports the thesis that in history horrors can indeed be repeated" (1975: 104).

Here I have arrived at the fourth and last aspect of the (dis-)connection between mourning and taboo. The Mitscherlichs explain that the "work of mourning can be accomplished only when one knows what one has to sever oneself from. And only by slowly detaching oneself from lost object relations—can a meaningful relationship to reality and to the past be maintained. Without the painful work of recollection this can never be achieved. And without it, the old ideals, which in National Socialism led to the fatal turn taken in Germany history, will continue to operate within the unconscious" (1975: 66). The work of mourning entails a process of detachment, and once it is accomplished it leads to the establishment of a meaningful relationship to reality. More precisely, it implies a testing of reality, which shows that the lost object no longer exists, and which requires the withdrawal of all libido from its attachment to the object.

However, since a person "never willingly abandons a libido-position," the work of mourning is "carried through bit by bit, under great expense of time and cathetic energy, while all the time the existence of the lost object is continued in the mind. Each single one of the memories and hopes is brought up and hyper-cathected, and the detachment of the libido from it accomplished" (Freud, 1917: 154). This means that when a person dies, we initially oppose reality and continue to cling to that person. However, eventually the person's death must at last "be dealt with realistically: internal acceptance of loss must be struggled for, learned, and accomplished. This is why in psycho-analysis we speak of the 'work of mourning'" (Mitscherlichs, 1975: 62).

If we take a closer look at the effects of the taboo, we can glimpse another element of the ways in which the taboo hinders the work of mourning. If a collectivity, such as a nation, observes a taboo in regards to past crimes, then it can soothe its conscience about individual and collective guilt and respon-sibility. However, the taboo has also a "paralyzing effect on the more highly organized capacities of the psyche, namely on the ability critically to work through reality" (Mitscherlichs 1995: 105). Insofar as the work of mourning entails a process and is accomplished over a long period of time, in which one learns, bit by bit, to accept the reality of the loss, the taboo, which paralyzes our ability to work through reality, has ample chances to interrupt the work of mourning in which one strives to work through the reality of the past horrors.

Tabooed Antigone: Mourning Denied

In a recent essay (Leeb, 2016) I discuss Antigone as the paradigmatic female example of what the Italian political philosopher Agamben termed *homo sacer,* the ambiguous legal figure first mentioned in Roman law, whom any-body can kill without committing homicide (Agamben, 1995), or, in Anti-gones' case, femicide, which challenges the dominant reading of Antigone as a transformative agent in feminist, critical and psychoanalytic theory.[7] Here I further develop the idea of Antigone as *homo sacer*, by showing that the tragedy points at a central aspect Agamben did not consider in his elabora-tion of different aspects that characterize *homo sacer*—that once you are in the position of *homo sacer*, you are not mourned for. Antigone stands as the paradigmatic example for the millions of people murdered during the Nation-al Socialist regime for whom mourning continues to be denied up until to-day.[8]

Why is the one who finds herself or himself in the position of *homo sacer* not mourned for? I answer this question by pointing at the peculiar position of *homo sacer*, who, first, as the living dead neither dwells among the living nor among the dead. Since the work of mourning can only be accomplished for those that belong properly to the world of the dead, Antigone is not mourned for. Second, *homo sacer* lives in the no-(wo-)man's land between the sacred and the profane, which is also the zone where the taboo is located. Antigone becomes the tabooed subject, because she mourns for her brother, himself a tabooed subject, which is why nobody stands by her side when she is buried alive, and her death remains not mourned for.

Because *homo sacer* finds herself in the zone in between life and death there is no need, or it is perhaps impossible, to mourn for her. Antigone finds herself living in the no-(wo-)man's land of the living dead, where she is dwelling neither among the living nor among the dead, which she laments *at the same time* she points out that she is not mourned for: "How I go unwept by loved ones, and with what ceremony to the newly raised mound of my strange tomb. Oh ill-fated woman, with no home among mortals nor as a corpse among corpses, neither with the living, nor with the dead (Antigone 2003: 808–812),

Here Antigone laments her peculiar position of *homo sacer*, who, as Agamben points out, is "defined solely by virtue of having entered into an intimate symbiosis with death without, nevertheless, belonging to the word of the deceased" (Agamben 1995: 100). It is no coincidence that she points out her position as the living-dead woman right after she points out that her death will be unwept—nobody will mourn for Antigone because she finds herself in the position as *homo sacer*. Since she neither belongs properly to the world of the living nor the world of the dead, and the work of mourning can only be accomplished for those who have entered the realm of the dead, mourning is denied to Antigone.

Contemporary readings dismiss that mourning is denied to Antigone and focus on Antigone's work of mourning for her brother Polineices, which mainly implies her capacity for transformative agency. As an example, Fanny Söderbäck suggests that Antigone's burial of her brother is a decisively public act, which "marks the inauguration of a public realm" (2010, 72). Similarly, Honig reads Antigone's lamentation as a deliberately political act (2013), and Gatta points out how Antigone's work of mourning can lead to political agency (2015). Such readings reinforce the dominant reading of Antigone as a transformative agent and veil the more unsettling side of the tragedy—Antigone's mourning for her brother puts her in the position of *homo sacer*, a tabooed subject, and as a result her own death is not mourned for.

Oedipus's and Jocasta's sons, and the brothers of Antigone, Eteocles and Polineices, had shared the rule of Thebes jointly until Eteocles, unwilling to share the rule with Polineices any longer, expelled his brother. Polineices left the kingdom, but raised an Argive army and attacked the city of Thebes. The civil war left both brothers dead. King Creon, who ascended to the throne after the death of the brothers, declared Polineices an enemy of Thebes, and decreed that Eteocles be buried as a war hero with full military honors, whereas Polineices was not to be buried and mourned for. His corpse was to rot in the city, lying open in its fields so that birds and scavenging dogs can feast on it.

Creon points at the principal prohibition of the taboo against touching when he announces his decree and turns Polineices (or his corpse) into a tabooed subject: "Polyneices, I say, is to have no burial: no man is to touch him or say the least prayer for him; he shall lie on the plain, unburied; and the birds and the scavenging dogs can do with him whatever they like." (Anti-

gone 2003: 44-49). Nobody was allowed to touch or be touched by Polineices's death in a double sense: physically, by handling his corpse in a
burial; and emotionally, by mourning for him. Creon made Polineices into a
tabooed subject, and all subjects of Thebes had to follow the taboo uncondi-
tionally. Here we can see the close connection between taboo and mourning,
insofar as Creon's tabooed subject (Polineices) is denied mourning.

"A taboo shared by many has a unifying effect, because it prescribes a
fixed and uniform verdict in relation to an area of conflict" (Mischerlichs
1975: 100). The area of conflict (struggle for the throne by the brothers) in
the Antigone drama was solved by the fixed verdict of Eteocles as a war hero
and Polineices as an enemy, which eradicated the memory of the more complicated aspects of the struggle (Eteocles's unwillingness to share the throne
with his brother and that Polineices was Creon's nephew/son), and had a
unifying effect on a society that was torn by civil war.

However, Antigone was not afraid of the taboo and did not subject herself
to it, and on two occasions both came in close physical contact with the
tabooed subject, by putting dust over the dead body as a gesture of burial,
and associated herself emotionally with the tabooed subject by openly
mourning his death in her attempts to bury him. Antigone's act to grant
Polineices funeral rites was not an attempt to either disrupt (Butler 2010:
143) or cleanse her family lineage (Mader 2010; Chanter 2007) that was
plagued by the incest taboo, insofar as Antigone was the offspring of the
incestuous relationship between Oedipus and his mother Jocasta. Rather,
Antigone's act of burying her brother and mourning for him was an act of
breaking the taboo set up by Creon to which everybody in Thebes was
subjected.

Taboos repress the desire to touch and be touched into the unconscious.
As such, "the prohibition is noisily conscious, while the persistent desire to
touch is unconscious and the subject knows nothing of it" (Freud 1989: 38).
Adorno points at the ways in which the child's fascination with carcasses and
the "repulsively sweet odor of putrefaction" is a physical moment where a
child is touched by the collectively repressed knowledge about the mass
murders committed during the National Socialist regime. In this physical
moment "an unconscious knowledge whispers to the child what is repressed
by civilized education," and the taboo can no longer repress her desire to
touch the taboo and she starts asking "'What is that?' and 'Where is it
going?'" (Adorno 2003: 366).

Perhaps it was also the stench of the rotting Polineices that touched the
people of Thebes and whispered into their ears the knowledge the taboo
aimed to foreclose—the knowledge of the injustices of civil war where former friends and once loved people (such as Polineices) are made into enemies. Antigone was so harshly punished because her mourning for the tabooed subject made the whispering of the repressed knowledge louder. Her

act implied the danger that in the people of Thebes, just like in the child Adorno invokes, the unconscious desire to touch the taboo surfaces and they start to ask questions that should not be asked.

Anyone who does what is forbidden, that is, who violates a taboo (Antigone by touching and being touched by her brother), becomes taboo herself. The reason for this is that that person "possesses the dangerous quality of tempting others to follow (her/) his example: why should (she/) he be allowed to do what is forbidden to others? Thus (she/) he is truly contagious in that every example encourages imitation, and for that reason (she/) he (herself/) himself must be shunned" (Freud 1989: 42). The reason Antigone turned into the tabooed subject whom everybody in Thebes had to shun was not because she touched the incest taboo, insofar as she mourned an incestuous love for her brother, as Brendese has suggested (2014), but because all subjects of Thebes were subjected to the taboo to not bury and mourn Polineices.

Antigone turned into the tabooed subject because she did what was forbidden to everybody—she came "in contact with" or touched what was taboo. The danger was here that she might arouse forbidden desires, the desire to touch the taboo, in others. Her transgression of the taboo prohibition might lead somebody else to do the same and then the problem (for Creon) is that "disobedience to prohibitions spreads like a contagion" (Freud 1989: 44), which helps to explain why Creon then had to punish her to prevent the disobedience from spreading to others.

The important aspect of Antigone's becoming a tabooed subject by touching the taboo herself is that, like her bother, she is denied any funeral rites and nobody will mourn for her, which underlines again the strong connection between the taboo and mourning, insofar as the taboo expresses itself here in the form of a denial of mourning. The height of the tragedy is when Antigone laments in the fourth episode after she learns that Creon has ordered that she will be buried alive for her act of transgression: "How I go unwept by loved ones, and with what ceremony to the newly raised mound of my strange tomb" (Antigone 2003: 850–853).

Antigone's lamentation on her death remaining unwept is confirmed by the unfolding of the tragedy. Antigone, unlike her brother, who receives at the end of the tragedy funeral rites from Creon, is not granted any funeral rites and nobody mourns for her death. At the end of the tragedy her uncle/ father Creon only mourns the death of his wife and son but not the death of his niece/daughter Antigone, which underlines that Antigone's lament about dying unwept has become a reality for her. As outlined in point three in the previous section, the taboo serves here to sever the emotional connection which is necessary for mourning.

Creon, at the end, lifts the taboo against touching Polineices by burying him. However, it seems that Creon is not truly touched by Polineices' fate, and his mourning is of a narcissistic nature, insofar as it is the result of demands by Tiresias, the seer, that Creon must bury Polineices to avoid his further downfall. No such demands to grant Antigone funeral rites are uttered by community members. Until the end of the story Antigone remains the tabooed woman bereft of any mourning, because she is the one who transgressed the taboo against touching Polineices. By not granting her funeral rites and not mourning for her, the memory of her transgressive act can be erased, and with that the danger that others in Thebes might imitate her.

Antigone was not only not mourned for, she also had no allies when she was buried alive, which she also laments: "What ally should I call upon?" (Antigone 2003: 886–887). Why does Antigone have no allies? Antigone dwells in the zone of indistinction between the sacred and the profane, which marks at the same time the zone of the taboo. Agamben points out that the taboo marks the Western experience of the sacred with its ambiguity: "The analysis of the ban—which is assimilated to the taboo—determines from the very beginning the genesis of the doctrine of the ambiguity of the sacred: the ambiguity of the ban, which excludes in including, implies the ambiguity of the sacred" (1995: 77). Antigone became the tabooed subject by her abandonment by the people and laws of Thebes, which exposed her to annihilation.

That the tabooed subject has no allies is connected to Antigone's particular position as *homo sacer*, behind which the ambiguous character of the taboo lurks. As Freud points out, "taboo" is originally a Polynesian word and was still used among the ancient Romans, whose "sacer" meant the same as the Polynesian "taboo." The "taboo" has a double meaning. On the one side it means "sacred," or "consecrated" and on the other side it means "uncanny," "dangerous," "forbidden, and "unclean" (Freud 1989: 24).

Nobody "touched" Antigone, in the sense that nobody showed solidarity with her and stood by her side, not because she was not equal and excluded from the public sphere (although this was also the case), as feminist thinkers such as Söderbäck (2010: 74) have claimed. Rather, nobody was an ally for Antigone because anyone who violates a taboo is in danger of becoming "infected" with the taboo, and with that become taboo herself. Furthermore, nobody was an ally because Creon needed to sever any emotional or physical bonds to Antigone, to keep others who might be tempted from also breaking the taboo. While Haemon was an ally of Antigone and was as such touched by her fate, this led to his death, which was perhaps a warning for the people in Thebes who contemplated violating the taboo. Furthermore, it underlines that it is not enough if one person is an ally to *homo sacer*, as the wider population needs to speak up against the violence unleashed upon her. As we can see in relation to National Socialism, the few people who were allies to its victims did nothing to bring down the regime. A wider population was needed who was not afraid to defy the taboo by becoming allies for *homo sacer*.

The work of mourning necessitates that one associates physically or emotionally with the lost object, which the taboo forecloses with its threat that any being touched by the fate of the tabooed subject leads to one's becoming dirty and thus shunned by the community oneself. Antigone's lament to not having an ally is connected to her lament of not being mourned for, insofar as mourning for a loss implies a painful touching of the loss, which the taboo forecloses. With that she is the ancient expression for all those who have found and find themselves in the position of *homines sacres*, such as the millions of victims of the National Socialist regime who did not have allies, because people were afraid that any solidarity with or "touching" them implies the danger of becoming "dirty" and with that *homines sacres* themselves. Furthermore, Antigone's lamentation about not being mourned for foreshadows the denial of mourning for tabooed subjects, insofar as mourning necessitates being touched by the victim's fate, which the taboo forecloses.

Taboo and Mourning in Austria's Genocide on Roma and Sinti

Agamben points out that, besides the Jews, the people who were "bearing the black triangle (i.e. Gypsies; this symbol of the genocide of a defenseless population ought to be remembered alongside the yellow star) are an example of *homines sacres* (plural of *homo sacer*)" (Agamben 1995: 155). Why has the Nazi genocide on Roma and Sinti been forgotten in Austria? Austrian postwar elites created a taboo in regards to Austria's enthusiastic support of and contributions to the Nazi genocide on Roma and Sinti, which was readily accepted by the broader population. The taboo threw a veil over this shameful part of Austria's history, and allowed Austrians to not feel guilty and responsible for it.

The taboo had the effect of erasing the memory, knowledge, and compassion for what happened to the Roma and Sinti. As a result, Austrians have failed to engage in the painful work of mourning for the loss of 90 percent of Austria's Roma and Sinti population murdered during the Nazi regime, and "the most ruthless crimes fade into oblivion, uncomprehended and unwept" (Mitscherlichs 1975: xvii). In this section I hope to counter some of the consequences of Austria's failure to mourn by providing the knowledge about the Austrian crimes perpetuated against its Roma and Sinti population, and by foregrounding the mechanisms that contributed to the circumstances in which such crimes could be forgotten.

Austrians did, to some extent, mourn the losses on their own side by erecting memorials for Austria's soldiers that fought in Hitler's Wehrmacht, and more recently (but not without controversy and resistance) also established some memorials to remember some victim-groups of the Nazi regime. Here we can see that taboos retain a certain psychic pressure even after they have started to be violated, insofar as the public establishment of the duty to mourn merely engenders a narcissistic form of mourning. In such mourning one does not need to be touched by the suffering of victims. Rather, one is allowed a quick movement from "we didn't do anything" to "we're all done with that (i.e. the mourning)" and we do not have to do anything more.[9]

In terms of the genocide on Roma and Sinti, signs of mourning remain strikingly absent, which underlines that the taboo remains firmly intact.[10] As a recent newspaper article from 2017 points out, "a central memorial for the in the NS-time persecuted and murdered Roma and Sinti is still missing in Austria" (DÖW Schnittarchiv).[11] Recently Austrian bishops released a statement where they demanded the establishment of a memorial for the murdered Roma during the Nazi regime, because says the statement: "only when we remember the victims can we cleanse the memory," and moreover every person has the "right to a grave, or at least a memorial" (DÖW Schnittarchiv).[12] Certainly the Austrian bishops have a lot of "cleansing" of their memory to do, because during the Nazi regime, Austrian bishops until the end of the war fully supported Hitler's Anschluss and the Nazi measures, including the genocide on Roma and Sinti.

The persecution of Roma and Sinti as *hominess sacres* has a long history that predates the Nazi genocide. When in 1498 "Gypsies" were declared as *vogelfrei* in the Freiburger Reichstag, the figure of the "Gypsy" as the paradigmatic example of *homo sacer* already emerges—the one who can be killed without committing homicide, yet he or she cannot be sacrificed, which means that he or she cannot be put to death via ritual practices, such as a trial. From now on anyone could persecute the "Gypsies" without punishment. Originally, the word *vogelfrei* meant "as free as a bird, not bound." However, by the 16th century it meant "free gallows fodder for predatory birds" (Bársony and Daróczi 2008: 116). Like Polyneices, whose corpse was left unburied to be devoured by birds, Roma and Sinti lives were devalued to the point of being seen as merely fodder for predatory birds.

Here the term *"vogelfrei"* becomes linked to a person being banned, insofar as several countries introduced edicts that advanced their persecution and elimination. In 1500, Maximilian I outlawed "Gypsies" throughout the Holy Roman Empire, and gave license to capture and kill them without any consequences. In 1715 a Silesian decree ordered "extermination of the *Vogelfrey* declared gypsy-vermin." Saxony released a decree that anybody encountering a "Gypsy" "has to immediately gun down or otherwise kill her or him." In 1749 Swabia decreed that all captured "Gypsies," "without any mercy and without any trial," are to be executed (Meuser 1996: 116). Frederick William I of Prussia issued a decree in 1725 under which any "Gypsy" caught within his realm was to be executed without trial. On July 20, 1749, the Spanish

Military, on the order of Ferdinand VI, rounded up all Roma and Sinti they could find and put 12,000 to death (Bársony and Daróczi 2008: 116).

Between 1933 and 1938 several laws discriminating against Roma and Sinti went into effect, which excluded them from access to jobs in public service, allowed their deportation into concentration camps, deprived them of citizenship, prohibited intercourse between German citizens and Jews and Roma and Sinti, and deprived them of voting rights. Such banishment by the law contributed to the politics of death of the Nazi regime, where between 1942 and 1945 about 600,000 Roma and Sinti were murdered in or en route to concentration camps. Most of them were murdered in the gas chapters upon their arrival. Those not murdered right away were subjected to deadly medical experiments (Bársony and Daróczi 2008: 116).

In the concentration camps Roma and Sinti were marked with both the black triangle, which meant "asocial" and was sewed onto their clothes, and with a Z—standing for *Zigeuner* (Gypsies), which was tattooed on their bodies next to the prisoner number. This double marking exposed those classified as "gypsies" to an unconditional capacity to be killed both as "*Asoziale* (asocials, black triangle)" and as "racially inferior (gypsies, Z)" (Schmidt 1996: 129). The double marking turned Roma and Sinti into tabooed subjects, with whom other people ought not to physically and emotionally associate. Such tabooing of Roma and Sinti also distorted and minimized the knowledge about them, from their long history of persecution that enforced their movement, to their efforts to become part of various societies hostile to them, for example by settling down and having regular jobs.

Also Austria's persecution of Roma and Sinti predates the Nazi genocide. On January 15, 1933, a "Gypsy conference" was held in Oberwart, Burgenland, a rural part of Austria, where about 80 percent (or roughly 9,000) of the Roma lived before their annihilation in 1938. Representatives of all parties of the national and regional Austrian governments discussed possibilities to deport and annihilate the Roma, to take away their rights and to force them into public labor. The aim of this conference was to rehabilitate the absolutist "Gypsy politics" that was practiced in Austria under Maria Theresia and Josef II (Baumgartner and Freund 2007: 212).[13]

Although the conference remained without consequence, the Austrian Anschluss (annexation) to Hitler's Germany in 1938 removed all barriers to annihilate Roma and Sinti, because racism and "racial hygiene" was introduced in Austria as state doctrine, which was supported by all sectors of Austrian society. Hitler found enthusiastic welcome and support in Austria not only because he promised, besides economic recovery, to solve "the Jewish question" as Bukey points out (2000: 22), but also because he promised to solve "the Gypsy problem" once and for all.

An Auschwitz survivor, a Roma from Oberwart, remembers that shortly after the Anschluss: "the Nazis went through Oberwart with the shout:

'Down with the Jews and Gypsies.' My father was a *Spengler*, and we children did not know any suffering. Right after it started our father wanted to leave, back to Hungary, where his brother lived back then. But our mother did not want to, 'where should we go with eight children,' she said "and with all our belongings, which we acquired so hard." Father packed the things, but then we stayed anyway. Once my father cried in a dream. In the morning mother asked him why he cried. 'Did you not hear how they shouted? Away with the Gypsies! We leave." But then my mother said: 'We did not commit any crimes, we are citizens and not foreigners'" (cited in Steinmetz 1966: 36). The family stayed in Austria and shortly after the Anschluss the father was taken away and murdered by the Nazis, and the witness and his sister were deported to Auschwitz.

The Nazi regime partially lifted the moral restriction against murder for some groups, including those they classified as "Gypsies." Austrian authorities and politicians provided several impulses to the Nazis to radicalize their "Gypsy policies" to advance their annihilation (Baumgartner and Freund 2007: 212). Right after the Anschluss, the persecution of Austrian "gypsies" escalated. Within a year, several thousand Burgenland Roma were deported into concentration camps, and the Reich established "Gypsy work camps" throughout Austria, from where they were deported to concentration camps.

In 1943, as a result of the continuing pressure of Austrian municipalities upon the Germans to have the rest of the remaining "Gypsies" in Austria annihilated, about 2,900 Austrian Roma and Sinti were deported to Auschwitz-Birkenau, where they were housed under the worst conditions in the "Gypsy collection camp" in Birkenau (Baumgartner and Freund 2007: 216). From here they were sent into other concentration camps in the Reich, where they became subject to deadly and maiming medical experiments. From the about 12,000 Roma and Sinti living in Austria before 1938, only about 10 percent survived the work camps and their deportation and murder in concentration and annihilation camps (Baumgartner 2015: 91).

How could Austrians forget their enthusiastic support and contributions to advance the genocide on Roma and Sinti? Austrian postwar politicians created a taboo around Austria as a perpetrator nation, which traveled over generations and is still in effect in Austria today. They accomplished this by defining Austria as "the first victim of Nazism," which at the same time established the taboo in regards to viewing Austria as a perpetrator nation, which Austrians readily accepted. The main aim of the taboo was to unify a fragmented nation (Berger 2012: 88). As explained earlier, a taboo that is shared by a nation has a unifying effect, because it prescribes a fixed verdict for an area of conflict (Mitscherlichs 1975: 100). The fixed verdict the taboo prescribed was an insistence on Austria's victim status and the conviction that Nazism was something largely alien to Austrian culture (Utgaard 2003: 27).

Insofar as Austrians themselves were only victims, the taboo stood in the service of forgetting the millions of murders of the National Socialist regime, and the Austrian support and contributions to such murders. The taboo created a new nation full of victims, who were free of guilt and responsibility for their contributions to the Nazi genocides. The taboo managed over generations to eradicate the memory and knowledge of the unprecedented violence unleashed upon Roma and Sinti in Austria, and it also eradicated compassion for these victims, which remains effective even today.

Here it is also important to point out that "the especially dangerous aspects of taboos is that they make not only for social association . . . but also for social dissociation, for exclusion: the two are inseparably linked" (Mitscherlichs 1975: 100). One reason for the disassociation aspect is that taboos create hostility and resentment, because those who must obey taboos are "left in the infantile position of children forbidden to ask questions" (Mitscherlichs 1975: 92). The hostility and resentment taboos create within ourselves are then displaced by projecting them upon groups that are different from us (Mitscherlichs 1975: 93).

The social disassociation is vividly apparent in Austrian's open hostility and resentment toward those 10 percent of Austrian Roma and Sinti who survived the Nazi genocide and returned to their villages after the liberation from National Socialism, as Austrians hindered or made it difficult for them to secure housing, buy land and build houses, and receive basic education (Baumgartner and Freund 2007: 222).[14] Moreover, Austrians were also hostile to those Roma and Sinti who attempted to receive reparations for the sufferings they endured in the camps. Those Roma and Sinti that applied for victim benefits were often rejected because Austrian officials continued to classify them as "asocial," which exposes their continued tabooed status in postwar Austria, and which eliminated any sympathy for their claims for reparations. Here the taboo also distorted knowledge, insofar as it was not their supposed "asocialty" that put them in a difficult position that made them apply for victim benefits, but Austria's victimization of them. Only when Roma and Sinti were acknowledged as an Austrian ethnic minority in 1993 did their social and economic situation improve and they received minor compensation for their losses and suffering during the NS regime (Baumgartner and Freund 2007: 225).

However, Austrian Roma and Sinti continue to be exposed to racial stereotyping and other forms of violence from the Austrian population, such as the bomb attack in Oberwart in 1995 in which four Roma died, which keeps them at the margins of Austrian society, and underlines that the past can indeed be repeated. Only if Austrians critically think through the tabooed past can they make the first necessary steps against the compulsion to repeat history. For this to happen they must touch two taboos at the same time—the taboo that covers over Austria as a perpetrator nation, and the taboo that perpetuates Roma and Sinti's status as "asocials," a Nazi ideology which remains unbroken until today, and distorts and eliminates knowledge about their history and Austrians victimization of them.

Only if Austrians really know what happened to Roma and Sinti, and what Austria contributed to that, can they start to defy the taboos, and start to feel compassion for them, and with that begin the work of mourning. Only mourning can bring back what the taboo aims to do away with—the physical and emotional association with Roma and Sinti, who have been and continue to be part of Austrian communities. As the Mitscherlichs put it, "discovering a capacity to feel compassion for people never before apprehended behind our distorting projections, would give us back our ability to mourn" (1975: 67).

Austrians must do everything to get rid of their distorting projections upon Roma and Sinti and rediscover their capacity to feel compassion for these victims of Nazi crimes, which has been foreclosed by the taboo. Only if Austrians and other European nations (as Austria is not the only country that has this problem) openly defy the taboo (much like Antigone did) and touch their shameful past can they rediscover their capacity to feel compassion for Roma and Sinti and engage in the painful work of mourning for their loss. The work of mourning is then the precondition that Austrians can take responsibility for their crimes upon Roma and Sinti, show solidarity with the survivors and their descendants (e.g., by being willing to pay reparations), and finally fight against the continuing violence upon Roma and Sinti that continues to plague Europe today.

NOTES

1. I would like to thank Matt Stichter, who has given me valuable feedback on various drafts of this chapter, and David McIvor and the anonymous reviewer, whose helpful feedback contributed to strengthen the chapter.

2. In the case of Roma/Sinti, which I will be discussing in this chapter, the crimes committed against them have a long history that pre- and post-dates National Socialism. Nonetheless some "delimitation" of specific crimes is needed if we are to mourn these crimes, which is why I retain the post-crime generation and complicate it with the "(post)". From here on out it will be assumed that those who need to mourn are those in the (post)-crime generations.

3. Of course some Austrians have mourned their loss, but that's more the exceptional case. I am concerned here with those still trying to master the past instead of work through it, and there are many indicators that the majority are still trying to master the past (see my book *The Politics of Repressed Guilt*, 2018 for examples). Present-day Austria instead resembles Germany in the 1960s that the Mitscherlichs wrote of, in terms of not having yet worked through the past, for example, lacking a Holocaust museum or other public memorials for victims, downplaying that part of their past in the educational system, or other institutions that would assist people in trying to work through the past.

4. In the last section of this chapter, for my general historical elaboration of the fate of Roma and Sinti in Austria, I am drawing on a section in the general introduction and a section in chapter three of my book, *The Politics of Repressed Guilt: The Tragedy of Austrian Silence*

(2018), reprinted with permission of Edinburgh University Press © Edinburgh University Press.

5. My specific interest in taboos is with respect to mourning and the guarding against guilt and responsibility, which is not the only function of taboos.

6. I will come back to this element of the taboo in the last section of the chapter, where I elaborate the subversive elements of the unconscious.

7. See as an example the collection of essays in Söderbäck 2010.

8. The main function of this section is to illustrate that mourning necessitates emotional ties between the mourner and the lost object, which the taboo aims to disrupt, which is the 3rd point outlined in the previous section. The following third section engages more with the ties between taboo and mourning in terms of memory, and knowledge, since it deals with collective wrongdoing in the past, which are the first and second points outlined in the previous section.

9. I am thankful for David McIvor for this insight.

10. While some Austrians have recognized the genocide of the Roma and Sinti, it takes more than a few people defying a taboo to undo the power that taboo has over the larger population. The continued violence against the Roma and Sinti, and the lack of memorials for their past persecution, show that the taboo is still in effect for Austrians in general.

11. Wiener Zeitung, *Romastrategie soll erweitert wereden*, 07.04.2017

12. Tiroler Tageszeitung, *Bischoefe fordern Gedenkstaette fuer in der NS-Zeit ermordeten Roma*, 11.11.2016; see also Wiener Zeitung, *Roma-Gedenkstaette*, 21.11.2016

13. In the eighteenth century the empress of the Austro-Hungarian Empire Maria Theresia released "Gypsy-mandates," which implied forced settlements and labor, complete subjection under their landlord, regulations what to wear, religious training, and the forced separation of children from their parents.

14. After 1945 licenses for their traditional incomes were revoked and they were forced into low-paying, part time and short-time unskilled rural labor. Also, in the after-war period, Austria continued its discrimination of Roma and Sinti by putting Roma and Sinti children into "special schools" for mentally and physically challenged children, a practice which was internationally challenged in the 1960s (Baumgartner and Freund 2007: 224).

WORKS CITED

Adorno, Theodor W. (2010), *Guilt and Defense: On the Legacies of National Socialism in Postwar Germany*, trans. J. Olick and A. Perrin, Cambridge: Harvard University Press.

Adorno, Theodor W. (2003), *Negative Dialectics*, trans. E. B. Ashton, New York, London: Continuum Press.

Agamben, Georgio (1995), *Homo Sacer: Sovereign Power and Bare Life*, trans. D. Heller-Roazen, Stanford: Stanford University Press.

Bársony, János, and Daróczi, Ágnes (2008), *Phjarrajimos: The Fate of the Roma During the Holocaust*, New York: International Debate Education Association.

Baumgartner, Gerhard (2015), 'Der Genozid an den österreichischen Roma und Sinti,' in *Romane Thana: Orte der Roma und Sinti*, Wien: Theiss G,bH, pp. 86–93.

Baumgartner, Gerhard, and Freund, Florian (2007), 'Der Holocaust an den österreichischen Roma und Sinti,' in *Zwischen Erziehung und Vernichtung: Zugeunerpolitik und Zigeunerforschung im Europe des 20. Jahrhunderts*, ed. M. Zimmermann, Stuttgart: Frank Steiner Verlag, pp. 203–25.

Berger, Thomas U. (2012), *War, Guilt, and World Politics after World War II*, Cambridge: Cambridge University Press.

Brendese, P. J. (2014), *The Power of Memory in Democratic Politics*, University of Rochester Press.

Bukey, Evan Burr (2000), *Hitler's Austria: Popular Sentiment in the Nazi Era*, Chapel Hill and London: The University of North Carolina Press.

Butler, Judith (2006), *Precarious Life: The Powers of Mourning and Violence*, Verso.

Butler, Judith (2010), "Promiscuous Obedience," in *Feminist Readings of Antigone*, Fanny Söderbäck (ed.), Albany: State University of New York Press, pp. 133–154.

Chanter, Tina (2007), "Antigone's Excessive Relationship to Fetishism: The Performative Politics and Rebirth of Eros and Philia from Ancient Greece to Modern South Africa," *Symposium* 11 (2): 231–260.

Freud, Sigmund (1989), *Totem and Taboo: Some Points of Agreement between the Mental Lives of Savages and Neurotics*, James Strachey (trans. and ed.), New York: London, W.W. Norton and Company.

Gatta, Giunia (2015), "Suffering and the Making of Politics: Perspectives from Jaspers and Camus," *Contemporary Political Theory* 14 (4): 335–354.

Honig, Bonnie (2013), *Antigone, Interrupted*, Cambridge: Cambridge University Press.

Leeb, Claudia (2016), "Female Resistance or the Politics of Death? Rethinking Antigone," in *The Persistence of Critical Theory* (Culture and Civilization, Vol. 8), Gabriel Ricci (ed.), Piscataway, New Jersey: Transaction Publishers, pp. 223–240.

Leeb, Claudia (2018), *The Politics of Repressed Guilt: The Tragedy of Austrian Silence*, Edinburgh: Edinburgh University Press.

Mader, Mary Beth (2010), "Antigone's Line," in *Feminist Readings of Antigone*, Fanny Söderbäck (ed.), Albany: State University of New York Press, pp. 155–172.

McIvor, David (2016) *Mourning in America: Race and the Politics of Loss*. Ithaca, NY: Cornell University Press.

Mitscherlich, Alexander and Mitscherlich, Margarete (1975), *The Inability to Mourn: Principles of Collective Behavior*, trans. B. R. Placzek, New York: Grove Press.

Schmidt, Erich (1996), "Die Entdeckung der weißen Zigeuner: Robert Ritter und die Zigeunerforschung als Rassenhygiene," in *Zigeuner: Geschichte und Struktur einer rassistischen Konstruktion,* ed. W. D. Hund, Duisburg: DISS, pp. 129–52.

Söderbäck, Fanny (2010), "Impossible Mourning: Sophocles Reversed" in *Feminist Readings of Antigone*, Fanny Söderbäck (ed.), Albany: State University of New York Press, pp. 65–82.

Sophocles (2003), *Antigone*, David Franklin and John Harrison (commentary and trans.), Cambridge: Cambridge University Press.

Steinmetz, Selma (1966), *Österreichs Zigeuner im NS-Staat*, Wien: Europa Verlag.

Chapter Five

Not in My Graveyard

Citizenship, Memory, and Identity in the Wake of the Boston Marathon Bombing

Osman Balkan

On May 6, 2013, a group of protestors gathered outside the Graham, Putnam and Mahoney Funeral Parlors in Worcester, Massachusetts. Inside the funeral home lay the corpse of Tamerlan Tsarnaev, who, with his brother Dzhokhar, had orchestrated the bombing of the Boston Marathon three weeks prior. The attacks resulted in three deaths and injured more than 250 people. In the citywide manhunt that ensued, Tamerlan was killed in a shootout with the police. His brother, Dzhokhar was apprehended and taken into custody.

Nobody knew what would happen with Tamerlan Tsarnaev's body, but the protestors were incensed about the possibility that it might be interred in the Boston area. Many brandished American flags and signs with messages like "Bury the garbage in the landfill," and "Boston Strong." A middle-aged man in a red WrestleMania XVI T-shirt held a placard with a graphic image of Tsarnaev's battered corpse that read, "Wrap his body in pigskin and dump it in the ocean—even that is too good for the shithead." Other protestors carried signs stating, "It's a disgrace to our military," and "Bury this terrorist on U.S. soil and we will unbury him—American Justice."

A smaller group of counter-protestors stood nearby. Among them were several nuns and priests. One man held a large wooden cross. Next to him, a woman prayed silently, clutching a string of rosary beads. Others bore signs that read, "Burying the dead is a work of mercy," and "We need compassion—not hate—in the face of tragedy."[1]

Contrary to the wishes of some of the protestors, Tsarnaev was eventually buried in U.S. soil, though not in Massachusetts. After much deliberation, his body was interred at a Muslim cemetery in Doswell, Virginia, a small town approximately twenty-five miles north of the state's capital, Richmond. As news about his whereabouts spread, another round of protests erupted, this time involving baffled Virginians who were distressed about the fact that the so-called "Boston Bomber" had been surreptitiously buried in their state. Why did the disposal of Tamerlan Tsarnaev's remains cause such a stir?

In this essay I want to consider the relationship between dead bodies and the politics of mourning by examining the public controversies prompted by the burial of Tamerlan Tsarnaev. In what follows, I trace the travels of his corpse, from the Chief Medical Examiner's Office in downtown Boston, to a series of funeral homes across the Greater Boston area, to its final resting place in a privately owned Islamic cemetery in rural Virginia. At each step of its itinerant journey, Tsnaraev's remains generated a flurry of political backlash and activity. To better understand the stakes involved in Tsarnaev's disposal and memorialization, I map out and analyze the perspectives of a range of different actors who shared an interest in the fate of his dead body. In doing so, I aim to show that dead bodies serve as perennial sites of political conflict because the treatment of the dead, including where and how dead bodies are buried, is an important means through which social actors express, enact, and contest the boundaries of national, political, and moral communities.

For scholars who write about the necropolitics of mourning, the assertion that burial practices are political or that dead bodies are sites of political contestation may well be taken for granted. Yet much of this literature tends to overlook the important connections between public mourning and material human remains. In her influential work on mourning and violence for example, Judith Butler offers important insights about how the differential exposure to death and violence faced by certain populations results from and is reinforced by the tendency to see certain lives as more valuable than others. In drawing attention to the conditions under which some human lives are more or less vulnerable than others and by extension, more or less grievable than others, she notes that "if a life is not grievable, it is not quite a life; it does not qualify as a life and is not worth a note. It is already the unburied, if not the unburiable" (Butler 2004, 34). For Butler, ungrievable life is by its very definition, unburied. Hence, what happens to the dead body is largely inconsequential, since it is prefigured as unburiable.

Yet even unburiable bodies must be buried or otherwise disposed of. And how this occurs is highly consequential for political life. As I aim to demonstrate with particular reference to the case of Tamerlan Tsarnaev, the very act of public mourning, grieving, or memorialization is to a large extent, dictated and structured by the actual treatment of material human remains. Of course, as I outline below, mourning can occur in the absence of a physical corpse. Yet when a body (or some other material object that is meant to represent the body) is present, the manner of its disposal is central to the possibilities and probabilities of political mourning. In developing this claim, my goal is to show that by paying closer attention to what happens to dead bodies, scholars of mourning will be better positioned to delineate the rituals, practices, and mechanisms through which mourning becomes political.[2] To better understand the place of the corpse in the work of mourning, I first turn to the ways that criminal, terrorist, or other unwanted bodies have functioned as politically charged sites of struggle and sovereign power across a range of historical and contemporary contexts.

Unwanted Bodies

Determining what to do with Tsarnaev's corpse was no easy matter. Public reactions were passionate and evinced a range of emotions, from indignation to exasperation to sympathy. Such reactions are common in the aftermath of political violence as survivors struggle to decide how to deal with the physical remains of the perpetrators of heinous crimes. Exceptional or unwanted bodies like Tsarnaev's have been subjected to a variety of treatments in different political contexts, but have always served as a potent force. As Richard Ward notes in his study on the global history of capital punishment, the criminal corpse "has been harnessed for the ends of state power, medical science, and criminal justice, amongst other things" (Ward 2013, 1). Violence directed at the criminal body (both dead and alive) was a crucial dimension of the spectacle of state power in Europe between the sixteenth and nineteenth centuries. Foucault's account of the torture and execution of Robert-François Damiens, condemned to death for his attempted assassination of King Louis XV in 1757, remains a stark testament to the gruesome nature of public punishment in the early modern era:

> Damiens the regicide . . . was to be "taken and conveyed in a cart, wearing nothing but a shirt . . . to the Place de Grève, where on a scaffold that will be erected there, the flesh will be torn from his breasts, arms, thighs and calves with red-hot pincers, his right hand . . . burnt with sulphur, and on those places where the flesh will be torn away, poured molten lead, boiling oil, burning resin, wax and sulphur melted together and then his body drawn and quartered by four horses and his limbs and body consumed by fire, reduced to ashes and his ashes thrown to the winds." (Foucault 1997, 3)

For political authorities in early modern Europe, the public desecration and disfigurement of living and dead bodies was intended as a form of deterrence and crime control, albeit one which fell out of favor as punishment ceased to be a visible spectacle and gradually became the most "hidden" part of the penal process (Foucault 1977, 9).

The question of what to do with a criminal corpse is a recurrent theme in ancient Greek tragedy, most notably in Sophocles' *Antigone*, written in the fifth century BC. The play's plotline pivots around the burial and unburial of Polynices, a traitorous rebel who dies during his attempt to seize the throne of Thebes. Creon, ruler of Thebes, forbids the burial of Polynices as punishment for his crime. His orders are defied by Antigone, sister of Polynices, who sets about burying her brother and is ultimately sentenced to death for her transgression. Antigone commits suicide, setting into motion a series of other deaths including the suicides of Creon's son and wife. The play has been interpreted in a number of different ways, with various commentators focusing on Antigone's civil disobedience as a democratic act of defiance in the face of excessive sovereign power or alternatively as an elite objection to Athenian democratic ideals (Butler 2002; Honig 2013; Hirsch 2014). Without wading into these debates, it is important to emphasize that *Antigone* successfully dramatizes some of the political stakes involved in the quotidian act of burial by showing how the treatment of corpses has attendant consequences for the community of the living.

In our own time, many states have faced dilemmas about what to do with the bodily remains of individuals that commit violent acts within their borders. In situations where the perpetrator's citizenship, legal status, or history of public service guarantees them the right to burial in a particular place, states have been caught in a contradictory position. On the one hand, they are obliged to adhere to and implement the law. On the other hand, there is a desire to punish the perpetrator posthumously by denying them burial rights. Such was the case with Timothy McVeigh, an army veteran who was awarded a Bronze Star and Combat Infantry Badge for his participation in the Persian Gulf War. On April 19, 1995, McVeigh orchestrated the bombing of the Alfred P. Murrah Federal Building in Oklahoma City, an attack which claimed 168 lives and injured nearly 700 others. Prior to the September 11 attacks, the Oklahoma City bombing was the largest terror attack on U.S. soil and remains the deadliest episode of domestic terrorism in American history.

McVeigh was convicted and sentenced to death for his role in the bombing. His execution took place on June 11, 2001. In the hours before his death, McVeigh asked for a Catholic priest to administer Last Rites, a ritual that normally involves some form of penance and absolution, receiving the Holy Communion, and an apostolic pardon from the priest (Broadway, 2001). Although prison authorities granted his request for religious rites, there was greater public concern over what would happen to his corpse. As an army veteran, McVeigh was entitled to military funeral honors and burial in a federally or state administered veterans' cemetery, such as Arlington National Cemetery. Yet the prospect that he would be buried alongside other servicemen and women angered legislators, including Senator Arlen Specter, a Pennsylvania Republican who, one week after McVeigh's execution, introduced a bill to prevent anyone who had been convicted of a federal capital crime from being buried in a veterans' cemetery.

McVeigh had committed "the most heinous criminal act in the history of the United States of America," noted Specter, and burying him in a national cemetery among veterans would be "unseemly" (Chronis, 2001). The bill's co-sponsor, Senator Robert Toricelli, a New Jersey Democrat, argued that "This is one further statement of national resolve," and warned would-be terrorists that, "we will deny you honor in death" (ibid.). The bill passed with a vote of 98–0 and in the end, McVeigh was not buried anywhere. His body was cremated at the Mattox Ryan Funeral Home in Terre Haute, Indiana, and his ashes were turned over to his lawyer who scattered them in an undisclosed location.

A similar debate took place in the aftermath of a series of terrorist attacks in France in 2015, targeting the offices of the satirical magazine Charlie Hebdo, and the kosher supermarket Hyper Cacher. The three perpetrators of the attacks, Saïd and Chérif Kouachi and Amedy Coulibaly, were killed in shootouts with the police. As French citizens, they were entitled to burial in France, but there was a great deal of resistance to local interment. Some politicians called for the mandatory cremation of all terrorists in an effort to prevent their graves from becoming "unhealthy sites of pilgrimage."[3] By destroying any trace of their bodies, the state could potentially foreclose the very possibility of mourning or memorialization.

Although this suggestion was not followed through, the French government initially sought to export their corpses to Algeria and Mali, countries from which their parents had emigrated to France decades earlier. When that plan also proved untenable, political authorities resigned themselves to burying the bodies in unmarked graves under the cover of darkness. The locations of the gravesites were kept secret and not disclosed to the public. Local officials took great pains to ensure that the entire process was conducted as discreetly as possible (Balkan, 2016).

In other national contexts, states and civil society associations have sought to prevent the extension of religious rites to the perpetrators of terror attacks and other crimes. Following a failed military coup in July 2016, Turkish authorities established a "Cemetery of Traitors," to house the remains of coup-plotters who were killed in their efforts to overthrow the government of President Recep Tayyip Erdoğan. The Turkish Directorate of Religious Affairs (the highest official religious body in the country) issued a directive to its imams in which it prohibited the extension of religious rites for coup plotters. "A funeral prayer is intended as an act of exoneration for the faithful," it read. "But these people, with the actions they undertook, have disregarded not just individuals but also the law of an entire nation, and therefore do not deserve exoneration from their faithful brothers and sisters" (*Bir Gün*, 2016).

Following a chain of terrorist attacks carried out by four young Muslim men in London and Manchester in 2017, the Muslim Council of Britain issued a statement denouncing the use of violence in the name of Islam. The Council, an umbrella organization established with the mission of promoting consultation, cooperation, and coordination on Muslim affairs in the United Kingdom, rejected the extension of religious services and funeral prayers for the perpetrators of the attacks. Urging other religious authorities to withhold prayers as well, it noted that, "such indefensible actions are completely at odds with the lofty teachings of Islam" (Muslim Council of Britain, 2016).

In all of these disparate examples, we can observe how the dead body itself becomes a heated site of political conflict over the possibilities and probabilities of public mourning and reconciliation. Neither person, nor thing, the corpse continues to exert a strange sort of agency and power in the world. It generates intense reactions from a broad array of social actors who have different ideas about what ought to be done to the body and why. For some, the severity of the crimes committed merit a form of posthumous violence directed at the corpse itself, either through cremation (a practice that is forbidden in Islam), the threat of unburial, or the withholding of religious rites. Others believe that these bodies should be buried irrespective of the person's actions, since burial is understood as a duty or act of mercy and charity. In either case, what is important is that the body is put in its "proper" place, though suffice to say, there is considerable disagreement about where that might be.

I return now to Tsarnaev and the controversies surrounding the disposal and memorialization of his politically charged corpse. In what follows, I chart out and analyze the perspectives of different actors and stakeholders who shared an interest in managing his dead body. These include Tsarnaev's immediate family, local politicians and public officials, concerned citizens, representatives of Muslim communities, and the death-care workers who took on the task of burying his corpse. I aim to show that dead bodies serve as perennial sites of political contestation because the treatment of the dead, including where and how dead bodies are buried, helps both to structure public mourning and memorialization, and is an important means through which social actors express, enact, and contest the boundaries of national, political, and moral communities.

In developing this argument, I am influenced by recent scholarship concerning dead body politics and the politics of mourning. Taken together, these literatures have drawn attention to the manifold ways in which mourning practices and the governance of the dead are consequential for political life. In his magisterial work on the cultural history of human remains, historian Thomas Laqueur observes that:

the dead body matters, everywhere and across time . . . in disparate religious and ideological circumstances . . . in the absence of any particular belief about a soul . . . across all sorts of beliefs about an afterlife or a god . . . [or] in the absence of such beliefs. . . . It matters because the living need the dead far more than the dead need the living . . . because the dead make social worlds. (Laqueur 2016, 1)

In a similar vein Simon Stow has recently argued that the stories that a political community tells about its dead can help shape the political outcomes of the living. "Mourning," he writes, can serve as "an important mode of critical-theoretical reflection and a rich resource for democratic innovation, education, and resilience" (Stow 2017, 2).

In both accounts, the dead are central actors in the process of world-making. The ways that we treat the dead and how we remember them through rituals of mourning help to define who we are as a political community. According to Bonnie Honig, "mourning practices postulate certain forms of collective life and so how we mourn is a deeply political issue" (Honig 2009, 10). Furthermore, mourning practices can be positively harnessed in the service of democratic ends. David McIvor has called for a democratic mourning, one which is not reducible to rituals of grief or eulogies for the dead, but rather, "an ongoing labor of recognition and repair—of recognizing experiences of social trauma and cultivating civic repertoires of response" (McIvor 2016, xii). In short, democratic mourning has the potential to help reframe and expand inherited notions of political community by attending to social traumas and losses that are not always registered as a loss.

Public mourning does not require the existence of a dead body, but the absence of one can generate additional grief and anxiety. Recall, for example, the "Madres de la Plaza de Mayo," a group of Argentine mothers whose children were "disappeared" during the years of military dictatorship between 1976–1983, who gathered publicly to demand justice and answers about the whereabouts of their bodies.[4] As Robert Pogue Harrison notes in his discussion of the "charisma" of the corpse, "the event of death remains unfinished or unrealized until person and remains have been reunified . . . and the latter disposed of ceremonially" (Harrison 2003: 147). In other words, the closure that comes through acts of mourning is forestalled or foreclosed when the corpse remains absent.

When there is a physical body, the terms of mourning are often dictated by what happens to the body. This is because, as Laqueur notes, the dead body is an enchanted object, "powerful, dangerous, preserved, revered, feared, an object of ritual, a thing to be reckoned with" (Laqueur 2015, 4). As anthropologist Katherine Verdery has observed, the materiality of the dead body is crucial for its symbolic efficacy. She argues that dead bodies are significant for politics because of their materiality (they can be moved around from place to place), their symbolic power (their meaning is ambiguous and polysemic), and because of their association with the sacred (they evoke awe, uncertainty, and fear associated with cosmic concerns) (Verdery, 1999). Dead bodies inspire awe and fear in part because they remind us of the limits of our own mortality. They must be attended to, often through funerary rites, what Arnold van Gennep calls "rites of passage," through which the dead are put in their proper place (van Gennep 1960). That is—out of our world, the world of the living—and into the realm of ancestors and the dead.

The improper handling of the dead, either through willful desecration of the corpse, the denial of proper funerary rites, or burial in the wrong place, is a problem for the living. This is in part because of beliefs about the dead's continued ability to exert influence in the world (through haunting or other forms of mischief) but also because such practices upset the given cultural order. As Mary Douglas famously observed, it is unsettling when persons and things do not conform to their ascribed category in the cultural order, an incongruity that she referred to as "matter out of place" (Douglas, 1966).

As we shall see, much of the disagreement around the burial of Tsarnaev hinged upon determining where his "proper" final resting place should be. If authorities made the wrong decision, it would have important consequences for the community of the living. To bury him in Boston, some argued, would not only disturb the dead, their families, and the tranquility of the city but also its ability to overcome and process the trauma generated by his actions. Unlike the disappeared in Argentina, the problem of Tsarnaev's corpse was not its absence but its excessive presence. Its materiality or "thereness" served as a reminder or residue of his crime. The political anxiety generated by the question of what would happen to his corpse was driven by the worry that he would remain a permanent fixture in Boston, forever reminding the city of his deeds and impeding the process of collective healing. In other words, the way in which Tsarnaev's body was handled had important implications for public mourning, closure, and reconciliation.

Burying Tsarnaev

On Monday, April 15, 2013, two bombs exploded near the finish line of the Boston Marathon, killing three and injuring 264 people. As authorities worked to identify the perpetrators, members of the public shared images of would-be suspects on websites such as Reddit and 4chan, noting why the individuals in question were suspicious—in some instances, merely stating "brown" (Volpp, 2014). The *New York Post* joined in on the speculation by running a full-page cover story featuring an image that had garnered 2.5 million hits on social media with the headline: "Bag men: Feds seek these two pictured at Boston Marathon." The photo erroneously identified sixteen-year-old Moroccan American high school runner Salaheddin Barhoum and his twenty-four-year-old friend Yassine Zaimi as the would-be bombers. Such misidentification is the result of what legal scholar Leti Volpp has described as "a new, technologically enabled vigilantism" in the post-9/11 era wherein "self-appointed avengers of justice . . . finger suspects based on their propensity to commit a crime—in this case, a propensity indicated by the descriptors "brown," "Muslim," or "looks Muslim" (Volp 2014, 2211).[5]

Three days after the bombing, the FBI released images of their two primary suspects, Dzhokhar and Tamerlan Tsarnaev, ethnic Chechens who had immigrated to the United States with their parents from Kyrgyzstan in 2002. That same day the brothers, aged nineteen and twenty-six respectively, shot and killed Sean Collier, an MIT police officer, hijacked a Mercedes-Benz SUV, and engaged in a shoot-out with police in Watertown, six miles northwest of Boston, ultimately resulting in the death of Tamerlan. Dzhokhar, who was wounded in the shoot-out, was captured and taken into custody the next day after a citywide manhunt involving helicopters, SWAT teams, armored vehicles, and hundreds of federal and state officers (Seelye et al., 2013).

As Dzhokhar sat in prison, his brother's corpse was in limbo. Massachusetts burial law states that "every dead body of a human being dying within the commonwealth, and the remains of anybody after dissection therein, shall be decently buried, entombed in a mausoleum, vault or tomb or cremated within a reasonable time after death" (Commonwealth of Massachusetts n.d.). Normally, the body is to be released "to the person with the proper legal authority to receive it, including the surviving spouse, the next of kin, or any friend of the deceased, who shall have priority in the order named" (ibid.). In Tamerlan's case, this would have been his widow, Katherine Russell. But Russell waived her right to collect and dispose of the body. Her family issued a statement disavowing Tsarnaev and asked that the media respect their privacy during this difficult time. "In the aftermath of the Patriots' Day horror, we know that we never really knew Tamerlan Tsarnaev," the statement read. "Our hearts are sickened by the knowledge of the horror he has inflicted" (Duke, 2013).

After his death, state officials took custody of Tsarnaev's corpse and brought it to a morgue at the Massachusetts Medical Examiner's Office, where it would be stored until an autopsy was conducted. In the meantime, Boston-area Muslim leaders publicly denounced his actions and weighed in on whether it was appropriate to conduct a religious funeral. Talal Eid, imam of the Islamic Institute of Boston, an organization that helps organize Islamic burials in the region, told reporters that he would be unwilling to perform religious rites for Tsarnaev. "This is a person who deliberately killed people. There is no room for him as a Muslim," he said (Kaleem, 2013). For Eid, Tsarnaev's actions placed him outside of the Islamic community. "He already left the fold of Islam by doing that," he said. "In the Qu'ran it says those who kill innocent people, they dwell in hellfire" (ibid.).

Suhaib Webb, imam of The Islamic Society of Boston Cultural Center (ISBCC), which temporarily closed its doors out of fear of reprisals after reports that the Tsarnaev brothers had worshipped at one of its affiliated mosques in Cambridge, argued that Tamerlan would be judged by God. "He should be buried according to the religious tradition that he adheres to. His case is with God. We can judge him as best we can according to the savage and insane actions he has done, but in the end, his soul is going to be brought before God," said Webb. "I don't think I could ethically lead a prayer for him, but I would not stop people from praying upon him" (ibid.).

Webb posted a message on his Facebook page stating, "We are all Bostonians—we mourn with the city." A week later, he coauthored an op-ed in the *New York Times*, entitled "No Room For Radicals in Mosques." In his op-ed, Webb criticized calls for increased surveillance of Islamic communities in the United States in the wake of the attacks. He argued that that "mediating" Islamic institutions across the country, including the ISBCC, were working hard to promote peace and prevent radicalization of "impressionable young Muslims" (Webb and Korb, 2013).

Such statements have become all too common at a moment where political leaders and large sectors of the public across many Western countries view Muslim communities with suspicion. What is striking here is the very banality of Webb's utterances, statements that must be repeated and rehashed ad nauseam by Muslim leaders and ordinary Muslims in the wake of every act of political violence committed in the name of Islam. My point is not that such acts should be condoned. Quite the contrary. Yet as many others have observed, the expectation that all Muslims ought to be effectively on-call to denounce acts of terror helps reinforce the "good Muslim"/"bad Muslim" binary, a binary that constructs the figure of the Muslim as always already in need of disciplinary intervention (Abu Lughod, 2013; Mamdani, 2004). In effect, it presents a false choice for Muslims, one in which social acceptance is predicated upon loyalty to the state and where critique of existing power relations is foreclosed in the interests of security. But back to Tsarnaev.

On May 2nd, several weeks after his death, officials at the state medical examiner's office turned Tsarnaev's body over to his uncle, Ruslan Tsnarni, a resident of Maryland, after conducting an autopsy which determined that the cause of his death was "gunshot wounds of torso and extremities" and "blunt trauma to head and torso" (Bidgood, 2013). The corpse was initially brought to the Dyer-Lake Funeral Home in North Attleborough, but it didn't stay there for long. Having learned about the whereabouts of Tsarnaev's body, a small group of protestors gathered outside of the funeral home to express their discontent. One local man interviewed by the *Boston Globe* said that, "to bring him here is a slap in the face." Elizabeth Poirier, a Republican member of the Massachusetts State Legislature, joined the protestors. When asked whether she was concerned that Tsarnaev was in North Attleborough she said that "we're a very happy wonderful community, very wonderful families, and this is not the kind of thing that we are used to having happen here, and I know it's very concerning to people who live in the neighborhood" (Anderson, 2013).

Barely four hours after it had arrived in North Attleborough, Tsarnaev's corpse was on the move again, this time to the Graham, Putnam and Mahoney Funeral Parlors in Worcester. The funeral home had agreed to accept the body after Tsarni approached its director, Peter Stefan, and asked if he would help bury his nephew. Stefan was no stranger to burial controversies. During the height of the AIDS panic in the 1980s, he became well known for burying many who had succumbed to the disease and whose bodies had been rejected by other funeral homes (Koczwara, 2013; Bidgood, 2013b). He has, by his own account, buried murderers and others at the margins of society, including indigents who could not afford funeral services (ibid.).

"I can't control the circumstances of someone's death, what they've done or how they died," Stefan told reporters. "If you look back, Lee Harvey Oswald, who buried him? What about Timothy McVeigh? Mr. Jeffrey Dahmer? And how about Mr. Ted Bundy?" he asked.

"[Tsarnaev] as a person doesn't deserve [to be buried], but we're not burying a person. We're burying a body," Stefan said (Koczwara, 2013). Here, Stefan weighs in on the curious ontology of the corpse. For the funeral director, Tsarnaev's corpse was just that—merely a corpse. In his mind, it was important to disassociate Tamerlan Tsarnaev, the person, from his mortal remains. While this position may be read as the detached approach of a professional who has spent a lifetime burying dead bodies, Stefan's arguments belie the concerns raised by protestors for whom the corpse represented much more than a body and served as an impediment for collective mourning and reconciliation. Nonetheless, Stefan tried to justify his actions by appealing to a sense of duty and American exceptionalism. "Somebody has to do it, and that's what it is. Nothing else. In this country we bury our dead regardless of the circumstances. And funeral directors here step up to the plate, and we should not be criticized," he concluded (ibid.).

When news about Tsarnaev's location spread, Stefan and his funeral home came under intense criticism as speculation mounted about where the body would ultimately be interred. The first group of protestors began congregating outside of the funeral home the next morning. They held signs proclaiming "Boston Strong" and "Bury this terrorist on U.S. soil and we will unbury him—American justice." In the ensuing days, the crowd grew larger, attracting more protestors and counter-protestors, who brought placards with the message "Burying the dead is a work of mercy." As the crowd swelled, police officers maintained a round-the-clock presence to keep the peace.

Inside the funeral home, Stefan was working tirelessly to find a cemetery that would accept the body. Tsarnaev's family hoped to bury him in a Muslim cemetery in the Boston area. "He lived in America. He grew up here and for the last 10 years he decided to be in Cambridge," Ruslan Tsarni told reporters. "His home country is Cambridge, Mass. Tamerlan Tsarnaev has no other place to be buried" (Lowery, 2013). "A dead person needs to be buried," he added. "That's what tradition requires, that's what religion requires, that's what morals require" (Seelye and Bidgood, 2013).

Tsarni's appeals to religious duty, tradition, and morality did not sit well with local political representatives. Cambridge City Manager Robert Healy issued a statement vowing to block any attempt to bury Tsarnaev in his city. "I have determined that it is not in the best interests of 'peace within the city' to execute a cemetery deed for a plot within the Cambridge Cemetery for the body of Tamerlan Tsarnaev," said Healy (ibid.). "The difficult and stressful efforts of the citizens of the city of Cambridge to return to a peaceful life would be adversely impacted by the turmoil, protests, and media presence at such an interment," he noted (Memmott, 2013).

For Healy, burying Tsarnaev among the citizens of Cambridge was an affront to the dead and their families. He observed that, "the families of loved ones interred in the Cambridge Cemetery also deserve to have their deceased family members rest in peace" (ibid.). Other politicians agreed. Representative Ed Markey, a member of the Democratic Party and, as of 2013, the junior United States Senator from Massachusetts, said, "I think that the people of Massachusetts have a right to say that they do not want that terrorist to be buried on the soil of Massachusetts" (Greenblatt, 2013). These statements attest to the idea that the Tsarnaev's corpse posed a threat to both the living and the dead. His proximity to Bostonians (both dead and alive) was understood as an undesirable pollutant that would disturb the public order, the peace of the dead, and the possibilities for public mourning and reconciliation.

Many ordinary citizens shared their representatives' concerns. Community activist William T. Breault, chairman of the Main South Alliance for Public Safety, established the "Body Transportation Fund," with the intent of crowdsourcing enough money to ship Tsarnaev's body to Dagestan. Speaking to reporters outside of the Graham, Putnam and Mahoney Funeral Parlors he took issue with Peter Stefan's insistence that the dead should be buried irrespective of their circumstances, stating that, "Tamerlan Tsarnaev is not a citizen of the United States and doesn't have to be treated as such." When asked what he thought the best course of action was, Breault said that he wanted to see the body repatriated. "I would like him to go back to his original country," he said. "Let the State Department, his parents get involved and take the body back and get rid of this phase of the controversy once and for all" (Koczwara, 2013). Like the political officials quoted above,

Breault wanted the body to be taken to its "proper" place, which for him meant as far away from the United States as possible.

In the end, Tsarnaev was buried in the United States, not in Massachusetts, but rather, at the privately owned Al-Barzakh Muslim cemetery in Doswell, Virginia. The burial was orchestrated by Martha Mullen, a forty-eight-year-old licensed professional counselor and Virginia resident, who said that she was upset by reports of the protests at the Graham, Putnam and Mahoney Funeral Parlors in Worcester. Mullen, who holds a degree from the United Theological Seminary in Dayton, Ohio, thought that the protests "portrayed America at its worst," adding that "Jesus says love our enemies" (Lowery, 2013b). She coordinated with the Islamic Funeral Services of Virginia and with the Worcester police, whose chief Gary Gemme had days earlier made a public appeal for help in finding a burial site for Tsarnaev, stating that "there is a need to do that right thing. We are not barbarians. We bury the dead" (NBC, 2013).

On the evening of Wednesday, May 8th, after a week of protests outside of the funeral home, Ruslan Tsarni drove his nephew's body to Virginia in an unmarked van (Croteau, 2013). The transfer was carried out in stealth and authorities revealed the whereabouts of Tsarnaev's body only after it had been buried. Public officials in Massachusetts were visibly relieved that the body was no longer in their jurisdiction. "There's a collective relief in the city," explained Konstantina Lukes, a Worcester city councilor-at-large and former mayor. "The trauma of the Patriots Day race was extended to the city of Worcester. It's something we weren't prepared for." (MacQuarrie et al., 2013). Lukes's statement points to the synecdochic qualities of certain corpses. The collective trauma of the terrorist attack is displaced on to the body of the perpetrator itself, which comes to stand for the vile act and thus must be expelled from the community. In doing so, the city achieves a sort of "collective relief," and repairs the wounded boundary that delimits its communal identity.

As the controversy over Tsarnaev began to subside in Massachusetts, a new one erupted in Virginia as news spread about his final resting place. Virginia officials claimed that they were blindsided by the burial in their state. Caroline County Administrator Charles M. Culley Jr. said that, "Caroline County was not consulted or given any input into the decision-making process for determining a burial site for this individual" (Dezenski and Viser, 2013). Culley noted that he had only learned about the burial after hearing it on the news, adding that, "We would much prefer to be associated with positive news reports from the national media, but unfortunately, we had no say in the matter" (ibid.).

Another local official, Floyd Thomas, Chairman of the Board of Supervisors of Caroline County, told reporters that he felt deep sympathy with the people of Boston and was upset that the perpetrator of a terrible crime was buried in his county. "This was a horrific event in Boston," he said. "We don't want the county to be remembered as the resting place for the remains of someone who committed a terrible crime." Thomas added that he and other officials were investigating into whether any laws were broken during the process of burying Tsarnaev but noted that, "as long as everything was done legally, there's really very little we can do" (Lowery and Viser, 2013).

Community members were equally surprised by Tsarnaev's burial in Doswell. Ammar Amonette, imam of the Islamic Center of Virginia, said that, "the whole Muslim community here is furious." Like the Massachusetts politicians quoted above, Amonette believed that the presence of Tsarnaev's corpse would disturb families whose relatives were buried in the Al-Barzakh Cemetery. "Now everybody who's buried in that cemetery, their loved ones are going to have to go to that place," he observed, adding that "it was all done secretly behind our backs," and that it "makes no sense whatsoever" that Tsarnaev was buried in Virginia (Aljazeera, 2013).

Other local residents expressed their anger more forcefully. James Lafferty, chairman of the Virginia Anti-Shariah (*sic*) Task Force, a group whose self-described mission is "to oppose and assist others in resisting the implementation of the radical, barbaric, and anti-Constitutional Shariah (*sic*) law in Virginia or anywhere in America," ("Mission Statement") was concerned that Tsarnaev's grave would serve as a sort of memorial. "I think it's the first step in establishing a monument to a jihadist," he said, pledging that he would "work within the law and within the political system [to] do everything we can to have this criminal disinterred and disposed of someplace else" (Shulleeta, 2013). The burial of Tsarnaev would have grave repercussions for local residents, he argued, adding that "just as innocent people in Boston were harmed by this man and his accomplices, innocent people in Doswell should not be forced to deal with the fallout of having this terrorist's body dumped in their midst" (ibid.). Although Lafferty did not elaborate on the specific threats that would be posed by the presence of Tsarnaev's corpse in Virginia, his outlook echoes the sentiments expressed by some Massachusetts residents. In fact, Lafferty draws a direct connection between the physical harm caused by the bombing and the psychic harm wrought on the people of Doswell because of Tsarnaev's dead body.

Not everyone was as worried about the potential repercussions of his burial in Virginia.

Those who were involved firsthand in the burial claimed that their actions were motivated by a sense of duty. Bukhari Abdel-Alim, vice president of the Islamic Funeral Services in Virginia, the funeral home that carried out Tsarnaev's burial, said in a statement that they opposed Tsarnaev's actions but were obligated to "return his body to the earth." "It's not a political thing. . . . Somebody needed to take responsibility, we were able to do so, and that's what we did," said Alim (Aljazeera, 2013). In a similar vein, administrators at the Al-Barzakh Muslim Cemetery told reporters that, "What Tsarnaev did is between him and God. We strongly disagree with his violent actions, but that does not release us from our obligation to return his body to the earth" (Lowery, 2013b).

Death workers like Bukhari Abdel-Alim and Peter Stefan sidestep the moral questions surrounding the burial of unwanted bodies by deferring to a different set of considerations and values. Stefan, like Bukhari, claimed that somebody has to bury the body. "In this country," he said, "we bury our dead regardless of the circumstances." Here, much like Worcester police chief Gary Gemme who observed that "we are not barbarians, we bury the dead," Stefan implicitly marks a civilizational difference between the United States and other nations, who might not be as attentive or friendly to the corpses of their enemies. Bukhari, on the other hand, defers to the authority and judgment of God. He himself is in no position to make a moral evaluation of Tsarnaev's deeds. That task will be left to those who have sovereign authority to judge in the afterlife. Consequently, Bukhari sees no problem with burying Tsarnaev, an act that he characterizes as an obligation.

Others would sidestep the difficult normative questions surrounding Tsarnaev's burial by appealing to the law. Asked about the burial, Virginia Governor Bob McDonnell, a Republican, said that he would have preferred otherwise but noted that no laws were broken in the process. "That wouldn't have been my choice," he said, "but it's a private cemetery—it's a religious cemetery. My understanding is we don't regulate those and it's really a matter of private property, and so that property owner made that choice" (Shulleeta, 2013). In spite of fears that the grave would become an attraction for would-be sympathizers and create a public disturbance, no incidents have been reported in the intervening years since Tsarnaev was buried in 2013 (Nelson, 2014).

CONCLUSION

So what should we make about the debates, protests, and emotions surrounding the burial of Tamerlan Tsarnaev? By way of conclusion, I'd like to circle back to where I started—the scene outside of the Graham, Putnam and Mahoney Funeral Parlors in Worcester, Massachusetts. The sign that I find most remarkable reads "Bury this terrorist on U.S. soil and we will unbury him—American justice." What kind of justice is at work in the exhumation of a corpse?

The Tsarnaev saga illuminates how competing notions of rights and justice are projected on to human bodies. For some, justice is akin to vengeance. The idea of unburying a corpse is meant as a form of posthumous punishment directed at a lifeless body. Historically, there have been numerous examples of violence directed at corpses, from the dragging of Hector's corpse by Achilles, to the desecration of Mussolini's dead body at the hands of a mob in a public square in Milan. For those who seek vengeance, the defiling of a corpse is meant to restore honor and repair social wounds. The treatment of the dead body helps structure collective mourning by sending a message about the values, ideals, and beliefs of a political community.

Such values are, of course, intensely contested. As we have seen, a model of justice as vengeance was countered by the notion of justice as mercy. Those who sought to bury Tsarnaev clung to a different understanding of human dignity, in which the body remains sacrosanct and should be treated with respect. The notion that burying the dead is a work of mercy and compassion alludes to the idea of restorative justice, wherein the task of public mourning is to overcome a given trauma not through redoubled violence, but through reflection and understanding. Here too, the physical treatment of a dead body is meant to send an unambiguous message about the shared values of a given community.

In a world where violence is imbued in the fabric of everyday life, political communities will have to make difficult choices regarding the disposal of unwanted bodies. As Tsarnaev's case demonstrates, the micropolitics of burial offers a rich lens to understand the rituals and practices through which social actors enact the boundaries of moral and political communities. It also shows how the possibilities and probabilities of collective mourning and healing are directly linked to the treatment and disposal of dead bodies. By following the corpse and the complex negotiations around it, we can better understand how our own self-understandings are intimately tied to the dead.

NOTES

1. For images of the protest see "Slideshow: The scene at Graham, Putnam & Mahoney Funeral Parlors," available online: http://www.telegram.com/photogallery/WT/20130509/NEWS/505009998/PH/1&Profile=1116?start=2 Accessed July 26, 2017.

2. Jessica Auchter has recently made a similar plea with regards to the field of international relations. See Auchter, 2016.

3. A similar logic was at work in the sea burial of Osama Bin Laden. According to U.S. officials, Bin Laden was buried at sea in order to prevent his grave from becoming a shrine for his followers. See Hersh, 2016.

4. Comparable actions have been undertaken by grieving mothers of the disappeared in Turkey and Peru. See Bargu, 2014 and Rojas-Perez, 2017. After the September 11 attacks, a great deal of effort was made to recover the remains of the victims (now reduced to ash) and to separate them from those of the perpetrators. See Aronson, 2017.

5. Barhoum and Zaimi later successfully sued the *New York Post* for defamation.

WORKS CITED

Abu-Lughod, Leila. *Do Muslim Women Need Saving?* Cambridge: Harvard University Press, 2013.

Anderson, Travis. "Protestors Outside Funeral Home in North Attleborough." *Boston Globe*. May 3, 2013. Accessed May 19, 2018.https://www.youtube.com/watch?v=Tz-WrytxeTo

"Anger over Burial of Boston Bomb Suspect." *Aljazeera.com*. May 10, 2013. Accessed May 18, 2017. http://www.aljazeera.com/news/americas/2013/05/20135111072214997.html

Aronson, Jay D. *Who Owns the Dead? The Science and Politics of Death at Ground Zero*. Cambridge: Harvard University Press, 2017.

Auchter, Jessica. "Paying Attention to Dead Bodies: The Future of Security Studies?" *Journal of Global Security Studies* 1, no. 1 (2016): 36–50

Balkan, Osman. "Charlie Hebdo and the Politics of Mourning." *Contemporary French Civilization* 41, no. 2 (2016): 253–271.

Bargu, Banu. "Sovereignty as Erasure: Rethinking Enforced Disappearance." *Qui Parle* 23, no. 1 (2014): 35–75.

Bidgood, Jess. "Autopsy Says Boston Bombing Suspect Died of Gunshot Wounds and Blunt Trauma." *New York Times*. May 4, 2013. Accessed May 18, 2018.http://www.nytimes.com/2013/05/05/us/autopsy-says-boston-bombing-suspect-died-of-gunshot-wounds-and-blunt-trauma.html

———. "Funeral Home Accepts Suspect's Body, and Problems." *New York Times*. May 3, 2013. Accessed May 18, 2018. http://www.nytimes.com/2013/05/04/us/funeral-home-accepts-tsarnaevs-body-and-with-it-problems.html

Broadway, Bill. "In His Final Hours, An Appeal to God." *Washington Post*. June 16, 2001. Accessed May 18, 2018.https://www.washingtonpost.com/archive/local/2001/06/16/in-his-final-hours-an-appeal-to-god/9c015727-da6–8e1-82f5-6e9b662dc5b1/?utm_term=.99fc512 14b14

Butler, Judith. *Antigone's Claim*. New York: Columbia University Press, 2002.

———. *Precarious Life: The Powers of Mourning and Violence*. New York: Verso, 2004.

"Chief Pleads for Burial Spot for Tsarnaev: 'We Are Not Barbarians.'" *NBC.com*. Accessed May 17, 2018.http://usnews.nbcnews.com/_news/2013/05/08/18125180-chief-pleads-for-burial-spot-for-tsarnaev-we-are-not-barbarians?lite

Chronis, Peter G. "Senate Moves Fast on McVeigh." *Denver Post*. June 19, 2001. Accessed May 17, 2018. http://extras.denverpost.com/bomb/bomb313.htm

Croteau, Scott J. "The Stealth Mission That Spirited Tamerlan Tsarnaev out of Worcester." *Boston.com*. May 10, 2013. Accessed May 18, 2018 https://www.boston.com/uncategorized/noprimarytagmatch/2013/05/10/the-stealth-mission-that-spirited-tamerlan-tsarnaevs-body-out-of-worcester

Dezenski, Lauren, and Matt Viser. "The Burial of Boston Marathon Bombing Suspect Tamerlan Tsarnaev Caught Virginia Officials by Surprise." *Boston.com*. May 10, 2013. Accessed May 17, 2018.https://www.boston.com/uncategorized/noprimarytagmatch/2013/05/10/the-burial-of-boston-marathon-bombing-suspect-tamerlan-tsarnaev-caught-virginia-officials-by-surprise

"Diyanet: Öldürülen Darbecilere Din Hizmeti Verilmeyecektir." *Bir Gün*. July 19, 2016. Accessed December 17, 2017. http://www.birgun.net/haber-detay/diyanet-oldurulen-darbecileredin-hizmeti-verilmeyecektir-120632.html

Douglas, Mary. *Purity and Danger: An Analysis of Concepts of Pollution and Taboo*. London: Routledge, 2002.

Duke, Alan. "Boston Bombing Suspect's Widow Is Assisting Investigation, Lawyer Says." *CNN.com*. April 23, 2013. Accessed May 15, 2018.http://www.cnn.com/2013/04/22/us/boston-suspect-wife/index.html

Foucault, Michel. *Discipline and Punish: The Birth of the Prison*. New York: Vintage Books, 1995 [1977].

van Gennep, Arnold. *The Rites of Passage*. Trans. Monika B. Vizedom and Gabrielle L. Caffee. Chicago: Chicago University Press, 1960.

Greenblatt, Alan. "In Boston, a Rare Rejection of the Dead." *NPR.org*. May 7, 2013. Accessed December 15, 2017. http://www.npr.org/2013/05/06/181678766/in-boston-a-rare-rejection-of-the-dead

Hersh, Seymour. *The Killing of Osama Bin Laden*. New York: Verso, 2016.

Hirsch, Alexander Keller. "Like So Many Antigones": Survivance and the Afterlife of Indigenous Funerary Remains. *Law, Culture and the Humanities* 10, no. 3 (2014): 1–23.

Honig, Bonnie. *Antigone, Interrupted.* New York: Cambridge University Press, 2013.

———. "Antigone's Laments, Creon's Grief: Mourning, Membership, and the Politics of Exception." *Political Theory* 37, no. 1 (2009): 5–43.

Kaleem, Jaweed. "Tamerlan Tsarnaev, Suspected Boston Bomber, May Not Get Islamic Funeral From Wary Muslims." *Huffington Post.* April 20, 2013. Accessed May 16, 2018.http:// www.huffingtonpost.com/2013/04/20/tamerlan-tsarnaev-funeral-boston-bomber_n_31237 98.html

Koczwara, Kevin. "Boston Marathon Bombing Suspect Tamerlan Tsarnaev's Funeral Arrangements Being Made by Worcester's Graham Putnam and Mahoney Funeral Home." *Masslive.com.* May 3, 2013. Accessed May 15, 2018.http://www.masslive.com/news/worcester/ index.ssf/2013/05/boston_marathon_bombing_suspec.html

Laqueur, Thomas. *The Work of the Dead: A Cultural History of Mortal Remains.* Princeton: Princeton University Press, 2015.

Lowery, Wesley. "Cambridge Won't Bury Marathon Bombing Suspect." *Boston Globe.* May 6, 2013. Accessed May 18, 2018.http://www.bostonglobe.com/metro/2013/05/05/cambridge-off icials-say-tsarnaev-can-buried-city-cemetery/cCsII4AnDxSxgI4s92qlCL/story.html#com-ments

———. "Virginia Woman Who Coordinated Tamerlan Tsarnaev's Burial Says Protests Showed 'America at Its Worst.'" *Boston.com.* May 10, 2013. Accessed May 17, 2018.https:/ /www.boston.com/uncategorized/noprimarytagmatch/2013/05/10/virginia-woman-who-coordinated-tamerlan-tsarnaevs-burial-says-protests-showed-america-at-its-worst

Lowery, Wesley, and Matt Viser. "Virginia County Officials Say They're Trying to Determine If Laws Broken in Marathon Bombing Suspect's Secret Burial." *Boston.com.* May 10, 2013. Accessed May 18, 2018. https://www.boston.com/uncategorized/noprimarytagmatch/2013/ 05/10/virginia-county-officials-say-theyre-trying-to-determine-if-laws-broken-in-marathon-bombing-suspects-secret-burial

MacQuarrie, Brian et al. "Bombing Suspect's Body Buried Outside Mass." *Boston Globe.* May 10, 2013. Accessed May 16, 2018. https://www.bostonglobe.com/metro/2013/05/09/body-bombing-suspect-tamerlan-tsarnaev-entombed-out-state/UWmxVKaid469DeHZtTHNSK/ story.html

Mamdani, Mahmood. *Good Muslim, Bad Muslim: America, The Cold War, and the Roots of Terror.* New York: Doubleday, 2004.

McIvor, David. *Mourning in America: Race and the Politics of Loss.* Ithaca: Cornell University Press, 2016.

Memmott, Mark. "Boston-Area Cemeteries Say No To Burying Bombing Suspect." *NPR.org.* May 6, 2013. Accessed May 16, 2018. http://www.npr.org/sections/thetwo-way/2013/05/06/ 181542151/boston-area-cemeteries-say-no-to-burying-bombing-suspect

"Mission Statement." *Virginia Anti-Shariah Task Force.* Accessed May 16, 2018. http:// virginiaantisharia.blogspot.com/

Muslim Council of Britain. "Over 130 Imams and Religious Leaders from Diverse Backgrounds Refuse to Perform the Funeral Prayer for London Attackers in an Unprecedented Move." *MCB.org.* Accessed May 17, 2018.http://www.mcb.org.uk/over-130-imams-religious-leaders-from-diverse-backgrounds-refuse-to-perform-the-funeral-prayer-for-london-attackers-in-an-unprecedented-move/

Nelson, Steven. "Bomber's Bones Haven't Stirred Trouble in Small Town Virginia." *USNews.com.* April 15, 2014. Accessed May 18, 2018.https://www.usnews.com/news/articles/ 2014/04/15/tamerlan-tsarnaevs-bones-havent-stirred-trouble-in-small-town-virginia

"Permanent Disposition of Dead Bodies or Remains." *MAlegislature.gov.* Accessed May 15, 2018.https://malegislature.gov/Laws/GeneralLaws/PartI/TitleXVI/Chapter114/Section43M

"Release of Body; Pronouncement of Death." *MAlegislature.gov.* Accessed May 15, 2018. https://malegislature.gov/Laws/GeneralLaws/PartI/TitleVI/Chapter38/Section13

Rojas-Perez, Isaias. *Mourning Remains: State Atrocity, Exhumations, and Governing the Disappeared in Peru's Postwar Andes.* Stanford: Stanford University Press, 2017.

Seelye Katharine Q et al. "2nd Bombing Suspect Caught After Frenzied Hunt Paralyzes Boston." *New York Times*, April 19, 2013. Accessed May 18, 2018.http://www.nytimes.com/2013/04/20/us/boston-marathon-bombings.html?pagewanted=all

Seelye, Katharine Q., and Jess Bidgood. "Man Accused of Lying Seeks Release as Cemeteries Reject Tsarnaev Family." *New York Times*. May 5, 2013. Accessed May 16, 2018. http://www.nytimes.com/2013/05/06/us/student-arrested-in-boston-bombing-seeks-release.html

Shulleeta, Brandon. "Tamerlan Tsarnaev's Virginia Grave Won't Become Memorial for Violent Jihadists, says Al-Barzakh Cemetery Leader." *Huffington Post*. May 14, 2013. Accessed May 17, 2018. http://www.huffingtonpost.com/2013/05/14/tamerlan-tsarnaev-virginia-grave_n_3271345.html

Stepputat, Finn, ed. *Governing the Dead: Sovereignty and the Politics of Dead Bodies*. New York: Manchester University Press, 2014.

Stow, Simon. *American Mourning: Tragedy, Democracy, Resilience*. New York: Cambridge University Press, 2017.

Verdery, Katherine. *The Political Lives of Dead Bodies: Reburial and Postsocialist Change*. New York: Columbia University Press, 1999.

Volpp, Leti. "The Boston Bombers." *Fordham Law Review* 82 (2014): 2209–2220.

Ward, Richard, ed. "Introduction: A Global History of Execution and the Criminal Corpse." *A Global History of Execution and the Criminal Corpse*. London: Palgrave Macmillan, 2013: 1–36.

Webb, Suhaib, and Scott Korb. "No Room for Radicals in Mosques." *New York Times*. April 24, 2013. Accessed May 17, 2018. www.nytimes.com/2013/04/25/opinion/no-room-for-radicals-in-mosques.html

Chapter Six

Reparations, Refusals, and Grief

Idle No More and Democratic Mourning

Vicki Hsueh

On December 10th, 2012, Attawapiskat Chief Theresa Spence announced her intention to hunger strike in protest of "continuing governmental abuses against First Nations" (Attawapiskat First Nation 2012). Attawapiskat Nation had recently declared a "state of emergency," which UN Special Rapporteur James Anaya had described as "dire," due to contaminated drinking water, broken sewage systems, and unheated and unlivable homes (Mackrael 2011).[1] Chronic underfunding of basic essential services and resource exploitation were far from the only issues at stake. Citing the government's attempt to erode indigenous rights and to remove protection of lakes and streams through C-45, a proposed omnibus bill, Chief Spence asserted that Canada has maintained "an aggressive, assimilatory legislative agenda without having first consulted, accommodated, and obtained the consent of First Nations as required by the United Nations Declaration on the Rights of Indigenous Peoples" (Attawapiskat First Nation 2012). Chief Spence committed to striking—taking in only fish broth and medicinal tea and living in a tipi on the land below Parliament Hill and the Supreme Court of Canada—until Prime Minister Stephen Harper and David Johnston, the Governor General of Canada, agreed to meet with First Nations Chiefs for a fundamental re-ordering of nation-to-nation treaty relations (CBC News 2012).

Chief Spence's strike quickly captured the public and international spotlight and also garnered widespread attention for the incipient Idle No More movement, a grassroots eruption of flash mob round dances and drumming, teach-ins, rallies, and blockages of logging roads and thoroughfares. The Idle No More movement started in 2012 in Saskatchewan, spread across the North American territories, and sprang up in places as far away as Australia,

Chile, Sri Lanka, Nigeria, and Egypt.[2] Prompted initially by four women (three indigenous and one non-indigenous—Nina Wilson, Jessica Gordon, Sylvia McAdam, and Sheelah Mclean) in response to Prime Minister Harper's violation of Section 35 (most notably through a series of proposed bills, including C-38 and C-45's proposed changes to the Indian Act, the Fisheries Act, and the Navigable Waters Act), Idle No More swiftly developed into a transnational grassroots assemblage of road and railway blockades, teach-ins, flash mob–style round dances, interruptions to the legislature, and a high-profile fast by Chief Spence (Coates 2015).

For supporters, Idle No More represented "the largest, most unified, and potentially most transformative Indigenous movement at least since the Oka resistance in 1990" (Denis 2012; Angus 2012). The movement brought together First Nations, indigenous and non-indigenous activists, and community members in a nonhierarchical structure aimed at protecting long-standing environmental protections, Aboriginal, and treaty rights. Groups, ranging from the Canadian Union of Postal Workers to the Nobel Women's Initiative to Canadian artists and academics, wrote and signed petitions in strong support of Idle No More and Chief Spence (Kino-nda-niimi Collective 2014).

Yet detractors were quick to call Idle No More a "failure." The flash mob round dances and blockades were described as "histrionic threats," "social-mediated mob scenes," and "dangerous delusion" (Foster 2013). The movement was critiqued as poorly organized and undisciplined. Chief Spence, in particular, became the target of increasingly personal insult. Her fast was derided as a "vanity project" and she was ridiculed for not losing enough visible weight. In the *National Post*, columnist Barbara Kay mocked Chief Spence's subsistence on fish broth and tea as a "detox diet," one that wouldn't do much harm to her health (Kay 2013). Conservative Senator Patrick Brazeau, an aboriginal Canadian born in Maniwaki, Quebec, referred to Chief Spence's forty-four days on Victoria Island as a "so-called hunger strike" (Hunt 2013). ""I was sick two weeks ago," Brazeau said. "I had the flu and I lost five pounds." "I look at Miss Spence, when she started her hunger strike, and now?" Brazeau added as a voice in the hall called out, 'She's fatter,' which drew laughter from much of the audience" (MacCharles 2013).

As I will argue in this essay, the mocking and dismissive responses to Chief Spence and the other Idle No More activists illuminates a crucial—and problematic—aspect of modern reparations discourse. In recent years, many have called for reparations discourse to expand beyond a strictly juridical approach and to incorporate more explicitly political and affective forms of reparations. However, even with these expansions, reparations continue to be haunted by colonial logics of expropriation and exclusion that see indigenous calls for change and transformation as threatening to the body politic. In doing so, colonial logics render indigenous forms of suffering, loss, and domination difficult to acknowledge and thus difficult, if not impossible, to genuinely grieve.

In what follows, I first trace the increasingly political and affective turn of modern reparation discourses, focusing especially on the distinctive redefinitions and expansions offered by Lawrie Balfour, Ta-Nehisi Coates, and others. As they persuasively argue, an expanded understanding of reparations as a political language provides a way to develop an *affective consciousness* that offers an opportunity for significant structural and political redress. Yet, despite these valuable and potent reconceptualizations, reparation discourse continues to retain significant colonial bias. What can be done to make indigenous lives and losses palpable? Can the affective circuitry of political consciousness be rewired to make such conditions sensible? What democratic arts of mourning and action are needed?

Through physical protest and occupation, the Idle No More movement offered a sustained and viscerally compelling political response to unjust rule over indigenous peoples in North America. In particular, I focus on the ways in which Idle No More made loss palpable to an audience habituated to overlooking or even mocking indigenous injury and grief. While a number of important recent studies have focused on the micro-practices of Idle No More protests and especially on the relationship between vitality and sovereignty in the Idle No More round dances, I emphasize a different but no less important dimension of body politics and affect. In turning to Chief Spence's body and the sympathetic strikes, marches, and rallies that arose to support her, I explore her corporeal presentation of grief and survival and I examine the ways in which bodies can spur and sustain political refusals and challenges. Her strike—along with the varied supportive actions of Idle No More— should be seen as part of democratic arts of mourning in which bodies are mindfully engaged to experience and to elicit a range of mixed affective responses (grief, love, anger) that can go "bone-deep" to challenge the colonial logic of overlooking and ignoring indigenous loss.

Idle No More offers a version of *reparative refusal* that makes visible the limitations of existing political frameworks as it also enacts a contestatory and democratic indigenous politics that seeks to interrupt and resist capitalist and settler logics by intensifying and collectivizing the processes of mourning. In shared practices in which the tempo of grief is crucially slowed down, the protestors called for greater and more precise attention, care, and beholding to indigenous suffering past, present, and future. In the space opened up by mourning, strikers spurred creative and diversified responses of solidarity, affirmation, and identification. These protests function, I argue in conclusion, as corporeal and affective ways to "unlearn" colonial norms and to make transnational networks through palpable forms of suffering and loss that have been systematically denied and dismissed by colonial governance.

REPARATION AND RHETORIC:
COLONIAL LEGACIES

Modern calls for reparation occupy fraught and increasingly contentious terrain. As Martha Minow notes, contemporary reparation discourses have cast slavery, "genocides, and regimes of torture as subjects for adjudication, a framework of human rights, reparation, and truth-telling" (14). But these reparative claims do not simply operate within the narrow confines of formal law and tort claims, where law is merely the "disinterested mediator" for aggrieved individuals and groups seeking compensation and/or apology for violence and aggression (Biondi 2003; Thompson 2001). Rather, in evocative and potent ways, modern demands for reparation—particularly in the American context—situate themselves as "political languages" that ask not only for redress but also for more systematic reconstruction. From Ta-Nehisi Coates's impassioned and visceral argument for racial reparations that encompasses "the full acceptance of our collective biography and its consequences" to Lawrie Balfour's reconceptualization of reparations as a "political language" that conjures "the heritage of the living past" for democratic education and politics, contemporary reparation discourses harness history, rhetoric, and affect to challenge systems of exploitation and conquest, mobilize alternative perspectives and myriad voices, and spur reconceived democratic political practice and ideals (Coates 2014; Coates 2017; Balfour 2015; Balfour 2014).

The stakes are significant. As Balfour points out, "[m]any commentators have argued that reparations advocacy is politically fruitless and even dangerous; and opinion polls affirm that white Americans overwhelmingly oppose the idea of cash payments to the descendants of slaves and the idea of apologizing for slavery. Even committed racial egalitarians maintain that framing arguments in terms of reparations will inflame anti-black animus and undermine the prospects for progressive politics" (2015, 682). Despite heavy and persistent opposition, modern calls for reparation persist and even deepen their willingness to affirm a contentious stance toward the status quo. "What I'm talking about," Coates clearly asserts, "is more than recompense for past injustices—more than a handout, a payoff, hush money, or a reluctant bribe. What I'm talking about is a national reckoning that would lead to spiritual renewal. Reparations would mean the end of scarfing hot dogs on the Fourth of July while denying the facts of our heritage. Reparations would mean the end of yelling 'patriotism' while waving a Confederate flag. Reparations would mean a revolution of the American consciousness, a reconciling of our self-image as the great democratizer with the facts of our history" (2017, 202).

In this way, Coates's call for a "reckoning"—a "revolution" of "consciousness"—helps to indicate how redress for past injury and crime serves as only one of the many different impacts of "political reparations." Balfour further affirms that reparations, when conceived of in political rather than narrowly legal or economic terms, can serve as a "discursive instrument" to articulate the claims of women and men who have historically been left unheard. Drawing on the writer and activist Ida B. Wells's incisive anti-lynching writings, Balfour illustrates how reparations discourse can and should focus greater attention on the intersectional dimensions of racial domination, refuse anemic apologies and impotent gestures of recognition, and fuel collective responsibility for transforming exploitation and violence (2014). Reparation, conceived in this way, does not simply identify individual injuries through empirical tabulation but rather offers political critique and transformation of larger systems and processes of injustice, oppression, and coercion.

Put even more strongly, what Balfour and Coates recognize in their collective call for a political language of reparations is the necessity of what we can describe as an *affective consciousness* that calls upon feeling and emotion to spur the transformation of laws, social structures, and historical understandings of cause and consequence. Coates's recognition of the need for "spiritual renewal" and Balfour's support for Wells's sharp sarcasm and wit affirm how affect can work to heighten the senses, to create opportunities to see and feel differently, and to register forms of frustration, outrage, and loss bypassed by a focus on restitution or formal legal processes of redress.

Yet the turn to an *affective consciousness* also carries its own thorny entanglements. Reparation claims often rely upon rhetorical strategies that marshal affective feeling to enhance their calls for recompense and restitution. However, in a reflection of their roots in the social contract tradition, these reparative demands tend to rely upon an exclusionary colonialist logic which positions indigenous and other noncolonial peoples as threatening outsiders to the security of the settler state. This commingling of reason and impassioned affect comes forward most clearly in one of the most widely cited and referenced characterizations of reparations, John Locke's account in the *Second Treatise*.[3] "The right to seek reparation," as Locke famously declares, develops as a consequence of egregious violations of the law by "degenerate" and "noxious" creatures (273). "Punishment" alone is not sufficient as a response to the "damage" caused. Rather, "reparation" calls for a more sustained and more comprehensive critique, one that recognizes the economic or physical loss as much as the political, moral, and psychic violence of the "transgressive" injury experienced (273). For many theorists tackling the long history of conquest and slavery, this passage has been critical in capturing the righteous and transformative possibilities of reparations. In one of the most notable of recent examples, Coates includes section 10, chapter 2 in Locke's *Second Treatise* as one of the opening epigraphs of his famous article in *The Atlantic*. Locke's references to the violations, injuries, and crimes done by those who have *"quit the principles of human nature"* frame Coates's account of the profound injustices of slavery, murder, corruption, and redlining (Coates 2014, 54).

However, this entanglement of reason and emotion in Locke's framing of reparation carries deeply troubling historical baggage. In Locke's argument, the terms of being seen as *human*—and by extension the power of reparation to secure human rights—have been powerfully shaped by the history of European colonialism. Most notably, the literary theorist David Eng identifies how the context of New World expansion influenced our conception of reparation as a response to unjust suffering (2012).[4] Namely, for Locke, suffering was cast in terms of the colonial experience of indigenous violence: Indigenous "Americans" behaved as the "brutal" and "noxious creatures" that put colonists in a state of war (273–4). Reparation thus arises in Locke's characterization as a process by which native genocide and the unfettered appropriation of indigenous lands can be pursued by colonists precisely in the name of justice. Far from serving as a moral response to violence *against* indigenous peoples, the *Second Treatise*'s framing of reparations instead helps reaffirm a long history of native exploitation and destruction.[5]

In chapter 2 of the *Second Treatise*, Locke primarily focuses on proportional reparation as an aspect of punishment in the state of nature. In the state of nature, the power to punish should be limited by "what is proportionate to his Transgression" (272). That is to say, when one seeks to punish another's transgression, it should be done not with "absolute or arbitrary power" and "the passionate heats, or boundless extravagancy of his own will" but instead only "so far as calm reason and conscience dictate, what is proportionate to his transgression, which is so much as may serve for reparation and restraint" (272). The exercise of "reparation" therefore calls for *individual control and temperance*, as should be expected in the state of nature, a realm of informal government and society. Although, to be sure, Locke also heightens the moral obligation to punish by characterizing transgressions as violations not just of a single individual but toward *society* as a whole:

> In transgressing the law of nature, the offender declares himself to live by another rule than that of reason and common equity, which is that measure God has set to the actions of men, for their mutual security; *and so he becomes dangerous to mankind, the tye, which is to secure them from injury and violence, being slighted and broken by him.* Which being a trespass against the whole species, and the peace and safety of it, provided for by the law of nature, every man upon this score, by the right he hath to preserve mankind in general, may restrain, or where it is necessary, destroy things noxious to them, *and so may bring such evil on any one, who hath transgressed that law, as may make him repent the doing of it, and thereby deter him, and by his example others, from doing the like mischief.* And in the case, and upon this ground, every man

hath a right to punish the offender, and be executioner of the law of nature
(274).

The representative nature of transgression, the way in which a violation to a
single individual can be interpreted as a threat to the "peace and safety" of
the "whole species," illustrates Locke's deployment of an affective register
to the procedure of reparation, which moves from a more placid account of
the processes of restoration to more dramatic and affective sensations of fear,
frustration, and anger.

Locke thus stages a theatrical spectacle of political injury in a Manichaean moral economy of good and evil, in which the colonial settler is the
victim of an indigenous aggression that aims for totalizing injury. Reparation
emerges in Locke's account not merely as a remedy for losses and wrongs
but rather as part and parcel of an ideological framework that relies upon the
"invasive," "unjust," and "unlawful" identity of natives to fuel its psychic
demand for redress. As James Tully has argued, Locke's conceptions of
political society and property were not only constructed "in contrast to Amerindian forms of nationhood and property in such a way that they obscure
and downgrade the distinctive features of Amerindian polity and property,"
they were also crafted to better position English settlements vis-à-vis other
European traders (1993, 165-6).[6] Indeed, Locke's characterization in the
Treatises not only fails to capture the complex realities of inter- and intra-
European competition for land in the Americas, it is also profoundly insufficient in recognizing the varied indigenous nations, tribes, and polities in the
Americas.[7]

Taken together, Eng's assessment of reparations and Tully's analysis of
Locke's conception of indigenous polities reveal how reparations discourse
has been shaped by a powerful colonial logic in which an oppositional affect
is deployed to demonize the "other," rendering differences in action or behavior as warlike, threatening, and even animalistic, while simultaneously
positioning colonial settlers as aggrieved injured parties. At the same time,
within this colonial perspective, indigenous theft, losses, and injury are minimized and at times made even imperceptible. While the recent turn to more
political and more affective conceptions of reparations discourse holds great
promise for accentuating the ethical and political necessity for response and
transformation, we should also be wary of slipping inadvertently into strategies of reparative mobilization that rely upon colonial logics which apprehend difference as threat, reinforce the social contract, and make certain lives
"ungrievable." To what extent can reparation discourse resist inherited colonial and settler frameworks of governance and identity? How should rhetoric
and affect be employed to make indigenous lives and injustices recognizable? Can rhetorical and affective deployments of mourning and loss facilitate transformations of long-standing colonial ideologies and norms?

As I will argue in the next section, the Idle No More movement enables us to see some of the ways in which rhetoric, affect, and refusal can resist some of the Manichaean dynamics of reparation and create spaces and resources for creative and participatory indigenous resurgence. The challenge is formidable. As Chief Spence and the activists of Idle No More make clear, the task at hand isn't simply to revise existing political structures or to include indigenous voices in electoral politics. Rather, Idle No More aims to politicize and highlight indigenous rights and sovereignty against a settler state that perceives indigenous protest as threatening and indigenous lives as ungrievable. To do so, protestors strategically engaged their bodies to pursue resistance and refusal on multiple fronts and in multiple dimensions: disrupting existing frameworks of political participation and recognition; rendering indigenous peoples and their suffering in real, visible, and palpable form; mobilizing indigenous and non-indigenous actors and groups in connection and solidarity. These are democratic arts of mourning that open up possibilities for resisting liberal settler governance and the psychic and political insinuations of the social contract, while creating connection and resilience in shared concerns and vulnerabilities.

RESISTANCE THROUGH GRIEF AND REFUSAL

Idle No More employed a combination of tactics, including road and railway blockades, teach-ins, flash mob round dances, interruptions to the legislature, and a high-profile fast by Chief Spence, to draw global attention and support for indigenous sovereignty and treaty rights (Coates 2015). In doing so, Idle No More protestors unleashed a vivid democratic energy, demonstrating both power in their corporeal resistance to settler government policies and pleasure in asserting an alternative form of political sovereignty. As the political theorist Ali Aslam contends, "For Idle No More, the first step to democratizing sovereignty involves addressing devitalized agency as one part of a larger norm of idleness associated with membership in the Canadian settler state" (2017, 20). In particular, as numerous theorists have noted, the spontaneous flash mob round dances were powerful rejections of this idleness and of the silencing, regulating, and corporatizing forces of the settler state.

In part, Idle No More activists reversed the flow of power by calling upon the state to account for the legitimacy of its action. But the protests also crucially built up fellow feeling, solidarity, and shared connection among protestors. "For the first time," Tanya Kappo, one of the early Idle No More organizers, recalled, "I saw a genuine sense of love for each other and for ourselves. Even if it was only momentary it was powerful enough to awaken in them what needed to be woken up—a remembering of who we were, who we are" (Kino-nda-niimi Collective 2014, 70).

In this section, I want to build on Aslam's and others' accounts by turning to a different yet equally distinctive aspect of the Idle No More protests. Unlike the dramatic bursts of kinetic energy unleashed by the round dances, Chief Spence's protest—and the numerous groups and individuals who came out to support her—revealed the temporal and affective intensities that could be released in *slowing* the body down and rendering it *still* but not silent. Hunger strikes and acts of sympathetic mourning, I argue, help to resist and overturn the colonialist logic of the settler state by insisting on forms of attention, understanding, and solidarity that can drill down and settle in "bone-deep," to draw on Eve Tuck's evocative phrase (14). Chief Spence's hunger strike presents a visceral performance of grief and survival that highlights the contradictory demands of the settler state as it also illuminates how the corporeal elicitation of affective responses opens up opportunities for shared grieving, affiliated practices of solidarity, and "unlearning" colonial norms.

Chief Spence's fast lasted for forty-four days, during which time she was hospitalized once and also endured one of the coldest winters in Ottawa in the past decade.[8] Many in the mainstream media belittled Chief Spence's strike. For example, as *Toronto Sun* newspaper columnist Peter Worthington sneered, "[t]he remarkable thing about Attawapiskat Chief Theresa Spence's celebrated hunger strike is that when she stopped it, after 44 days of fish broth, she looked as plump as she did when she started it" (2013). Moreover, as the strike proceeded, critics increasingly tried to distinguish Chief Spence's "indulgent," "vain," and "self-serving" strike from the other Idle No More actions. In fact, Chief Spence was accused by some of using the hunger strike to distract the public from pending investigations of band financial mismanagement. For example, after visiting Chief Spence during her strike, Ottawa-Orléans Conservative MP Royal Galipeau disparaged her appearance and criticized her spending habits, "I noticed that manicure of hers. I tell you Anne can't afford it," he said, referring to his wife (Patriquin 2013).

These crude jokes about Chief Spence "cheating" with her "liquid diet" and "gaining weight" revealed settler ideology's failure to see and value indigenous life. "Mainstream Canada," the Anishinaabeg writer and theorist Leanne Betasamosake Simpson lamented, could not understand the multiple resonances of Chief Spence's fast. As Simpson further clarified:

> My Ancestors survived many long winters on fish broth because there was nothing else to eat—not because the environment was harsh, but because the land loss and colonial policy were so fierce that they were forced into an imposed poverty that often left fish broth as the only sustenance. . . . Fish broth sustained us through the hardest of circumstances, with the parallel understanding that it can't sustain one forever. We exist today because of fish broth. It connects us to the water and to the fish who gave up its life so we could sustain ourselves. Chief Spence is eating fish broth because, metaphorically,

colonialism has kept Indigenous Peoples on a fish broth diet for generations
upon generations. (154–157)

For many Idle No More activists, it was clear that Chief Spence's subsistence
on fish broth and tea—and the mainstream media's mocking coverage of her
fast—highlighted precisely this division between lives "considered valuable"
and "lives considered ungrievable." As Judith Butler has powerfully suggested, "One way of posing the question of who "we" are in these times of
war is by asking whose lives are considered valuable, whose lives are
mourned, and whose lives are considered ungrievable. . . . An ungrievable
life is one that cannot be mourned because it has never lived, that is, it has
never counted as a life at all. We can see the division of the globe into
grievable and ungrievable lives from the perspective of those who wage war
in order to defend the lives of certain communities, and to defend them
against the lives of others—even if it means taking those latter lives" (38).

This "ungrievability" was more than mere misunderstanding of indigenous practice or simple skirting over the presence of indigenous nations. The
attempts by mainstream media and Conservative leaders to ridicule Chief
Spence and to deride the Idle No More actions as "disorganized" and "chaotic" reveal the intersecting biases of a neocolonial settler state that used crude
insults and mockery as tools of misogyny and racism to minimize and neutralize indigenous power and agency. In part, the jokes relied upon a familiar
sexist set of dismissals of female leadership and authority: focusing on her
appearance and weight, they attempted to disparage Chief Spence and to
eliminate the moral and mortal significance of her protest. Yet, the jokes also
went beyond chauvinism: they were part of a larger affective colonial logic,
one which simultaneously bypasses indigenous loss as it also identifies indigenous agency, power, and leadership as threats which needed to be neutral-
ized as quickly as possible. As the theorist Audra Simpson bluntly states,
Chief Spence's body failed "to do what it was supposed to do—perish"
(2016). On multiple levels, her body was seen as a threat to the state—
because of its female-ness, its Chief-ness, and, perhaps most of all, because
of its Indian-ness. Thus, following this logic, conservative MPs and media
pundits tried to code Chief Spence's actions as, on the one hand, "vain" and
"ridiculous," and, on the other hand, as also "dangerous" and "threatening."
Recalling Locke's description of those who threaten civil society as "noxious" to the "whole species," the insults and jokes about Chief Spence can be
viewed as a form of compulsive defending against colonial responsibility for
conquest, appropriation, and injury and, as a consequence, a way to avoid
any real confrontation or engagement with reparation and transformation.

In such contexts, can indigenous demands and lives be realized and made
visible and palpable? In refusing to eat, Chief Spence's fleshy yet starving
body—a body that persisted in surviving *and* speaking—offered a profound

refusal of the desires and urges of the Canadian settler state. As the activist and writer Pamela Palmater noted, the strike "is symbolic of what is happening to First Nations in Canada. For every day that Spence does not eat, she is slowly dying, and that is exactly what is happening to First Nations, who have lifespans up to 20 years shorter than average Canadians" (Kino-nda-niimi Collective 2014, 40). Chief Spence's duality in dying and surviving served as a form of what I want to describe as *reparative refusal*, a concept that draws on both Audra Simpson's account in *Mohawk Interruptus* and Rebecca Tsosie's study of intercultural indigenous reparations.

Reparations need to have critical and transformative goals that go beyond claims for monetary compensation. As Tsosie explains, "reparations should respond to the need to heal wounds that relate to past wrongdoing, as well as contemporary forms of injustice against Native peoples" (44). Like Balfour and Coates, Tsosie focuses on a "political" and interrogative understanding of reparations. "The measures used to redress these harms," Tsosie notes, "will require a significant restructuring of America's basic institutions, including its political and legal institutions" and any understanding of "reparation must be flexible and account for the different historical experiences of particular groups" (56). And yet as we have seen, pursuing reparation in a settler colonial context is difficult precisely because the demands of indigenous peoples and nations are reflexively and defensively read as threats that require elimination while simultaneously indigenous suffering is treated as inconsequential. As a result, an additional measure of *refusal* is also a needed tactic for navigating reparative projects. As Simpson notes, refusal can enable resistance to colonial and settler norms while also illuminating key points of coercion and oppression. For example, the Mohawks of Kahnawa:ke, in Simpson's account, employ "grounded refusal"—of passports, of American and Canadian citizenship, of recognition, of incorporation, of rights, of gifts—not only to resist and critique the bureaucratic and legal machinations of various colonial states (U.S. and Canadian) but also to "insist upon the integrity of Haudenosaunee governance" and to speak to the "geographic alterity" and "radical past as Other in the history of the West" (2014, 7). Refusal, that is, clears away lies and misconceptions in its rejection of normative conceptions of identity, state, and legitimacy. Most of all, "refusal," Simpson notes, "raises the question of legitimacy for those who are usually in the position of recognizing: What is their authority to do so? Where does it come from? Who are they to do so?" (11). Refusal thus politicizes the exposure of injustices, misconceptions, and betrayals through the layered and repeated accretion of rejections to colonial states and systems.

When calls for reparations are linked to tactics of refusal, key opportunities are opened up not simply for creative forms of consciousness-raising but also visceral and sustaining forms of solidarity that cross over the parameters of the settler state and its affective exclusionary consciousness. What makes Chief Spence's form of *reparative refusal* particularly distinctive is its attention to tempo, permeation, and affect. Through her body, Chief Spence embodied multiple refusals—a refusal to die, a refusal to stay silent, a refusal to move, and a refusal to accept an illegitimate political process. Hunger strikes in other contexts have illustrated the potent ways in which the "hungering" body lodges resistance to coercive authority. For example, as Maud Ellmann argues in her well-known study of the 1981 IRA hunger strikes in Long Kesh, the strikers offered indelible protest against institutional and political authority; their refusal to eat served as a rejection of compliance. On the one hand, Ellmann finds, "the protestors transform their bodies into the "quotations" of their forebears and reinscribe the cause of Irish nationalism in the spectacle of starving flesh" (14). On the other hand, their bodies become living catalogs of the present and former struggle and "by making theater of their own starvation . . . the prisoners brought shame on their oppressors and captured the sympathies" of supporters (72).[9] The hunger fast and shared support for Chief Spence similarly served as a way to "refuse" the settler state's willful blindness, shame oppressors, and also "make present" what are often treated as "ungrievable" losses of generations of indigenous peoples and nations. As Chief Isadore Day noted, Chief Spence's hunger strike served as a powerful demonstration of how the Canadian government kept native peoples in the realm of bare life for generations: "fed" "enough food and water to keep us alive," Day contends, but still not "let in" "in any substantive way" (Kino-nda-niimi Collective 2014, 75).

Yet Chief Spence's "starving flesh" also did not stand as a solitary or silent "spectacle." Instead her strike spurred numerous supporters to participate in affective and permeating forms of resistance. Almost immediately after Chief Spence first announced her strike, numerous groups and individuals pledged their support and solidarity, engaging in sympathetic hunger strikes with Chief Spence, some lasting only one day and others matching the duration of Chief Spence's action. In early January 2013, Raymond Robinson (Cross Lake First Nation in northern Manitoba) and Mi'kmaq activists Jean Sock and Shelley Young treated Chief Spence's action as a "sacred petition" to be honored by shared "fasting" (Francis 2012; CBC News 2012). A worldwide day of fasting brought together people from South Dakota to Egypt to strike in solidarity.[10] Still others showed their support through marches and rallies. For example, in the middle of January 2013, six Cree youth from the Whapmagoostui First Nation began a 1,600-kilometer walk from the northernmost Cree village on Hudson Bay to Parliament Hill (the Journey of Nishiyuu/Human Beings) in support of Chief Spence (CBC News 2013). Along the way, the walkers were joined by hundreds of others and then met more than 5,000 supporters at Parliament Hall in March 2013. In addition, a diverse set of supporters participated by testifying to Chief

Spence's action through social media. Chief Spence's Twitter feed was updated almost daily and the account's handle ("voice of #chieftheresa and her team") reflected the communal nature of the action (@ChiefTheresa 12/22/2012). "Voice of #chieftheresa and her team," Chief Spence posted, "I am on my 13th day and not stopping until the meeting takes place. Grassroots pple keep making noise" (@ChiefTheresa 12/22/2012). Throughout the fast, aides and allies helped to update a far-flung community on Chief Spence's condition and many offered their support, love, thoughts, and solidarity in the comments. "Chief Spence woke up feeling rested and strong," her aides posted, "She expressed her gratitude for all the support and sends her love to everyone even #PMHarper" (@ChiefTheresa 12/24/2012). Indeed, even while "[h]er physical state has been weakened," supporters noted that she "is strong in spirit and remains steadfast in her position" (@ChiefTheresa 1/11/2013). As the strike progressed, the feed even began to blur the distinction between "I" and "we," and the commentary on Chief Spence's status reflected this overlapped and intermeshed community (i.e., "I am not leaving"; I am "not stopping"; we will "not be silent no more").

The marches, FB testimonials, and Twitter support served as actions of shared mourning—and these were forms of mourning that ranged from bone-deep participation to more episodic acts of witnessing and supporting. Tuck describes "bone-deep participation" as collective processes of witnessing, thinking, and feeling, which take place in "unseen moments" "far off screen" and open up possibilities for a variety of transformations, ranging from a "re/newed epistemology" to "nodes and networks and pathways to be activated episodically for more explicit political participation" (14). Building on Tuck's powerful description, I want to further elaborate upon the ramifications of "bone-deep" participation as a form of *democratic mourning*. With their collective response to Chief Spence, Idle No More supporters demonstrated a desire to affirm and attend to the specific conditions of Chief Spence's tenuous life. Some did so through social media (Facebook and Twitter, especially), sending messages of care, support, and concern for Chief Spence's physical, spiritual, and emotional condition. Particular attention was given to Chief Spence's daily needs and demands, offering careful consideration of her body, her perspective, and her feelings on every day of the fast.[11] Those who supported Chief Spence by joining in sympathetic hunger striking and marches participated even more viscerally, seeing their exertions as an analogous but certainly not identical experience of Chief Spence's tolls and hardships. As Megan Rice, a supporter in England, explained, "The idea that people in this modern world are still willing to do that for something they believe in very deeply is something that just really moves me and it's something I find extremely noble beyond words and so for me a one-day fast is really the least I can do when you consider the fact Chief Spence is risking her life" (Francis 2012). In witnessing and responding to

Chief Spence's daily and essential modalities of life and survival, the Idle No More protestors offered responses of care and investment which not only rebuked the colonial ideology that treated indigenous lives as ungrievable (namely, by looking for the public "to open your heart and mind"), but also offered up a self-aware conception of political responsiveness which sought to resist the co-optive terms and expectations of the settler state by forging transnational alliances, affirming solidarity, and practicing resistance.

These are democratic arts of mourning that refuse indigenous invisibility. Through public dialogue and response, supporters demonstrated that Chief Spence's body would not be ignored or overlooked as they put forth their bodies and words in solidarity. "I don't want her to die for this. We should all be there for her," explained Janie Kapaquapit-Ramos, a protestor who joined a one-day sympathy fast with Chief Spence. "For me fasting represents prayer, when you pray for others to find their way because we see too much suffering by our people and they need to find their way back, so for me that's the highest thing you can do to help others," she said (Francis 2012). Meanwhile, those who could not pursue a hunger strike or do the long march to Parliament Hill turned to other forms of corporeal action. For example, as one of the Facebook pages noted, "[t]hose that are sick, disabled, or who are breastfeeding may join with prayer and smudging."[12]

In a complication to Tuck's assessment, these actions of solidarity were not hidden away out of public examination. They were freely communicated and discussed on social media and in blogs and they provided a visible and active refusal of the characterization offered up by the settler state and its representatives, namely that Chief Spence's action was a sham. Characterized in this way, mourning required paying attention to time, to feeling, to the conditions necessary for life and to threats to health. As Simpson explained:

> We support. We pray. We offer semaa. We take care of the sacred fire. We sing each night at dusk. We take care of all the other things that need to be taken care of, and we live up to our responsibilities in light of the fast. We do these things because we know that through her physical sacrifice she is closer to the Spiritual world than we are. We do these things because she is sacrificing for us and because it is the kind, compassionate thing to do. (155)

Through accretion and persistent attention, Chief Spence's supporters gave heft and substance to indigenous demands and rendered indigenous life grievable, demonstrating how such lives mattered, how integral they were to the community, and thus how much they *counted*. We can see this as a way to "unlearn" the colonial logic of exclusion through the intensification of both affective and physical attention. As Jacques Rancière observes, "unlearning" involves scrutinizing "everyday" practice and examining the ways in which those practices, acts, sensibilities, and movements relate to received knowledge. Through a "multiplicity of practices, inside and outside dominant institutions, that extend the community of equal speaking beings," activists can challenge received knowledge and "open new paths for the circulation of thought," undoing regulatory norms and requirements (Rancière 2016, 604). By bringing together a diverse community of witnesses/participants, Idle No More calls forth a "we" that refuses to ask the state for permission to grieve, rejects the misogyny and insults of mainstream politicians and press, and knits together a transnational network of care and protest. In doing so, Idle No More offers a form of reparative refusal that sets its own standard for grievability.

Just as powerfully, Chief Spence's hunger strike and the actions of Idle No More also indicate the insufficiency of simple apology or financial restitution as a way of overturning the affective logic of colonialism and establishing reparation for stolen land and lost lives. As Spence's supporters demonstrate, the political processes and structures that need to be transformed require democratic and grassroots responses that are open-ended, associational, and exceed the boundaries of the state. Idle No More's mourning created a decentralized and far-flung grassroots community—a form of transnational repair—that established a visible and palpable alternative to colonial logics and the formal structures of the settler state.

CONCLUSION

Amplified by social media and technology, *Idle No More* represents a multimodal way of staging reparative claims in which resistance, refusal, and affect highlight the shape-shifting and opportunistic dimensions of colonial engagement and recognition. In that sense, the focus of the movement wasn't simply a response to Harper's persistent violation of Section 35, but rather an attempt to identify *and* combat a settler infrastructure in which unfair and disproportional representation, the abuses of residential schools, the colonial illegitimacy of *terra nullius* and the discovery doctrine, violence and abuse of indigenous women, and the theft of indigenous land and wealth are all intertwined. This is a rhizomatic grassroots response that aims to tackle the tentacular and shifting powers of the modern colonial state by offering up critique of the settler state and by simultaneously forming an alternative transnational network of response.

Nonetheless, challenges remain. Disagreement, contention, and dis-unity all threaten the solidarity of the movement. Most notably, at the end of Chief Spence's fast, the Attawapiskat Nation issued a 13 Point Declaration of Commitment on January 24, 2013, that called for full recognition and implementation of treaty and non-treaty rights, legislation with the "free, prior, and informed consent of First Nations," "sustained environmental oversight," and a "National Public Commission of Inquiry on Violence Against Indigenous

Women of all ages" (Kino-nda-niimi Collective 2014, 323-4). Many responded positively to the Declaration, affirming its insistence on Canada's implementation of the UN Declaration of the Rights of Indigenous Peoples (UNDRIP) and for greater indigenous participation and control. Still, the 13 Point Declaration was not uniformly supported by indigenous activists, Métis, Inuit, and First Nations. A number of activists expressed frustration with the heavy emphasis on representations by Native chiefs and the circumscribed role for grassroots activists (Galloway 2013). Others, such as Taiaiake Alfred, questioned the Declaration's commitment to indigenous sovereignty and self-determination and argued for the reoccupation of "Indigenous sacred, ceremonial, and cultural use sites to re-establish our presence on our land and in doing so educate Canadians about our continuing connections to those places" (347–9).

The post–13 Points Declaration disagreements reflect how indigenous politics must grapple with divergent and contested perspectives. The work of resistance is necessarily continuing and difficult (Belleau 2014). Yet, as the activists and activities of Idle No More made clear, reparative refusal demarcates and makes visible not simply the limitations of existing political frameworks on reparations but also the possibilities of creative and participatory indigenous resurgence.

NOTES

1. Located at the mouth of the Attawapiskat River at James Bay, Attawapiskat Nation, an isolated community of less than 2,000 (with 3,500 band members in total), was thrust into the national spotlight in the previous year for a severe housing shortage in which nearly 100 people were living in unheated homes, trailers, and tents without electricity or running water.

2. For example, the Idle No More Global Action Day (http://www.idlenomore.ca/story) took place in Australia, Chile, Colombia, Egypt, Finland, Germany, Italy, Mexico, New Zealand, Nigeria, Poland, Sri Lanka, UK, and in about eighty locations throughout the United States.

3. See, for example, Coates 2014; Magee 1993; Perugini and Gordon 2015; Boxill 1972; Boxill 2003.

4. While Eng's broader ambition in the project is to address the possibilities and limits of repairing twentieth-century injuries of war, violence, and colonialism especially in the transpacific region, he views Locke as central both to shaping the ideological assumptions of liberalism and the colonial history that structures reparation discourse. In particular, by drawing on the work of Freud and Klein, Eng identifies how the context of New World expansion influenced Locke's conception of human suffering (Eng 2012 and forthcoming).

5. Further complicating this dynamic, "liberal" European settlers in the American context, as Michael Rogin points out, combined their repulsion and violence toward indigenous peoples with projections of indigenous innocence and immaturity, enabling settlers to situate themselves in the roles of both justifiable aggressors *and* paternal guides—a situation perhaps not all that different from the domineering role adopted by Harper (Rogin 1988).

6. See also Ivison 2003; Armitage 2004; Arneil 1996.

7. A number of studies recognize that Locke had a complicated and nuanced understanding of indigenous peoples in other works, including the *Essay, Letters on Toleration*, and other political writings. See, notably, Turner 2011; Farr 2009.

8. Chief Spence's tent was on Victoria Island (below Parliament Hill), in the traditional territory of the Algonquian Peoples (Ottawa, Ontario).

9. See also Feldman 1991; Bargu 2014.

10. For information on the global one-day fasts, see Hunger Strike in Solidarity with Attawapiskat Chief Theresa Spence, https://www.facebook.com/events/448271678567106/ accessed: July 11, 2017.

11. On the indigenous and feminist dimensions of these forms of care, see Suzack 2010.

12. For discussion on feminist activism through social media, see Rentschler 2017.

WORKS CITED

Alfred, Taiaiake. 2014. "Idle No More and Indigenous Nationhood." In *The Winter We Danced*, ed., The Kino-nda-niimi Collective, 347–349. Winnipeg: ARP Books.

Angus, Charlie. 2012. "Harper: Act Now Before Chief Theresa Spence Dies," *Huffington Post*, December 21, 2012. Accessed 2.6.17. http://www.huffingtonpost.ca/charlie-angus/chief-theresa-spence-hunger-strike_b_2346601.html.

Armitage, David. 2004. "John Locke, Carolina, and the Two Treatises of Government." *Political Theory* 32: 602–27.

Arneil, Barbara. 1996. *John Locke and America: The Defence of English Colonialism*. New York: Oxford University Press.

Aslam, Ali. 2017. *Ordinary Democracy: Sovereignty and Citizenship beyond the Neoliberal Impasse*. New York: Oxford University Press.

Attawapiskat First Nation. 2011. "Housing Crisis in Attawapiskat." Bulletin, December 1, 2011.

———. 2012. "Chief Spence Announces Hunger Strike in Ottawa." Press release, December 11, 2012. Accessed 2.15.17. http://www.chiefs-of-ontario.org/sites/default/files/files/Chiefpercent20Spencepercent20Presspercent20Releasepercent20-per-cent20Finalpercent20approved.pdf.

Balfour, Lawrie. 2015. "Ida B. Wells and "Color Line Justice": Rethinking Reparations in Feminist Terms." *Perspectives in Politics* vol. 13, no. 3: 680–95.

———. 2014. "Unthinking Racial Realism: A Future for Reparations?" *Du Bois Review* 11:1: 43–56.

Bargu, Banu. 2014. *Starve and Immolate: The Politics of Human Weapons*. New York: Columbia University Press.

Belleau, Lesley. 2014. "Pauwauwaein: Idle No More to the Indigenous Nationhood Movement." In *The Winter We Danced*, ed., The Kino-nda-niimi Collective, 349–354. Winnipeg: ARP Books.

Biondi, Martha. 2003. "The Rise of the Reparations Movement." *Radical History Review* 87: 5–18.

Boxill, Bernard R. 1972. "The Morality of Reparation." *Social Theory and Practice* 2:1: 113–123.

———. 2003. "A Lockean Argument for Black Reparations." *The Journal of Ethics* 7:1: 63–91.

Butler, Judith. 2016. *Frames of War: When Is Life Grievable*. London and New York: Verso.

CBC News. 2011. "Attawapiskat Crisis Sparks Political Blame." December 1, 2011.

———. 2012. "Attawapiskat Chief 'Willing to Die' to Force Harper Meeting." December 11, 2012.

———. 2012. "Manitoba Elder Takes Hunger Strike to Ottawa." December 31, 2012.

———. 2013. "'Journey of the People' Ends with Crowds Cheering Aboriginal Youth on Parliament Hill." March 25, 2013.

Coates, Ken. 2015. *#IdleNoMore and the Remaking of Canada*. Regina: University of Regina Press.

Coates, Ta-Nehisi. 2014. "The Case for Reparations," *The Atlantic*, May 21, 2014: 54–71.

———. 2017. *We Were Eight Years in Power: An American Tragedy*. New York: One World.

Denis, Jeff. 2012. "Why 'Idle No More' Is Gaining Strength, and Why All Canadians Should Care." *The Star*, December 20, 2012.

Ellmann, Maud. 1993. *The Hunger Artists: Starving, Writing, and Imprisonment*. Cambridge: Harvard University Press.

Eng, David. 2012. "Reparations and the Human." *Columbia Journal of Gender and Law* 21.2: 159–181.

Eng, David, Teemu Ruskola, and Shuang Shen. 2011. "Introduction: China and the Human." *Social Text* 29: 1–27.

Farr, James. 2009. "Locke, 'Some Americans,' and the Discourse on 'Carolina'." *Locke Studies* 9: 17–96.

Feldman, Allen. 1991. *Formations of Violence: The Narrative of the Body and Political Terror in Northern Ireland*. Chicago: University of Chicago Press.

Foster, Peter. 2013. "Misguided Hunger Strike Is Manufacturing Dissent." *Financial Post*, January 3, 2013.

Francis, Annette. 2012. "Sympathy Hunger Strikes Begin in Support of Attawapiskat Chief Theresa Spence." *APTN National News*, December 14, 2012.

Friesen, Joe. 2013. "What's Behind the Explosion of Native Activism." *The Globe and Mail*, January 18, 2013.

Galloway, Gloria. 2013. "With Hunger Strike Over, Chief Spence's Polarizing Legacy." *The Globe and Mail*, January 24, 2013.

Hunt, Nevil. 2013. "Senator Knocks Theresa Spence During Orléans Dinner," *Ottawa East News*, Jan 30, 2013.

Ivison, Duncan. 2003. 'Locke, Liberalism and Empire.' In Peter R. Anstey, ed., *The Philosophy of John Locke: New Perspectives*: 86–105. London and New York: Routledge.

Kay, Barbara. 2013. "You Call That a 'Hunger Strike'?," *The National Post*, January 4, 2013.

Kino-nda-niimi Collective, eds. 2014. *The Winter We Danced: Voices from the Past, the Future, and the Idle No More Movement*. Winnipeg: ARP Books.

Locke, John. 1988. *Two Treatises of Government*, ed. Peter Laslett. Cambridge: Cambridge University Press.

MacCharles, Tonda. 2013. "Conservative MP and Senator Belittle Chief Theresa Spence, Idle No More Movement." *Toronto Star*, January 30, 2013.

Mackrael, Kim. 2011. " UN Official Blasts 'Dire' Conditions in Attawapiskat." *Globe and Mail*, December 20, 2011.

Magee, Rhonda V. 1993. "The Master's Tools, from the Bottom Up: Responses to African-American Reparations Theory in Mainstream and Outsider Remedies Discourse." *Virginia Law Review* 79: 876–92.

Minow, Martha. 2002. "Breaking the Cycles of Hatred." In *Breaking the Cycles of Hatred: Memory, Law, and Repair*, ed., Nancy Rosenbaum. Princeton: Princeton University Press.

Patriquin, Martin. 2013. "43 Days and for What? Theresa Spence and the Status Quo." *Macleans's*. January 24, 2013.

Perugini, Nicola, and Neve Gordon. 2015. *The Human Right to Dominate*. New York: Oxford University Press.

Rancière, Jacques. 2016. "The Un-What?" *Philosophy and Rhetoric*, vol. 49, no. 4: 589–606.

Rentschler, Carrie A. 2017. "Bystander Intervention, Feminist Hashtag Activism, and the Anti-Carceral Politics of Care." *Feminist Media Studies* 17:4: 565–584.

Rogin, Michael. 1988. *Ronald Reagan, the Movie and Other Episodes in Political Demonology*. Berkeley: University of California Press.

Simpson, Audra. 2014. *Mohawk Interruptus: Political Life Across the Borders of Settler States*. Durham: Duke University Press.

———. 2016. "The State is a Man: Theresa Spence, Loretta Saunders, and the Gender of Settler Sovereignty." *Theory and Event*, vol. 19, issue 4. Accessed July 10, 2017. https://muse-jhu-edu-ezproxy.library.wwu.edu/article/633280.

Simpson, Leanne Betasamosake. "Fish Broth and Fasting." In *The Winter We Danced*, ed., The Kino-nda-niimi Collective, 154–57. Winnipeg: ARP Books.s

Spence, Richard. 2013. "Attawapiskat's Housing Crisis: A Ground-Level Perspective." *CBC News*, December 12, 2013.

Spence, Theresa (@ChiefTheresa). 2012–3.

Suzack, Cheryl. 2010. "Indigenous Women and Transnational Feminist Struggle: Theorizing the Politics of Compromise and Care." *CR: The New Centennial Review* 10:1: 179–193.

Thompson, Janna. 2001. "Historical Injustice and Reparation: Justifying Claims of Descendents." *Ethics* 112: 114–135.

Tsosie, Rebecca. 2007. "Acknowledging the Past to Heal the Future: The Role of Reparations for Native Nations" in Jon Miller and Rahul Kumar, eds., *Reparations*, 43–68. Oxford and New York: Oxford Press.

Tuck, Eve, and K. Wayne Yang, eds. 2013. *Youth Resistance Research and Theories of Change*. New York: Routledge.

Tully, James. 1993. *An Approach to Political Philosophy: Locke in Contexts*. Cambridge: Cambridge University Press.

Turner, Jack. 2011. "John Locke, Christian Mission, and Colonial America." *Modern Intellectual History* 8:2: 267–297.

United First Nations of Turtle Island. 2012. *Hunger Strike in Solidarity with Attawapiskat Chief Theresa Spence*. December 24, 2012. Accessed July 11, 2017. https://www.facebook.com/events/448271678567106/.

Worthington, Peter. 2013. "Starved for Attention." *Toronto Sun* January 27, 2013.

Chapter Seven

Burning Rage

Disenfranchised Mourning and the
Political Possibilities of Anger

Shirin S. Deylami

In the days after a white police officer murdered an unarmed African American student named Michael Brown the small city of Ferguson, Missouri was transformed from a relatively quiet suburb to a space of open grieving and protest. As peaceful protests were interspersed with more aggressive forms of rioting, the unrest in Ferguson came to epitomize the complicated emotional and affective experiences of Blacks who have found little positive institutional response to their suffering and vulnerability. Expressions of grief and loss were punctuated by righteous anger over not only the conditions that precipitated Brown's death (racial profiling, the militarization of the police, lack of political representation and continued racial segregation) but also the ways in which his suffering and the mourning of his family and community were disenfranchised.[1] Brown's death and the Ferguson uprising will no doubt come to function as only one nodal point in what will surely be a lengthy resurgence of a social movement for the radical transformation of the structures that produce racial vulnerability and suffering. But Brown's death at the hands of police and the ultimate mourning and rage of the Black community of Ferguson also signals the ways in which politics rooted in mourning are imbricated in other affective political responses, including anger and outrage. This essay attempts to think more deeply about the role of rage in the politics of mourning through the contemporary constellation of anti-racist and police-accountability activism that falls broadly under the Black Lives Matter movement.

Many political theorists have urged a democratic politics of affective display and ethical responsiveness in which the suffering and grief of subjects is explored in order to produce new political coalitions and alliances (Connolly 1995). In one of the most powerful and influential accounts, the feminist philosopher Judith Butler argues, "Open grieving is bound up with outrage and outrage in the face of injustice or indeed of unbearable loss has enormous political potential" (Butler 2010, 39). As Butler argues, mourning has an affective political presence, something transformative for both those who grieve publicly and for those who recognize and apprehend the loss of others. More specifically, public mourning relies on a symbiotic relationship between those who act publicly in their grief and those who apprehend that grief and the structural and normative conditions through which suffering is made possible. However, despite Butler's prescient claim about the role of outrage in political life, her work on the political possibilities that emerge out of grief and public mourning only tangentially engage with the bad and unruly feelings that are in response to experiences of vulnerability and suffering, specifically those of anger and outrage.

The consequence of this lack of attention is that Butler's theorization of political mourning: (1) acknowledges but does not substantively examine the differential ways in which some lives are rendered as worthy and grievable and others are not[2] and (2) does not sufficiently analyze the way in which anger and outrage or born out of the insufficiencies of this form of public (mis/un)recognition. This essay asks: How have these expressions of mourning been disenfranchised and what are the political effects of this disenfranchisement? What role does rage play in a specifically racial politics of mourning? And what work do expressions of rage and anger do to make recognizable the racial suffering necessary for a politics of mourning?

By focusing directly on the issue of anger, this essay supplements and amplifies an account of political mourning in order to think about the ways in which specific structural conditions of precarity function to make some forms of mourning illegible, even to others who might acknowledge an ethical responsiveness toward the vulnerability of others. It then looks at the ways in which expressions of anger and outrage over the experience of vulnerability and suffering work to both bring the racially precarious out of, what Frantz Fanon has called, the "zone of nonbeing" and to expose, challenge, and reimagine the structural conditions that contribute to the precarious life of millions of people (Fanon 1952). To do this, I look to one contemporary manifestation of a politics of mourning/anger in the response to racialized police violence in order to understand the connections between the varying political and affective experiences of mourning and anger and to push theorists of political mourning further in thinking about the nature of recognition in suffering.

MOURNING, VISIBILITY, RECOGNITION

In her recent work on precarity and the politics of mourning Judith Butler has argued for an ethical and political reception of subjective and bodily vulnerability as a model for connection in moments of deep instability. She asks, what might it look like politically to understand ourselves and others as fundamentally vulnerable; as subject to the psychic and physical undoing of ourselves by others? This question animates Butler's argument for a connective politics of mourning against a reactive politics of violence and isolationism. This political mourning not only assuages violence as a technique of subjectivity but also, she contends, opens up the possibility of reconstituting the power relations that determine whose lives are worthy of grief and recognition.

In her groundbreaking article, "Violence, Mourning, Politics," and in her later book *Precarious Life: The Powers of Mourning and Violence,* Butler puts forward a theory of public mourning that is grounded in the recognition of bodily and psycho-social vulnerability. For Butler, our very condition as human beings is contingent on our vulnerability to others. From the bodily necessities connected to birth and death to the social contingencies of recognition endemic to life (love, desire, need) in society, all human beings experience vulnerability. But unlike the repercussions of bodily vulnerability experienced in a Hobbesian state of nature, whereby vulnerability leads to a fight to the death or one's eventual demise, or a realist conception of power as one that must always be used and articulated for dominance, Butler understands shared human vulnerability as a possible ethical point of connection between disparate socially constituted subjects. We all experience some form of vulnerability just by virtue of being human, she contends, and in having that experience are able to connect with and see ourselves in others.

Butler acknowledges that these experiences of vulnerability are differential and rightly argues for a distinction between experiences of precariousness and precarity. She writes, "Lives are supported and maintained differently, and there are radically different ways in which human physical vulnerability is distributed across the globe. Certain lives will be highly protected, and the abrogation of their claims to sanctity will be sufficient to mobilize the forces of war. Other lives will not find such fast and furious support and will not even qualify as 'grievable'" (Butler 2006, 32). In this way, precarity is the experience of precariousness not simply because of natal and human ties but instead because of the conditions of a social and political system that target specific bodies as more vulnerable. Although the levels of violation and experiences of vulnerability differ because of our gender, sexuality, ability, race, religion, socioeconomic positions, and simple life circumstances, Butler imagines that recognition of shared vulnerability can forge connections between those who are often cast as enemies.

Through the articulation of public mourning, Butler argues, those who experience loss demand recognition for their loss as loss and make public the disparate ways in which lives are rendered as (un)grievable. In turn, to publicly grieve those lives is to reject their ungrievableness—to make them real in a world in which they have been erased—and in doing so challenge the social and political authority that makes those lives unrecognizable and ungrievable in the first place. In this way, Butler sees political mourning as a practice that both exposes norms of sovereignty, vulnerability, and grievability but also can challenge these norms and thus disrupts the very subject articulations constitutive of such norms. As David McIvor has argued, following Elena Lozidou, "by connecting with voices of suffering, subjects can revise the norms that prescribe both *who* can be mourned and *how* those others can be mourned" (McIvor 2012, 411).[3] This expression of political mourning thus functions to express a form of grief that is often ignored and to make visible a loss that is obfuscated from and by others and in turn, Butler argues, this transforms the very normative parameters of subjectivity and recognition.

At the heart of Butler's theory of political mourning, then, is a two-sided coin. First, those who mourn demand visibility for the ungrievable and recognition of themselves as those who grieve. Second, others, including those with significantly more power, she hopes, will respond ethically to that vulnerability. As I suggested above, Butler conditions this ethical response on our own experiences of vulnerability and intersubjectivity. We are all vulnerable to the words and deeds of others and in this way, can be undone by an Other.[4] In fact, who we are is always contingent on others. In turn, our capacity to link with others who experience differential forms of precarity is predicated on our ethical capacity to reject the instantiation of a sovereign self and instead tap into the human condition of vulnerability as the connective force of political and ethical affiliation. In this way, Butler's political-ethical demand is predicated on a complex form of political visibility and recognition. This is not a form of liberal recognition, she contends, that focuses on the acknowledgment of the sovereign autonomous liberal subject but rather she understands this recognition of the subject as always partial and contingent and wholly predicated on the social and personal conditions one is subject to.

While Butler offers a powerful theory of the necessary ethical-political response to mourning and vulnerability, she does not offer a description of the content or terms of these varying forms of visibility or responsiveness. How do those with differential levels of precarity or who benefit from the precarious experience of others come to respond to the vulnerability of the further marginalized? Do they acknowledge their grief as worthy of recognition? In what ways do they see the loss of those lives as connected to the structures they shore up and support? And most importantly, for this essay, how do they come to distinguish the recognition of some lives as grievable rather than simply perpetuating the fetishization or spectacularization of that grief as a form of power in itself? I ask these questions as a way to frame how visibility and responsiveness to Black suffering from structural violence has come to challenge the conception that public mourning and the visibility of grief might challenge the normative conditions of grievable life. Put slightly differently, it is not clear that what has come to be the hyper-visibility of Black death and Black mourning has functioned to produce more responsiveness or reoriented the structures that produce that vulnerability and grief. In fact, it might be that some of these (un)ethical responses have functioned to delegitimize the political and social conditions that produce this precarity and, in fact, might even intensify this precarity and the suffering of those who are mis/un-recognizable as sufferers. In turn, as I will argue in the rest of the essay, the focus on the punctuated and spectacular visibility of particularly forms of racial suffering and public mourning have been in many cases apprehended in such a way as to obfuscate the structural conditions of racial precarity.

SPECTACLE, DISENFRANCHISED GRIEF, AND THE CONDITION OF BLACK PRECARITY

In recounting a conversation with a friend, the poet/activist Claudia Rankine writes: "The condition of Black life is one of mourning" (Rankine 2015). Rankine interweaves the joys of motherhood with the sense of imminent loss every Black mother feels bringing a child to life in the United States. In describing her friend's experience she writes,

> For her, mourning lived in real time inside her and her son's reality: At any moment she might lose her reason for living. Though the white liberal imagination likes to feel temporarily bad about black suffering, there really is no mode of empathy that can replicate the daily strain of knowing that as a black person you can be killed for simply being black: no hands in your pockets, no playing music, no sudden movements, no driving your car, no walking at night, no walking in the day, no turning onto this street, no entering this building, no standing your ground, no standing here, no standing there, no talking back, no playing with toy guns, no living while black. (Rankine 2015)

In Rankine's description we do not see a form of mourning in response to the immediacy of loss nor is it a grief that can resolve itself overtime or through psychic work. Rankine describes mourning as a *condition* of precarity; an experience of subjectivity in which the very practices of Black maternality are imbricated with the imminence of loss, constituted through the possibility of mortal grief at any moment. The Black mother is on edge because she knows that there is no suffering worse than losing one's child and that the greater odds of this loss are conditioned by a state and a culture that renders Black death as inconsequential and necessary for white supremacy. Rankine posits that no matter how many white people are outraged or mourn the loss produced by systemic racism and the violence that goes along with that system, they cannot understand this form of precarity, the quotidian nature of experiencing Black life as always possible death and Black motherhood as always possible loss. Even white supporters—in her language, "white liberals"[5]—those who imagine themselves as racially conscious, cannot attend to this mourning and precarity as a constant condition of life itself. Instead, they assume that the grief and mourning of Black motherhood is in response to moments of spectacular violence. This form of violence is spectacular in that is understood to be both out of the ordinary and visible to a broader white audience. In her analysis of Black mourning, Rankine reflects on how the racism that fueled the deaths of four young girls in the Sixteenth Street Baptist Church bombing in 1963 Alabama is continued in the actions of the white supremacist Dylan Roof's massacre of nine Bible-study attendees in 2015, yet both are treated as spectacles, as "events out of time" (Rankine 2015). These spectacular incidents that make news headlines and are condemned by politicians are treated as punctuated moments rather than as a constant condition of structural racism in a white supremacist society.

While Rankine thinks about Black death in terms of its (a)temporal uptake and as a reflection on white society's inability to fully comprehend the condition of Black mourning, it is also worth analyzing the contours and character of Black death and Black mourning as spectacle. Put slightly differently, it is necessary for us to understand the way in which the experience of precarity and the mourning of those who grieve are also made into a kind of spectacle that is both consumed and interpreted by a dominantly white audience. From Diamond Reynolds's Facebook Live feed in the aftermath of Philando Castile's shooting by a Minnesota police officer to the hours Michael Brown's bullet-ridden body was left uncovered in the streets of Ferguson, Missouri for all to view, we are inundated by the constant and explicit depictions of Black death at the hands of police[6] and white society.[7] And yet, rather than waking up to the suffering and grief caused by these deaths and connecting them to the broader structural conditions that make it possible, image after image of these deaths first turns the everyday violence against Blacks into a spectacle and then simultaneously renders that spectacle into the mundane, perhaps because of the repetitive nature of the violence.

Fleeting in its impact and ignorant in the way in which these incidents are connected, the spectacle of Black death is treated as ineluctably consumable by and sometimes shocking to white audiences, yet often causes no awaking to the structures that make the death of Black citizens acceptable. In fact, in many cases, discourses surrounding those deaths are articulated in terms of

Black culpability: Why did he wear a hoodie? Why did he have a toy gun? Why did she run? What the consumption of the spectacle of Black death and the concomitant justification of those deaths tell us then is that, to put it in Butlerian terms, Black lives are ungrievable lives.

In turn, public mourning over these deaths too functions as a visual spectacle. One cannot forget the images of sorrow and grief we have seen in so many of these cases in which Black men and women have been killed and shooters have not been charged or acquitted. Indeed, one could argue that in the last three years the mourning of women, particularly mothers and partners, who suffer through the deaths of their children and lovers has come to take a particularly overt political manifestation. [8] Their lives must be made grievable so that other lives like theirs can be protected. They are grieved in public, on television and the internet, for people to watch and see and hopefully feel. Grief too is made into a spectacle for others to apprehend and to enliven a response. And yet, despite Butler's normative desires to see otherwise, the publicizing of those deaths and the grief of those connected does not enlist an ethic of responsiveness to their suffering or a critique of the structures of white supremacy. Instead, the visibility of the deaths of Black bodies at the hands of state actors is read as either terribly unfortunate or justifiable and their grief is disenfranchised.

To fully understand how outrage might facilitate the political potential of public mourning, it is important to analyze more specifically how the contemporary condition of Black political mourning is predicated on a form of social disenfranchisement that renders African Americans as precarious and ontologically erased. I use the language of disenfranchisement to not simply reflect the lack of recognition for the mourning, suffering, and vulnerability of others. Disenfranchisement here signals the way in which grief and mourning are both ignored or unacknowledged and in the ways in which vulnerability and experiences of precarity are rendered invisible. It marks a kind of dehumanization or what Frantz Fanon has called a "zone of non-being" in which Blacks are not simply the Other but are marked in relation to a whiteness that objectifies them and renders them non-agents who are not fully recognized as human (Fanon 1952, xii). This "zone of non-being" is manifested in the homology between Blackness and violence and thus the consequent inability to appear politically as a public being without being pathologized (Gordon 2007).

The disenfranchisement of grief functions as one of many ways that Blacks experience racial precarity and ontological erasure. Psychologists have conceptualized disenfranchised grief as a form of grief in which experiences of loss are not openly acknowledged, socially sanctioned, or recognizable as a loss by the broader public. [9] More recently, a small number of scholars have focused on the experiences of grief under unequal racial structures and have argued that the structural conditions of racism as well as the larger inability to see Black lives as worthy of grief has had a deleterious psycho-social effect on these racial minorities. In her work on African Canadian grief over gun violence, for example, Erica Lawson argues that Black men's perceived criminality and the experiences of structural violence African Canadians endure often translate into a broader denial of the grief experienced by family members and communities in deaths by gun violence (Lawson 2014). The result of this social invalidation and the pathologizing of victims and those who grieve them produces more social and psychological precarity and vulnerability in the racialized liberal nation-state. Lawson's ethnographic work and analysis convincingly argue that the experience of disenfranchised grief in the context of racist social structures has the effect of producing an increase in the psychological fragility and social stigmatization of those who grieve the casualties of gun violence.

This disenfranchisement of grief over the death of Black Americans through police violence functions in two simultaneous and sometimes competing ways. The first way in which this mourning is disenfranchised is in the way the victim is cast in the shadow of culpability; their very being is rendered as violent. Michael Brown was cast as a thug and a robbery suspect. Eric Garner was criminalized for selling cigarettes and for his large Black body. Philando Castile was carrying a (licensed) firearm while Black. His very bodily movement was seen as a threat. For many the presumption in these cases was that their deaths were only possible because of their actions, but these actions are always already preconceived through a conception of the Black body (particularly the Black male body) as inherently violent. If their deaths were, at least in part, if not all, caused by their behavior than the presumption is that police were simply doing their duty in a very difficult job and the victims should have acted differently. Such a claim fully rejects racial injustices like racial profiling and also sees each incident as individualized rather than part of a structure of racism. But, secondly, it also renders those who mourn those victims[10] as having lost someone less worthy of grief or not grievable at all because of an inability to recognize their very subjectivity. Indeed, the victim's worthiness for life is brought into question, and thus their very existence of humanity is challenged, and consequently the grievers' authenticity as people who mourn is refused. The private emotional experience of such a disenfranchisement of grief by the media, police narratives, and the broader white public is no doubt psychologically difficult, producing a double grief in which one must both suffer loss and resist the "thingification" of one's loved one.

This disenfranchised grief might also precipitate a political and social effect worth exploring. There is no doubt that after experiencing this explicit form of disenfranchisement and racial stigmatization many might feel even more loss. But Lawson also reflects on the ways in which some of those who mourn rejected the notion that they must get over their losses because they were not real losses and instead "engaged in activities of willful remembering," thus demanding the recognition of lives lost as grievable lives (Lawson 2014, 2102). This willful remembering could surely look like public mourning as described by Butler but given the ways public mourning continues to be disenfranchised, this willful remembering, I argue, necessitates the expression of public anger and outrage. These public expressions of outrage alongside mourning set the stage for political alliances, political disruption, and the radicalization of people who feel that their constant experience and expression of mourning is not only ignored but has come to be seen as a spectacle that reaffirms the pathologizing of Black life without attending to the structural and political conditions that make such vulnerability possible. In this way, their public anger not only makes them visible but challenges their very condition of nonbeing.

ANGER, BECOMING, AND THE POLITICS OF GRIEVANCE

In his writings on Blackness and colonialism, Frantz Fanon has suggested that expressions of anger, including that of violence, not only reject the social order that only partially permits people of color to exist but also simultaneously reform the self and the conditions through which the subject of colonialism experiences their precarity. Expressions of anger reaffirm one's humanness against the structural project of bodily violence and catalyze precarious subjects into being. For Fanon, the colonized body vibrates in its rage and it is this energy that inaugurates the destruction of the structures of inequality and allows the colonized to reform their psyches and become whole again (Fanon 2004). Every experience of racial precarity is one in which a demand for the recognition of humanity is rejected. It is a disenfranchisement of being itself. Only through anger and the rejection of racialization can the subject emerge. It is worth quoting Fanon at length here.

> I don't believe it! Whereas I was prepared to forget, to forgive, and to love, my message was flung back at me like a slap in the face. The white world, the only decent one, was preventing me from participating. It demanded of me that I behave like a Black man—or at least like a Negro. I hailed the world and the world amputated my enthusiasm. I was expected to stay in line and make myself scarce.

> I'll show them! They can't say I didn't warn them. Slavery? No longer a subject of discussion, just a bad memory.[11] My so-called inferiority? A hoax that it would be better to laugh about. I was prepared to forgive everything, provided the world integrated me. My incisors were ready to go into action. I could feel them, sharp. And then . . .

> I don't believe it! Whereas I had every reason to vent my hatred and loathing, they were rejecting me? Whereas I was the one they should have begged and implored, I was denied the slightest recognition? I made up my mind, to assert myself as a BLACK MAN. Since the other was reluctant to recognize me, there was only one answer: to make myself known. (Fanon 1952, 9–10)

Fanon's assertion of Blackness and his ability to make himself known were only possible through a rejection of the structures that built him as inferior. Rather than rely on the ethical responsiveness of the dominant Other, rage bursts apart that power relation that requires the recognition and legitimation of the dominating Other for being. It demands the demise of the relations of precarity by making the body more vulnerable, more nimble, more confrontational. It rejects the precarity imposed by the political and social order by tearing it down, by screaming, by standing against those who wish to intimidate the precarious subject into nothingness. In this way, it rejects the power of the dominant to give meaning to Black subjectivity. For Fanon, this lashing out has both psychological and structural consequences for the Black subject. While expressions of anger and rage in the wake of systemic racial violence can be seen as ethical or moral objections to a social order that produces precarity, they are not limited to that. These expressions can also reflect an affective limit; a desire to be seen and for grievances to be heard in their own right without consent from those who dominate or benefit from the domination of others. For Fanon, expressions of anger, and even violence, are both political and ontological in that they both demand a change in the structural conditions of precarity and allow the colonized and/or Black subject to emerge out of the "zone of non-being" and thus participate in a dialectic of recognition and transformation. This is not recognition in the traditional liberal sense of demanding equal dignity or recognition of the specificity of one's difference (Taylor 1994). Instead, the expression of rage brings the Black subjects into being and allows them to articulate a set of grievances that lay bare the conditions of precarity. This enlists others in an engaged reformulation of the conditions of social and political entry.

While Fanon provides us a compelling account of the way expressions of anger bring Black subjects into being on their own terms, it is still crucial for us to understand how the expression of anger as part of a politics of mourning and grief function to produce new forms of political affiliation and coalition. In her book *Sing the Rage*, Sonali Chakravarti argues that we can understand political anger in three dimensions: the cognitive-evaluative, the confrontational and the kinetic (Chakravarti 2014). The cognitive-evaluative is an informative expression of anger that allows the speaker-subject to express their needs in the context of their suffering or frustration. Often focusing on "righteous anger" these expressions of emotion allow the aggrieved to "bring injustices to light" (Chakravarti 2014, 129). In the context of violence by a racialized and carceral state, the cognitive-evaluative helps mourners connect their experience of grief to an expression of grievance, where grievance is understood as legitimized grounds for political complaint for the wrongs suffered. In turn, Chakravarti describes the confrontational dimension of anger as one in which "the confrontation contained in the term refers to anger that goes beyond the contained adversarial quality of righteous anger by eschewing obvious solutions or reparations" (Chakravarti 2014, 143). Its expression is not intended to change the minds of the dominant order or to demand redress. Rather, it can be described as an affective necessity born out of the subject's desire to express the intensity of emotions that take over her body and mind. Finally, Chakravarti argues that a third and interrelated dimension of anger should be seen as kinetic. "It is not connected to the conceptual issues of redress or contradiction as found in the cognitive-evaluative and the confrontational dimensions. Instead, the kinetic dimension operates on the level of visceral experience and the recognition of shared humanity" (Chakravarti 2014, 149). Put simply, the kinetic dimension is the energy produced by the expression of anger in political life that can lead to creative and dynamic change and political connection. What connects a politics of mourning with a politics of rage is this kinetic energy. Like mourning it functions as a condition of humanity. Yes, we all feel grief and vulnerability (although these experiences are differential) but we also experience unfathomable anger at the conditions that produce that grief. Yet while a politics of mourning focuses on the political expression of the inward experience of the sufferer in order to show that all lives are grievable and to transform the norms of grievability, a politics of rage exposes the other side of the coin—it challenges the structures and conditions that have caused the loss in the first place. This kinetic form of anger turns the subjective experience of precarity to one that enlists others to respond to injustice.

In this way, expressions of anger have two functions that are necessary supplements to political mourning. First, expressions of anger allow the speaker to alleviate (not eliminate) the pressures and pains of precarity.[12] As Fanon suggests, expressing anger releases tension and functions as a punctuated form of unrest that unsettles the conditions of everyday life. While Fanon tends to advocate the articulation of this rage through the use of violence by the colonized, there is ample psychological evidence to suggest that the expression of anger and outrage are sufficient in helping the subjects affirm their humanity and challenge the conditions of precarity. It allows the subject to express the visceral energy s/he experiences in the archipelago of racist experiences as well as other intersecting conditions such as sexism, homophobia, and ableism. This leads to the second important outcome of expressing political anger over the conditions of racism. Those at the margins are often told or conditioned to internalize their sorrow and repress their anger, to smile, to brush it off, to get over it. As bell hooks so aptly notes in

the context of racial domination, "to perpetuate and maintain white supremacy, white folks have colonized black Americans, and part of that colonizing
process has been teaching us to repress our rage, to never make them the
targets of anger we feel about racism" (hooks 1996, 14). In this context, to
express one's rage is to reject the social pressures that force those at the
margins to hold their emotions in so as not to offend. It is a release—a
punctuated moment of liberation, no matter the costs. It gives voice to the
experience of precarity without a desire to enlist others in recognizing one's
suffering alone. Instead, it manifests as a model of self-recognition and consciousness that demands structural accountability. Claudia Rankine describes
this moment of expression in moments of racial interaction as follows,

> Hold up, did you just hear, did you just say, did you just see, did you just do
> that? Then the voice in your head silently tells you to take your foot off your
> throat because just getting along shouldn't be an ambition. (Rankine 2014, 55)

Rankine, here, is writing about an interpersonal racist experience in which
the expectation is that she, as a Black woman, must be silent and suppress her
anger for the comfort of others. But as she points out, "getting along
shouldn't be an ambition." And further, silence, in an attempt to get along, is
a condition and contour of the structures of racism itself. It reflects a systemic condition in which white comfort is the norm and Black respectability is
about not making people too uncomfortable. To fear or repress that anger is
to lose oneself and to stay stagnant in a system that rejects the affective
conditions that make change possible. As Audre Lorde so aptly writes,

> My response to racism is anger. I have lived with that anger, on that anger,
> beneath that anger, on top of that anger. Ignoring that anger, feeding upon that
> anger, learning to use that anger before it laid my visions to waste, for most of
> my life. Once I did it in silence, afraid of the weight of that anger. My fear of
> that anger taught me nothing. Your fear of that anger will teach you nothing,
> also. (Lorde 1997, 278)

To speak then, to express anger over racism, to express anger over loss,
allows for the expression of the emotion that challenges the very norms that
make racial hierarchy possible, all while allowing the subject to demand
recognition of the structures of inequality and releasing their own repressed
anger. It enlists a messy visceral experience for the both those who express
their anger at injustice and those who perpetuate or benefit from it.

These expressions of anger can produce new kinetic forms by enfranchis-
ing the feelings of others and allowing them the space to express their mis-
trust, anger, and revulsion and consequently, embedding their personal experiences in a broader structural account. Politically, expressions of rage, both
at the level of the individual and at the group level, can alter the conditions

that contributed to the feelings of rage in the first place. They burst through the quotidian by laying bare the conditions that have become so everyday that they become almost unnoticeable—the racism, sexism, and classism that undergird social relations as well as the structural inequalities ignored or furthered by the state apparatus. By invoking outrage against that which is habitually producing precarity, the speaker has the capacity to spark a radical stance[13] toward the social and structural realities that undergird that precarity and also politically grieve for their loss. These political expressions of anger and mourning have no clear outcome but no doubt can engage others in a structural account of the limits of the racialized liberal state.

One might counter that such articulations of anger would foster the antithesis of what those who advocate a politics of mourning are encouraging. Anger, one might argue, produces distinction rather than coalition. It rejects vulnerability and thus the ethical conditions that foster connections between all humans. In realistic terms, engaging the anger of others might have the effect of a kind of destabilization. It can produce resentment by those who do not experience or understand the vulnerability of others. It does function as an outlaw emotion,[14] one that is often rejected in democratic politics, particularly when articulated by racial and gender minority groups who are characterized as being suffused with anger in their very construction. As George Ciccariello-Maher right puts it, "For those relegated to nonbeing and condemned to invisibility, to even appear is a violent act—because it *is* violent to the structures of the world and because it will inevitably be treated as such. Black subjects are thereby trapped in a catch-22: condemned either to accept inferiority or be demonized as violent" (Ciccariello-Maher 2017, 61). Yet, the expression of anger is both internally necessary as part of the grieving process and politically necessary in articulating a political critique of the structures that produce precarity.

In turn, we might also worry that the convergence of anger and mourning can be all-consuming; that it can fetishize the pain experienced by the precarious. It can, as Wendy Brown has warned, create a culture of injury and woundedness, that leads to a politics of *ressentiment* and even revenge (Brown 1995). This is clearly detrimental to a democratic political culture should it mobilize those precarious subjects to impose their own forms of pain if or when they might come to power. However, as Sara Ahmed convincingly argues in her account of feminist anger, "Anger does not necessarily require an investment in revenge, which is one form of reaction to what one is against. Being against something is dependent on how one reads what one is against (for example, whether violence against women is read as dependent on male psychology or on structures of power)" (Ahmed 2015, 174–5). In this way, like other emotions including grief, the very circulation and performance of political mourning and anger can either foreground the possibilities of political action or can be debilitating depending on the ways in which it engages in the conditions that produce pain and suffering. But as I have tried to argue in this chapter, the political expression of anger in and against racialized police violence brings to the fore the structures of racism that make the killing of Black subjects not only normal but justifiable. It does this by making viscerally visible the condition of Black mourning that Rankine talks about, by connecting the historical experiences of Black suffering to contemporary Black precarity, and by envisioning a future in which the Black body is freed from violence.

To elaborate this argument, I want to briefly turn to one critical example of how such articulations of mourning and anger might function together to demand redress and challenge the conditions of racial precarity; how they use anger to illuminate the structures that produce the conditions of Black suffering. As I recounted in the introduction to this chapter, in the summer of 2014 an unarmed Black student named Michael Brown was gunned down by a white police office, Darren Wilson, in Ferguson, Missouri. A series of events precipitated angry protests in Ferguson: Brown's body was left uncovered on the streets for half a day in the hot summer sun; his parents were later denied requests to view their son's body in private; public memorials devoted to Brown were destroyed by police, with one account suggesting that a police officer allowed his police dog to urinate on one makeshift memorial. These police actions together triggered multiple nights of protests by Ferguson's citizens, who simultaneously mourned Brown's death and angrily connected that death to a history of racist policing in Ferguson. Swiftly, the grief of Brown's family, friends, and community was disenfranchised. He was painted by police and media as a criminal who stole from a corner store; a Herculean thug who attacked Wilson (despite being shot with his hands up); and a drug-using loser who contributed nothing to society. Brown's death and the mourning of that death were delegitimized by many in power with the final blow being a grand jury decision to not indict Wilson for murder.

Righteous anger erupted in Ferguson and people took to the streets in varying forms, from peaceful protests to property destruction challenging the police state's legitimacy and bearing witness to the structures of systemic racism in policing. Their anger, if only briefly, penetrated the mundanity of Black death. Importantly, that anger and energy were not limited to the specific conditions of Brown's death but were connected to a broader indictment of the carceral state and policing. As Keeanga-Yamahtta Taylor has argued, the Ferguson incident showed a remarkable shift in the way in which these singular protests were now understood. "The young activists were beginning to politically generalize from the multiple cases of police brutality and develop a systemic analysis of policing. Many began to articulate a much broader critique that situated policing within a matrix of racism and inequality in the United States and beyond" (Taylor 2016, 162). They developed a consciousness of the experience of Blackness that moved from the specific moment of violence to violence as the condition of Black life. And as James Baldwin so aptly puts it "To be a Negro in this country and to be relatively conscious, is to be in a rage almost all of the time" (Baldwin 1962, 205) It was through the capacities to express, despite violent police attempts to stop the protests, that rage, mourning, and anger over their disenfranchised mourning that slowly a movement that centers Black experiences of suffering and death at the hands of police has come to fruition. While the continued state violence against Black bodies has been a spectacle, the connective work of political anger and mourning over these deaths has refused to see these deaths in their singularity. From these experiences, many different forms of Black resistance movements have emerged, including the Black Lives Matter movement,[15] that articulate their righteous anger and grief in order to expose and damage the structures that make racial precariousness possible. Through these articulations, they not only have made the death of Black subjects more visible but also more seen. And, in turn, they refuse to let each incident be seen alone but rather connect them together in the form of urgent grievance that must be attended to.

CONCLUSION

As I write this another Black American has been murdered by police. Charleena Lyles. Philando Castile. Michael Brown. Eric Garner. Brendon Glenn. Freddie Gray. Walter Scott. Rekia Boyd. The list of names goes on and on. It could take up pages and pages. These names are etched in the brains of communities across the United States. These are names of the dead written on walls, sidewalks, and Facebook posts. Their names are screamed and whispered. We are reminded to "say their names"; to feel them roll off our tongues; to make them visible—recognizable in death. For some of us these are just names and news headlines but for others these names refer to children, siblings, neighbors, and community members; people dispossessed and oppressed by the structural racism of American society. People mourn these lives. They are filled with rage by the wanton killings of black men and women across the United States. And yet, their wails of suffering and anger are funneled through a political echo chamber and their public grief is used as a political punching bag; reflecting a long history since the origins of American slavery in which Black grief is rejected, ignored, disenfranchised.

In almost all of these cases of state-sanctioned murder, families, friends and supporters have had to turn to nonjuridical models of justice because the legal system has treated Black lives as expendable. In these contexts Black citizenship is treated as an oxymoron and the precarious place of African Americans is a constant reminder that their experience of the state and society is vastly different than their White counterparts. Mothers, activists and community members have spoken out, protested, shut down freeways, prayed en masse, and even in some cases rioted because their collective mourning, their demand for justice, and a desire for the state and white society to see that Black lives do matter has not been truly acknowledged. In their public articulations of grief and their angry expressions of grievance they have sought to transform a structure that centers on white experience and together have made visible and recognizable the lives of others.

This chapter has attempted to think about the political potential of outrage and mourning in the racial politics of America in order to understand its democratic possibilities. It has argued that a turn to politics of mourning must more fully engage with the ways in which mourning as a democratic practice relies on expressions of rage and anger as instrumental to both the challenging of the racial status quo and the reformulation of the contours of citizenship. There is not much that is positive that we can glean from the current racial violence that permeates American life but the hope that the outrage over suffering will grow and that the structures that produce racial precarity may be seen and challenged.

NOTES

1. Two incidents particularly struck a nerve: First, Brown's bullet-ridden body was left uncovered in the middle of the street for hours and secondly, multiple reports indicated that a Ferguson police officer allowed his canine to urinate on a makeshift memorial of candles and flowers dedicated to Brown.

2. It is clear that Butler is more than aware of this. From her analysis of AIDS activism to her work on Antigone, she pursues political mourning as a messy and fractured politics—one that challenges forms of dominant power and reimagines and re-performs citizenship differently. And in her more recent work, she has proffered a normative political theory of performative assemblage that relies on coalition building among those who experience precarity and who reorganize the very meaning of the political field through their political activity. See (Butler 2015).

3. My emphasis.

4. In her description of precariousness Butler writes, "Let's face it. We're undone by each other. And if we're not, we're missing something. If this seems so clearly the case with grief, it is only because it was already the case with desire. One does not always stay intact. It may be that one wants to, or does, but it may also be that despite one's best efforts, one is undone, in the face of the other, by the touch, by the scent, by the feel, by the prospect of the touch, by the memory of the feel" (Butler 2004, 19).

5. Rankine castigates white liberals for their inability to see the long-standing structures of racism particularly because they see themselves as allies with the African American community but continue to be blind to the overarching narrative of white supremacist society.

6. We might even think about the push for police cameras as not simply a form of police accountability but as an attempt to make visible the precarious existence of African Americans in the context of police overreach.

7. While no doubt the publicity of lynching also functioned as a spectacle to discipline both Black and white society in the context of contemporary forms of social media and the capacity to go viral with video and image the range of viewership has expanded. See (Wood 2011).

8. Both the groups Mothers of the Movement (which includes the mothers of Sandra Bland, Eric Garner, Trayvon Martin, Michael Brown, Dontre Hamilton, Jordan Davis, and Hadiya Pendleton) and Black Lives Matter predicate their activism on their own experiences of

losing their relatives and friends to police and gun violence precipitated by racism. Their essential goal is to make visible these losses and demand recognition for the lives lost and for their mourning. Black lives matter, they contend. They are worthy of grief.

9. The vast majority of this psychological literature focuses on the bereavement experiences of those whose loss is unrecognizable by others, for example, same-sex lovers whose relationships of love had not been historically accepted by families and society at large. Some of the literature also focuses on other forms of loss including pet bereavement, the experience of children who are moved around a lot, transitional grief, etc. For an overview of this psychological theory see (Doka 1989).

10. It's worth noting that those who grieve over the lives of the Black men and women who succumb to police violence may not have intimate relationships with the deceased. While there are individuals who mourn the intimate and proximate loss of someone they love to police violence, there is also broader movement of mourners who grieve both for the life of the individual but also for the life lost as part of and representative of racial injustice. These mourners may not have an intimate connection with the lost subject but experience the loss as one of subjective affiliation, as in a Black mother who mourns for the loss of a young life because of her recognition of the bonds of maternity, or experience the specific loss as one in a long history of racialized violence by a white supremacist state and society. These mourners too experience a disenfranchised form of mourning from the framing of the victims as having acted in such a way that deserves police violence to the rejection of criminal accountability of violent cops to a broader white rejection of the acknowledgment of the structural conditions which link such deaths to the historical violence of slavery and to the contemporaneous precarity of Black lives.

11. One could rewrite this in our contemporary moment as "Racism? No longer a subject of discussion, just a bad memory."

12. There is significant psychological evidence that expressing anger is both a positive expression of mental health and in tends to reduce episodes of violence.

13. It is worth noting that Black Lives Matter has challenged the notion of piecemeal reforms to the police system and has embraced a more radical stance in abolishing the police system as we know it.

14. Alison Jagger defines outlaw emotions as "unconventional emotional responses," "that are distinguished by their incompatibility with the dominant perceptions and values" (Jagger 1989).

15. Black Lives Matter precedes the death of Michael Brown as it emerged in 2013 as a response to the acquittal of George Zimmerman for the murder of Trayvon Martin.

WORKS CITED

Ahmed, Sarah. *The Cultural Politics of Emotion.* New York: Routledge, 2015.
Baldwin, James. "The Negro in American Culture." *Cross Currents* 11, no. 3 (Summer 1961): 205–224.
Brown, Wendy. *States of Injury.* Princeton, NJ: Princeton University Press, 1995.
Butler, Judith. "Violence, Mourning, Politics." *Studies in Gender and Sexuality* 4, no. 1 (2003): 9–37.
———. *Undoing Gender.* New York: Routledge, 2004.
———. *Precarious Life: The Powers of Mourning and Violence.* London: Verso Books, 2006.
———. *Frames of War: When is Life Grievable.* New York: Verso, 2010.
———. *Notes Toward a Performative Theory of Assembly.* Cambridge, MA: Harvard University Press, 2015.
Chakravarti, Sonali. *Sing the Rage: Listening to Anger after Mass Violence.* Chicago: University of Chicago Press, 2014.
Ciccariello-Maher, George. *Decolonizing Dialectics.* Durham, NC: Duke University Press, 2017.
Connolly, William. *The Ethos of Pluralization.* Minneapolis, MN: University of Minnesota Press, 1995.

Doka, Kenneth J. (ed). *Disenfranchised grief: Recognizing Hidden Sorrow*. Lexington, MA: Lexington Books, 1989.

Fanon, Frantz. *Black Skin, White Masks*. New York: Grove Press, 1952.

———. *The Wretched of the Earth*. New York: Grove Press, 2004.

Gordon, Lewis. "Through the Hellish Zone of Nonbeing: Thinking Through Fanon, Disaster, and the Damned of the Earth," *Human Architecture* 5, no. 3 (Summer 2007): 5–11.

hooks, bell. *killing rage: Ending Racism*. New York: Holt Paperbacks, 1995.

Jaggar, Alison. "Love and Knowledge: Emotion in Feminist Epistemology," *Inquiry* 32 no.2 (1989): 151–176.

Lawson, Erica. "Disenfranchised Grief and Social Inequality: Bereaved African Canadians and Oppositional Narratives About the Violent Deaths of Friends and Family Members," *Ethnic and Racial Studies* 37 no.11 (2014): 2092–2109.

Lorde, Audre "The Uses of Anger," *Women's Studies Quarterly* 25 no. 1/2 (Spring–Summer 1997): 278–285.

McIvor, David. "Bringing Ourselves to Grief: Judith Butler and the Politics of Mourning," *Political Theory* 40 no. 4 (August 2012): 409–436.

Rankine, Claudia. *Citizen: An American Lyric*. Minneapolis, MN: Graywolf Press, 2014.

———. "The Condition of Black Life is One of Mourning." *New York Times,* June 22, 2015. https://www.nytimes.com/2015/06/22/magazine/the-condition-of-black-life-is-one-of-mourning.html.

Taylor, Charles. *Multiculturalism: Examining the Politics of Recognition*. Princeton, NJ: Princeton University Press, 1994.

Taylor, Keeanga-Yamahtta. *From #BlackLivesMatter to Black Liberation*. Chicago, IL: Haymarket Books, 2016.

Wood, Amy Louise. *Lynching and Spectacle: Witnessing Racial Violence, 1890–1940*. Chapel Hill, NC: University of North Carolina Press, 2011.

Chapter Eight

The Funeral and the Riot

#BlackLivesMatter, Antagonistic Politics, and the Limits of (Exceptional) Mourning

David Myer Temin[1]

In August of 2014, thousands of protestors came together under the banner of #BlackLivesMatter in Ferguson, Missouri, to mourn the murder of Black teenager Michael Brown by Officer Darren Wilson and to call for Wilson's indictment. Militarized police responded with massive repression of the protestors, creating a dynamic that would unfold again upon the deaths of Freddie Gray in Baltimore, Eric Garner in New York, Jamar Clark and Philando Castile in the Twin Cities, John Crawford in Columbus, Tamir Rice in Cleveland, and Sandra Bland in Texas, among many others. One lens through which to view the protests is through their heavy affinity with the practice, rhetoric, and iconography of mourning: In St. Paul, the young students at the elementary school at which Phil Castile worked led a somber and poignant vigil and spoke of their admiration for the soft-spoken cafeteria worker (Woltman 2016). Across North America and internationally, protestors, medical students, and others staged "die-ins," which juxtaposed the affirmation of the inherent value of Black life with the reality of state-sanctioned deaths. Such deaths, it might be said, required constant waves of grieving—of mourning in public.

Yet another interpretation of these same events would focus less on the practice of mourning and more on the disruptions of traffic and property damage by protestors that unsettled municipal, state, and federal authorities and racked cities with the threat of even greater disorder. As Juliet Hooker observes, some celebrated these actions as "uprisings" and others demonized them as "riots" depending on the perspective of the speaker (2016, 449).

Such disruptive actions—both planned and relatively spontaneous—embodied the militant rage of an emerging movement coalescing around an inclusive, intersectional, anti-racist politics aimed at the collective liberation of all Black people. This latter interpretation fits with the language of war, survival, and resistance that is one important feature of the political practice of #BlackLivesMatter. By referring to "war, survival, and resistance," I am glossing a language and practice of critique present within #BlackLivesMatter that focuses on resisting the state-sanctioned social control and violence exercised over Black bodies and working toward the eventual collective liberation of all Black people. #BlackLivesMatter draws on a language of state violence as a central way of crystallizing their critique of systems of policing, criminal justice, as well as disinvestment and uneven economic exploitation and abandonment. As #BlackLivesMatter co-founder Alicia Garza argues:

> What we are dealing with right now is a disease that has plagued America since its inception. Convicting a few cops isn't going to deal with that disease. We've been trying hard this year to be clear that state violence is bigger than police terrorism. Although police terrorism plays a specific role on behalf of the state, it is not the totality of what state violence looks like or feels like in our communities. We've been shifting the narrative to talk about state violence being structural racism. Given that, what we are lifting up here is that we need a bigger vision than just Band-Aid reforms—we need to move towards a transformative vision that touches on what's at the root of the problems we are facing. (Denzel Smith 2015)[2]

Such a frame of police terrorism and survival informs questions of strategy for the movement, which has embraced disruptive tactics such as blocking highways and occupying police precincts as one mode among others of creating a sense of crisis and disorder over the constant reality of this war against Black people.[3] The aim, Garza argues, is to go beyond questions of individual culpability for police shootings and to see these individual events as surfacing interconnections between different nodes of a punitive, carceral system in order to move toward a "transformative vision" based on "a redistribution of resources from militarization to community needs" (Denzel Smith 2015).

Despite the setback and precarious situation now represented by the Trump administration, such protests have produced some results: Though it is difficult to say for sure, it seems unlikely that then–Attorney General Eric Holder would have initiated the Department of Justice (DOJ) investigation of Ferguson without the perceived need to respond to escalating, high-profile clashes between police and protestors Yet, despite the release of the Obama DOJ's Ferguson Report, which points to Ferguson's predatory local policing aimed at extracting wealth from poor communities of color as typical—not exceptional—little has changed to disrupt the system of which policing serves as a central cog (United States Department of Justice Civil Rights Division 2015; Page and Soss 2018). Aside from the consciousness-raising that has accompanied the #BlackLivesMatter movement, the punitive "carceral state" that connects policing, incarceration, class subjugation, and systematic disinvestment in working-class Black communities remains in place.

Scholars from Michelle Alexander (2010) to Naomi Murakawa (2014) have recently theorized how the punitive turn against which #BlackLivesMatter organizes shapes the post–civil rights reality of contemporary North American white supremacy. Vesla Weaver and Amy Lerman's work in particular documents how the expanding carceral state makes (especially) working-class communities of color into second-class citizens whose interactions with and access to the "state" are profoundly mediated by predatory policing and the criminal justice system (Lerman and Weaver 2014; Soss and Weaver 2017). If the problem is that politics within the bounds of elections and reforms—such as, e.g., illusory reforms of "police-community relations"—have failed for working-class Black communities especially, then how might political influence and even the repair of these conditions emerge otherwise? With these conditions and this practical question in mind, this chapter tries to make sense of some of the interpretive frames used to theorize the democratic potential of the politics of movements like #BlackLivesMatter through a sympathetic critique of the turn to mourning in political theory. This chapter explores the political upshot of adopting either of these two initial interpretations of #BlackLivesMatter—which I gloss here as the "funeral" and the "riot."

Political theorists as diverse in approach as Simon Stow, David McIvor, Bonnie Honig, Judith Butler, and Heather Pool have taken to mourning as an exemplary democratic practice, a practice that initiates the repair of wounds and divisions within democracies produced through lasting forms of domination and oppression. I turn to an unlikely figure to illustrate the limits of the politics of mourning as a force expected to transform contemporary forms of white supremacy: the Reverend Dr. Martin Luther King, Jr. King's early political thought has been read through the lens of mourning, yet such an analysis downplays problems of hierarchy, responsibility, and resistance that King's later thought poses. The reason I turn to King is that the shifts in his own thought resonate with many of the challenges that #BlackLivesMatter continues to starkly confront in the contemporary moment. I argue that the turn to foreground mourning as an exceptional, democratic form of political action is poorly equipped to handle the conceptual and political challenges bequeathed by King. By examining the transition in King's own thought from a politics of tragedy, loss, and redemption to one that more profoundly interrogated the resilience of white supremacy, my analysis offers an admittedly skeptical perspective on the interpretive and political purchase gained in foregrounding the politics of mourning in the post–Jim Crow, nominally post-racial, and differently white supremacist society that began to emerge after King's death.

This chapter asks: If theorists attach themselves to the first interpretation with which I began, one that focuses on the politics of mourning and down-plays the more aggressive expressions of rage at white supremacy, what is lost and what is gained? Does the expression of Black suffering through a practice of public mourning act as a form of democratic repair or does it merely exacerbate the unjust burden of needing to dramatize one's suffering and death at the hands of white supremacy? Who must bear the work of mourning? Moreover, does making *mourning* in particular the exceptional activity of democratic repair risk sliding into a form of "respectability poli-tics" that would rule out of bounds other forms of resistance like the "riot" that might be—at least indirectly—effective ways of exerting political pres-sure?[4]

Theorizing Mourning

Those who have turned to mourning have seen in it several positive features from the perspective of a politics aimed at generating sympathy, solidarity, and renewed responsibility across long-frozen social and political divides that enable—and are enabled by—relations of domination and oppression. As agonistic theorists of mourning like Simon Stow have argued, public mourning can amplify unheard, marginal voices, creating a militant yet am-bivalent perspective on the past. For Stow, public mourning in such Black "counter-memorial" practices responds to the losses imposed under white supremacy by telling stories about the dead that create a "pluralistic, critical, and self-consciously political" perspective (2010, 2017). Across several works, Judith Butler turns to Antigone as a figure of grief and mourning who relentlessly challenges the norms of who can be grieved and of what counts as the proper expression of grief, unsettling illusions of sovereign mastery and opening space for a collective responsibility founded on a pre-political relation between all human beings as vulnerable beings (2000; see also, 2003, 2004, 2009). While Bonnie Honig (2013) rejects what she casts as Butler's too un-textured reading of Antigone as interrogating the limits of normativity itself, Honig retrieves "economies of mourning" as central fea-tures of political orders than can neither entirely occlude nor internalize the often-competing meanings of grief. Heather Pool (2015) has argued that public mourning as a practice can publicize suffering and remake once-racialized lines of solidarity between oppressed and privileged audiences, such as the open funeral Mamie Till-Bradley staged when white supremacists killed her son Emmett for reportedly winking at a white woman in the Jim Crow South. More recently, David McIvor (2017) has referred to keeping mourning an "open dynamic" in democratic societies, meaning one conducive to the creation of "intermediary" social spaces neither premised on friend-enemy antagonisms nor on consensus. Mourning in spaces such as truth and reconciliation commissions allows multiple parties to create an open and ambivalent dialogue in relation to past traumas seen through multiple perspectives, yet controlled by no one account, whether militant or (relatively) unmoved in orientation. For McIvor, mourning is thus a "means of speaking about loss in the name of establishing crosscutting relationships amidst social plurality and diversity" (2012, 430). Crystallizing much of the aim of this turn to mourning, McIvor calls on mourning as potentially an exemplary starting point for "democratic repair."

Nancy Luxon (2016) points to two troubling aspects of the turn to mourning, the second of which I pick up on here by turning to King. First, Luxon argues that the focus on mourning often too quickly conflates the process of mourning in the individual psyche as it takes place on the psychoanalyst's couch with the aims of political resistance.[5] The point of working through one's emotions in politics is not—as it often is in psychoanalysis—to let go of or integrate such emotions but rather to hold on to anger and resentment that can be channeled into a political work that sustains the formation of new solidarities (and enmities, as well). Second, and as a result of this first point, the mapping up of individual psychic dynamics onto collective action may end up prescribing terms of collective agency that are themselves the result of hierarchies (such as the racialized terms I am focusing on here).[6] For my purposes, Luxon's point shows how an openly antagonistic politics might be ruled out of bounds as pathologically connected to "bad," rageful forms of militancy, whereas certain forms of mourning become exceptional stand-ins for a politics with relatively more ambivalent and pluralistic (thus "democratic") tendencies.

On the one hand, movements such as Black Lives Matter draw on anger to drive a strategically disruptive politics.[7] On the other hand, critics may plausibly suggest that anger often functions in movements as unproductive catharsis, even to the point of undermining the means-ends calculations that political action necessitates. In this latter case, though, the frame of analysis ought to shift to an irreducibly structural one: Namely, what structural conditions, what conditions of power and powerlessness, produce and occasion such anger? My focus in this chapter, then, will be on the conditions under which mourning might be effective within social and political movements that already embrace a diversity of tactics to confront the conditions of white supremacy I described above, especially in relation to idioms and practices of political struggle pitched much more in embodiments of war, survival, and resistance. I argue that these are languages in a sometimes tense but intertwined relation with this narrower sense of mourning and equally constitutive of the Black freedom struggle. I turn to King to reframe this relation away from a politics that risks sliding into the too-easy embrace of mourning as the central motor of democratic repair and toward one that engages the more complex relations between interwoven accounts of political transformation in the struggle against white supremacy.

More specifically, I draw out from King three pitfalls of the turn to mourning that become more apparent when contemporary struggles against white supremacy are framed in relation to ongoing debates within the Black radical tradition. First, I argue that the turn to mourning risks ascribing distinctively liberal boundaries to democratic life by pathologizing aggressive responses to loss—responses that do not easily adhere to the ambivalence and pluralism characteristic of even the contestation-driven practice of agonistic mourning. I gloss the latter as "exceptional" forms of mourning, and I describe the former riot-like responses as antagonistic. Second, I illustrate how the turn to mourning as a form of democratic exemplarity relies on questionably optimistic assumptions about white moral psychology that drive expectations about what mourning can do to transform persistent hierarchies.[8] I argue, by contrast, that forms of antagonistic politics that work through disruption may breach liberal norms and operate under a different theory of transformation motivated by the need for unsettlement and external coercion as a condition for change. Finally, I suggest in the conclusion that the turn to mourning might benefit from greater attention to questions of responsibility, division, and strategy within movements like #BlackLivesMatter that do adopt a diversity of tactics of resistance to oppression and domination—including more confrontational ones. Rather than solidarity with those defined as mourners, I ask, what would it look like to take up the problematic of solidarity with rioters?

King on Nonviolence and the Limits of Prophetic Mourning

MLK might seem an unlikely candidate for carrying the brief for the limits of mourning as opposed to militant anger. Indeed, in an early article published shortly after his election as the first president of the Southern Christian Leadership Conference in February 1957, King delineated the characteristics of his famed philosophy of nonviolence by contrasting the "external physical violence" and "internal violence of spirit" of violence with the disciplined and directed militancy of nonviolent action: "In struggling for human dignity the oppressed people of the world must not allow themselves to become bitter or indulge in hate campaigns. To retaliate with hate and bitterness would do nothing but intensify the hate in the world" (King Jr. 1986g, 8). King thus expressed an early and acute sense that anger and violence can only encourage hate and deepen the stances of victim and perpetrator.

The King I will refer to as the early King, from 1954 through 1963, can be understood as the carrier of a Black prophetic tradition pointedly expressed through the practice of public mourning. Simon Stow points out that for

King, "the connection between mourning and politics was especially tight" (Stow 2010, 690). Death and loss became an occasion for staging politics: King and other activists generated the idea of the Selma to Montgomery March at activist Jimmie Lee Jackson's funeral. As Stow argues, King drew on the "black funeral tradition," as "a powerful weapon in the fight for equality," especially in his famous eulogy for the young girls slain in the Sixteenth Street Baptist Church Bombing in August of 1963 (2010, 690). In that speech, King casts the four girls as "martyred heroines of a holy crusade for freedom and human dignity" who "have something to say . . . to each of us, black and white alike, that we must substitute courage for caution" (King Jr. 1986b, 221). Speaking of these unthinkable losses, King affirms a "democracy about death" that might yet move into the realm of the living. In essence, the eulogy "undermin[es] claims about racial differences in suffering" and interpolates a number of different audiences who might find meaning and resolve in these unmerited, innocent deaths (2010, 690). Stow rightly places King in a longer sweep of Black counter-memorial practice typified in public funerals that exemplify an ambivalent and critical relation to the past. If not the central theme in King's rhetoric, mourning, then, does figure importantly as a feature of what George Shulman calls King's "prophetic office," which blends a tragic sensibility at the immeasurable losses of slavery and Jim Crow with a redemptive hope against hope that these can be overcome through the transformative power of "suffering without retaliation" (King Jr. 1986g, 9; Shulman 2008, 97).

Bringing together these readings of mourning and prophecy, I argue that King's early politics represents a form of prophetic mourning that dramatizes suffering and loss and transmutes that suffering into the possibility of redemption. The early King brilliantly fashions a transformative mission in which Black Americans become the exemplary redeemers of American principles—a "redemptive protagonist," in Shulman's words (2008, 117). This project cohered around the idea that the losses eulogized and mourned in the struggle against white supremacy could be redeemed by the latter's eventual transformation and overcoming. Indeed, King's writings and speeches from 1954 to early 1963 invest the nonviolence of Black Americans with a democratic significance that binds Christian precepts of righteous suffering and loss with collective action aimed at forging the "beloved community" in the ashes of white supremacy.

But my focus here ultimately will be on how King moved away from this early model of transformation in ways that are illustrative of some of the *weaknesses* of a politics of mourning: While the brilliance of King's early rhetoric lies in his artful stretching of the boundaries of constitutional liberalism to accommodate this mournful yet redemptive politics, I will show how King's later engagements with questions of loss and violence reveal a different story about the limitations of a politics of mourning. If a politics of mourning is to remain contextually sensitive to contemporary forms of white supremacy, then it must consider questions of political strategy and these limits of liberal representation that King himself increasingly began to question by 1963. These questions necessitate more attention to activities that strain the limits of even deeply agonistic politics, including those that cross over from agonism into outright antagonism and violence.

King's focus on redemptive suffering is not unique: Examining Ralph Ellison and Danielle Allen's reflections on Black suffering as a form of democratic exemplarity, Juliet Hooker (2016) has questioned how a focus on exceptional sacrifice may ultimately reinscribe the very hierarchies that force racialized subjects to sacrifice in the first instance.[9] King sees Black sacrifice as an exemplary vehicle "to bring into full realization the American dream." Blacks serve as the "conscience of America—we are its troubled soul," exemplifying an unfulfilled yet latent "heritage of our nation" (King Jr. 1986a, 105). By solemnly suffering violence at the hands of racist police and other white mobs, Black demonstrators interrupt the eye-for-an-eye cycles of violent revenge and redeem American ideals violated under Jim Crow oppression. Nonviolent demonstrators have their suffering transmuted into a form of exemplary democratic activity. Where the U.S. polity has been incapable of living up to ideals of equality, Black Americans take up the burden of realizing those ideals through a nonviolent militancy aimed at "awaken[ing] a sense of moral shame in the opponent" (King Jr. 1986g, 8). Nonviolence in this sense enables a form of democratic repair in which a particular group's response to loss carries within itself the sacrifice necessary for transforming the social order by awakening the now-deadened moral sensibilities of whites.

As we have seen, the turn to mourning in political theory promises a critical and ambivalent relation to loss that transforms moments of suffering and trauma into occasions for democratic repair. Yet the early King's theory in particular demands more than that Blacks take up a disproportionate burden of the work of such democratic repair. It demands, for George Shulman, suffering with the "promise that such suffering is redemptive" (2008, 105). King argues that whites are also victims of white supremacy whose personalities are distorted by its pathologies. Because of this distortion of oppressor and oppressed alike, King inveighs that practitioners of nonviolence must distinguish between white supremacy's evil and injustice as abstract forces and the being of those citizens who participate in upholding white supremacy. In King's writings during the Montgomery Bus Boycott, for example, he describes the conflict as one between the "forces of light and the forces of darkness" (King Jr. 1986k, 83). In this sense, "the real tension," King insists, "is not between Negro citizens and the white citizens of Montgomery" (King Jr. 1986d, 82). Those who practice nonviolence must treat the violence of white supremacy as exceeding the individuals who participate in them for two reasons: First, to equate whites with their actions alone assumes that they are immune to ethical change, thus severely limiting their capacity to respond to Black suffering. Such an assumption would dehumanize them by treating individuals acting on "blindness, fear, pride, or irrationality" as incapable of moral and ultimately of spiritual redemption (King Jr. 1986i, 149).

Second, this equation would send resisters down the track of blame and bitterness that would lead to spirals of escalating violence. Rather than fighting for the negation of injustice that would create structures of equality for former victims and oppressors, resisters would become trapped in a desire for eventual domination. In other words, the very nonviolence aimed at cutting off the cyclical quality of revenge-tinged violence would slide into this pattern, merely reversing the position of victim and oppressor. Both the basic social and political structure and its theological valences of evil manifested would remain the same, King argues.

This twofold justification of the method of nonviolence depended on a set of moral and political calculations whose half-successes would generate later conflicts, in particular in later mid-1960s debates over the content and form of "Black Power." More specifically, these claims amount to wagers about the malleability of white moral psychology and the goals of anti-racist political action: First, King develops an account of white moral psychology that relies on an awakening of the opponent from their white supremacist "sleep" that tests their ability to sustain a belief in American ideals of equality and freedom while supporting a racial state in which the de facto conditions are the denial of these ideals (King Jr. 1986d, 149). Awakening this sense of moral shame through exemplary suffering would bring those in an uncommitted middle over to the side of righteous political action in the service of realizing founding ideals. Vulnerability, sacrifice, suffering—the core reference points of a politics of mourning—bring out especially to Northern whites the systematic susceptibility of Black bodies to violence and suffering to which the former have never been exposed. Such practices dramatize the evils of Jim Crow rule. The goal is to awaken a deep and unsettling sense of moral shame in the opponent and thus to bring them over—if not immediately, then eventually—to the side of righteous action.

It follows from this claim secondly that King's early writings insist on the notion that whites can eventually internalize the norms of fellowship with their Black fellow-citizens. For King, the goal of political action is not merely to draw on the coercive power of the state—the federal government—in order to enforce the laws. Politics has a cosmic purpose and that is to bring into being the "beloved community" and to reconcile oppressors with their victims. Through this process, both parties find redemption in different ways: The oppressed become the agents of this redemption and receive the protections of law and the rights they have long been denied. The oppressors become whole, stripped of the hatred and prejudice they needed to harbor deep within them in order to participate in the lynch mob. While King recognized that the (federal) law was needed to "restrain the heartless" during the struggle for voting and civil rights, he held out hope that the activities of everyday citizens could breathe flesh into the bones of law by making integration into "usual and ordinary in human conduct" (King Jr. 1986a, 100, 102).

Thus far within this account of the process by which white supremacy would be destroyed, King defines violence as a form of anti-politics that would forgo the discipline required to dramatize injustice and to communicate the evils of Jim Crow. Violence is by definition an emotive and undisciplined lashing out. In this sense, the resort to violence, King writes, does not even amount to a politics that could meaningfully transmute loss into democratic repair. Instead, the choice to rely on violence is "no more than a confused, anger-motivated drive to strike back violently, to inflict damage"—less a choice than an instinctive, reactive impulse (King Jr. 1986j, 32). According to this set of claims, the turn to violence is not only ineffective as a political strategy. It represents a kind of acquiescent repetition in which the oppressed can do no more than lash out arbitrarily and sporadically in anger to inflict the same kind of extra-legal vengeance characteristic of Jim Crow. Driven by resentment that surges into the desire for revenge, violence is no more than an affective and expressive outlet that has little of the directedness and intentionality that organized politics necessitates. Prophetic mourning thus requires that discontent be channeled toward nonviolent direct action in order to dramatize the conditions of injustice that haunt the Jim Crow South and transform the distorted humanity of the oppressor. This exemplary sacrifice and suffering thus makes possible the kind of confrontation with police that would force a crisis of conscience in liberal elites and establish a coalition capable of sustaining transformative change in the South.

From Mourning to "Chaos": The Changing Calculus of Nonviolence

Reflecting on the Watts riots of summer 1964, King argued in an essay for the *Saturday Review* in 1965 that:

> the cohesive, potentially explosive Negro community in the North has a short fuse and a long train of abuses. Those who argue that it is hazardous to give warnings, lest the expression of apprehension lead to violence, are in error. Violence has already been practiced too often, and always because remedies were postponed. (King Jr. 1986d, 193)

King implies that he is giving a "warning." He argues that to warn is not to incite violence. To anticipate how white supremacy's "long train of abuses" leads to a potential for counter-violence is not to incite violence. King continues to reject violence in terms akin to the above, yet he warns that such spontaneous violence (like a fuse that might quickly explode) happens because of the failure of political elites to enact reforms. He inveighs that riots can be averted—"urban slums need not be destroyed by flames"—if the responsibility is placed back on those who originally caused these explosions (King Jr. 1986f, 194). While King retains the focus on violence as a primarily reactive phenomenon, he imputes a (social) logic to riots that pins the resort to violence on the failure of nonviolence to reach receptive ears and thus to drive the kind of moral transformation that King had earlier imagined as part and parcel of bringing an end to Jim Crow.

Two factors explain the changing tenor of King's speeches and writings around 1963 to 1965: First, King turned his sights to the North, which suffered from problems of *covert* racial violence that would test "the limit," James Cone writes, "of white interest in the plight of blacks" (2001a, 232). Whereas King had thought that the North would organically change in lockstep with the emergence of a "New South" out of Jim Crow, he admitted to the "miscalculation" of believing that "opposition in the North was not intransigent, that it was flexible and was, if not fully, at least partially hospitable to corrective influences" (1968, 20).[10] As he pointed out, "White America stopped murder, but that is not the same thing as ordaining brotherhood; nor is the ending of lynch rule the same thing as inaugurating justice" (King Jr., 1967). That King found equal intransigence to racial justice in the North tested his views on the capacity of moderate whites to embrace more substantive policies aimed at equality and thus forced him to question the transformative logic of prophetic mourning. Second, Cone offers, "It was much easier to advocate nonviolence when there were concrete victories and few serious challenges to its advocacy" (2001b, 177). With the passage of the Civil and Voting Rights Acts in 1964 and 1965 respectively alongside the Watts riots in the summer of 1965 and the rise of Black Power in summer of 1966 at the Meredith March through Mississippi, "King's views on nonviolence were seriously challenged by young movement activists who became disillusioned with the relevance of nonviolence for bestowing self-esteem and eliminating poverty in the black community of the urban ghettoes of the North" (Cone 2001b, 177). Instead, for King, nonviolence became an *open question* in a way it had not been for him since the beginnings of the Montgomery Bus Boycott in 1954. In 1965, he argued that "the insistent question is whether the movement will be violent or nonviolent," whether the future would culminate in "chaos or community" (King Jr. 1986f, 192–93).

As the political calculus began to change, King's strategy increasingly transformed to accommodate such new realities not well captured by the framework of prophetic mourning that focuses on exemplary suffering as a vehicle of redemption. This changing political scene forced King to question his previously optimistic assumptions about white moral psychology and thus the very calculus of nonviolence and violence. I foreground these features of this familiar shift in King's thought towards a deeper confrontation with capitalism and militarism by examining the politics of his engagement with riots throughout the North.[11] This later King, even as he clung to nonviolence in principle, shifted his assumptions about the malleability of white moral psychology to value strategically forms of coercion and threat arising from an antagonistic politics—not from a politics of mourning narrowly construed.

As August Nimtz (2016) argues, King's questioning of what I call prophetic mourning was already visible in his "Letter to Birmingham Jail" (1963) when he was still seeking to pressure JFK and after him LBJ to get behind the Civil Rights and Voting Rights Acts. Echoing earlier writings in which King rejects violence as a force for "bitterness" and "hatred," in the letter he actually names that force in the "various black nationalist groups that are springing up across the nation," most notably Elijah Muhammad's Black Muslims. Without the philosophy of nonviolence, King argued, "by now many streets of the South would, I am convinced, be flowing with blood" (King Jr. 1986d, 298). Putting the point of MLK's sincere yet strategic rhetoric sharply, Nimtz writes, "It was as if he was saying, in other words: 'It's either me and my nonviolent course or them, the [Nation of Islam] and other potentially violent extremists'" (Nimtz 2016, 7). Nonviolence steps in not only as a force of moral suasion and political organization, but also as a way of disciplining the unruly emotions that might otherwise lead to more systematic (counter-)violence against whites.[12]

With the Northern riots and the radicalization of CORE and SNCC in 1966 and its emergent calls for Black Power, King transformed the abstract opposition between violence and nonviolence into a rhetoric with these concrete political consequences. As King shifted his attention from the Jim Crow South to conditions in Northern cities, his assessment of the possibilities of nonviolence also shifted. In addition to placing even greater emphasis on nonviolence as a tactic and a practice and not (just) a moral stance, King also began to reevaluate the victories nonviolence had won thus far. Writing in 1968 in an essay composed just before his assassination, King observed: "Only a few years ago, there was discernable, if limited, progress through nonviolence. . . . The fact is inescapable that the tactic of nonviolence, which had then dominated the thinking of the civil rights movement, has in the last two years not been playing its transforming role" (1986g, 64). King's changing assessment of nonviolence also poses a set of political and ethical dilemmas for the focus on mourning, since King's rhetoric worked in counterpoint to the openly antagonistic politics typified in the riot.

To clarify and provide grounding for the claim that the riot serves as a coercive counterpoint to King's nonviolent politics post-1963, let me now turn back to King's comments on riots.[13] King's rhetoric threatens authorities that violent riots will hasten and intensify if they do not come to the negotiating table. In particular, as King began to focus increasingly on questions of labor, welfare, and militarism as intimately tied to white supremacy, his rhetoric on riots becomes comprehensible as a leverage point to exact greater and broader concessions. Such a rhetoric of crisis and threat made sense in a context in which riots were of such concern that LBJ would eventually establish the National Advisory Commission on Civil Disorders (the Kerner Commission) to investigate the causes of rioting in July 1967.[14] King presents nonviolence as a viable alternative while using its (relative) quiescence and appeal to moral suasion as a leverage point to coerce the "white moderate" or "white liberal." He does so by placing responsibility for counter-violence back onto "white leadership": "The white leadership—the power structure— must face up to the fact that its sins of omission and commission have challenged our policy of nonviolence" (King Jr. 1986e, 176). The alternative is dire for King: "The urban outbreaks are 'a fire bell in the night,' clamorously warning that the seams of our entire social order are weakening under strains of neglect." This "neglect" points a finger of responsibility back at the "white leadership" for the unraveling seams of the social order (King Jr. 1986h, 71).

King's nonviolence here functions within a political context in which the threat of violence is a necessary prerequisite to the persuasiveness of nonviolence: "We have learned from bitter experience that our government does not correct a race problem until it is confronted directly and dramatically. We also know, *as official Washington may not*, that the flash point of Negro rage . . . close at hand" (King Jr. 1986h, 65). King, again, poses this as a binary "choice" pitched as a warning to reticent elites about the consequences of their inaction rather than a sui generis affirmation of the redemptive suffering of prophetic mourning:

> I think we have come to the point where there is no longer a choice now between nonviolence and riots. It must be militant, massive nonviolence, or riots. The discontent is so deep, the anger so ingrained, the despair, the restlessness so wide, that something has to be brought into being to serve as a channel through which these deep emotional feelings, these deep angry feelings, can be funneled. There has to be an outlet, and I see this campaign as a way to transmute the inchoate rage of the ghetto into a constructive and creative channel. It becomes an outlet for anger. (King Jr. 1986h, 69)

King's argument casts nonviolence less in terms of a redemptive, moral necessity that would appeal to white conscience than a pragmatic avenue through which to channel otherwise troubling and chaotic emotions that form through conditions generated by white supremacy. Even more bluntly, he contends: "if we do not get a positive response in Washington, many more Negroes will begin to think and act in violent terms" (King Jr. 1986h, 70).

King frames the context in this way because elites have stacked the choices available to Black activists by failing to alleviate social misery and thus forcing many into a "despair" that "made them active participants" in the riots that threaten the unraveling of the social fabric (King Jr. 1986e, 177).

In other words, it is not the relative vulnerability and finitude of Black bodies in the racial polity that brought potentially amenable elites to the bargaining table via a practice of public mourning but the posing of dire alternatives to reticent and fairly immoveable elites that might, ultimately, threaten *white* lives should the government fail to deliver concessions. To be sure, King argued that a renewed commitment to nonviolence in an even deeper and more militant form in the North could dismantle white supremacy. Yet his argument on behalf of nonviolence only could prove persuasive and become a motor of change in dynamic counterpoint to the alternative embodiment of struggle in the riot. The latter's emphasis on a credible threat to white bodies as opposed to the transformation of white conscience becomes the necessary backdrop to substantive transformation of the racial order.

King's sympathetic understanding and strategic deployment of the riot can also be seen in his analysis of the riot as a serious and enduring protest phenomenon. King developed an account of the causes of riots that consistently moved the blame from Black criminality and disorder onto white liberals who failed to avow the connections between racial and economic justice. The riots, he argued in 1964, "are caused by nice, gentle, timid white moderates who are more concerned about order than justice" (qtd. in Cone 2001a, 232). While it may be "understandable that the white community should fear the outbreak of riots," "social justice and progress are the absolute guarantors of riot prevention" (King Jr. 1968, 22). In his address to the American Psychological Association in September 1967, King argued further that "into the vacuum of inaction, violence and riots flowed" (1967). Rather than dismissing riots as passing events, King sensed that "urban riots must now be recognized as durable social phenomena" with particular forms of (group) intentionality behind them. As a "special form of violence," they are neither "insurrections" nor efforts to "attain control of institutions." Instead, they are "mainly intended to shock the white community" by violating property laws in just the way that "the police make a mockery of the law" (King Jr., 1967). In other words, they are aimed at democratic repair through "shock." Though in King's logic riots remain a "distorted form of social protest," he nonetheless does not dismiss this distortion as anything less than a durable form of violence that will not disappear so long as the conditions of the "ghetto" persist.

In invoking the specter of riots and Black Power, King plays two rhetorical chords at once. On one hand, he sings the praises of nonviolence and its continued capacity for moral suasion in the North while acknowledging as "understandable" the fears of whites. King argues: "This really means making the movement powerful enough, dramatic enough, morally appealing enough, so that people of goodwill, the churches, labor, liberals, intellectuals, students, poor people themselves begin to put pressure on congressmen to the point that they can no longer elude our demands" (King Jr. 1986h, 66). These protests are based on the ongoing validity of using mass actions to "dramatize" problems, in this case "the economic problem of the poor" (King Jr. 1986h, 66). Protests work as a form of pedagogy, creating mass events so that others can be educated and witness the real conditions of poverty in the affluent society. Moreover, he assuages the "white liberal" by assuring them that—though advocates of Black Power receive the most media coverage— the latter "represent a very small minority in the Negro community." In fact, "Most Negroes are still committed to the principle of white and black cooperation" (King Jr. 1968, 100).

On the other hand, though, King's rhetoric poses a dire alternative to liberal elites should they refuse to learn the lessons of this protest pedagogy and fail to concede to the movement's demands. He describes them as "nice, gentle, timid white moderates" who are instinctively conservative in their preference for order over justice. Arguing on behalf of creating an economic bill of rights, King addresses anxieties that pose the stark possibility that Northern Blacks will become ungovernable. Jobs and basic income programs "could minimize—I don't say stop—the number of riots that could take place this summer" (King Jr. 1986h, 67). This latter, more jarring rhetoric transforms white anxieties not by conjuring the dream of mournful unity and its tragic, untimely deferral—and, thus, of the nation's failure to achieve its promises—but rather by threatening the specter of anomie and of racial terror in reverse. In other words, King strategically draws on idioms of respectability, sympathy, and commonality that necessarily rely on both the figurative and literal presence of rioters to issue visceral threats to white power. King was gambling that the former mode of dramatizing injustice becomes significantly more appealing when the latter threats are also in play. By striking both of these chords, King places himself in a "militant middle between riots on the one hand and weak and timid supplication on the other hand" (1967). King's militancy is made possible in these later years by investing his audiences with dire choices that make militant nonviolence a more attractive option if the only other choice is a form of politics willing to express itself through illiberal, antagonistic means.

It may sound surprising at first blush to read King in sympathy with the riot as a form of political activity that is written out of the focus on a tragic, critical, and prophetic politics of mourning. To be sure, King finds in rioting no long-term political solutions to white supremacy and laments the arbitrary and spontaneous nature of riots since they forgo the discipline of nonviolence he had earlier championed. He never let go of his ardent opposition to violence as a form of "emotional catharsis" that leads ultimately to more violence (King Jr., 1967). In his final book, *Where Do We Go From Here: Chaos or Community?* (1968), King argued that Black Power was understandable as a slogan capturing the "disappointment" of young activists with the failures of the earlier movement but continued to lack a sustained, systematic political program.[15] King thus attributed minimal creative energy and agency to rioters and in a sense saw them as primarily reactive and explicable in naturalistic, even mechanistic, terms as an outgrowth of the structural situation to which they reacted.

In the above sense, I believe King's analysis to be somewhat limited as a "theory" of the riot, and am less interested in exploring its function as a free-standing account of the riot. For my purposes in this chapter, however, analyzing the way he later positioned himself in relation to the riot does prove useful as a means of identifying a tense meeting place between the different sensibilities and underlying assumptions of different sides of the Black radical tradition. In particular, read as a rhetoric in relation to the political strategy of the broader Black freedom movement, King's writings on riots function as more than a lament or a symptomatic reading posed against the more ambivalent and tragic sensibilities of Black counter-memorial practice: However sincerely meant, King's later writings resonate as a warning and even a threat to anxious liberal elites about the potential of coming disorder—of a "chaos" that King himself hoped to ward off. In this sense, his proclamations are themselves driven by a different theory of change that relies on more disruptive forms of political practice in order to force concessions from reticent white elites. In other words, the goal here is no longer to create a common grammar of shared loss—or even a plural and agonistic dissensus about losses. His later politics mount a more confrontational strategy of disruption and coercion as a way of exerting power with relatively little certainty about the malleability of white moral psychology.

Responsibility and the Impasse of Respectability Politics

I have made two central claims thus far about the pitfalls of the turn to a politics of exceptional mourning, which I have illustrated by way of a reading of this oft-noted shift in MLK's political thought: First, the turn to mourning risks ascribing distinctively liberal boundaries to democratic life by pathologizing aggressive responses to loss. Put more sharply, it might pathologize forms of political action born of deep injustice that refuse the kind of ambivalent and pluralistic approach that—as King would come to acknowledge with a mix of embrace, disgust, and strategic engagement—is characteristically difficult to sustain under conditions of domination and oppression. Second, I show how the turn to mourning as a form of democratic exemplarity relies on questionably optimistic assumptions about white moral psychology that drive expectations about what mourning can do to transform persistent hierarchies. I contrast the (relatively greater) emphases on a grammar of finitude and common suffering—the aspirational imagination of a "democracy about death"—with a practice more girded by the acknowledgment of lasting blindness and disavowal, if not outright investment in domination that can only be confronted through disruption, threat, and coercion.

While it would be somewhat trivial and commonplace to marshal figures such as Malcolm X—or, in a different register, contemporary Afro-pessimist thinkers—in support of such a critique of anti-racist politics as primarily a form of soulcraft, the case of King is more edifying because of his own historical and biographical arc that led him to question the very assumptions that also tend to buttress the turn to mourning. King's later movement-building found political efficacy in relation to the side of the movement that cultivated a more antagonistic politics. The former's power partly lies in this dynamic opposition rather than in the power of prophetic mourning to transform the conditions of white supremacy of itself. The first two arguments made in the foregoing lead to a third claim: Given King's response to the divides within the Black freedom movement in his own context, the turn to mourning might today benefit from greater attention to questions of responsibility, division, and strategy within movements like #BlackLivesMatter that do adopt a diversity of tactics of resistance to oppression and domination—including more confrontational ones pitched in the language of war and survival. I thus open up this problem more directly to today's post–civil rights version of white supremacy, with attention especially to the circulation of discourses of respectability that continue to haunt gestures toward a politics of loss and trauma.

While political theorists have turned to mourning to identify a practice that sustains an ambivalent and critical relation to the past without collapsing too quickly into friend and enemy, this chapter poses a dilemma: Given the ways in which the racial order has been reproduced since the civil rights movement through the expansion of the carceral state, what kind of practices could both sustain this open dynamic yet also get enough of a resistant critique off the ground so as to produce some space for lasting transformation?[16] The answer is not straightforward for two reasons. First, solidarity itself is often split along racial lines (Hooker 2009). Since solidarity is racialized, pointing to the ways in which an openly antagonistic politics that breaches liberal boundaries might generate white resentment and perhaps fail to elicit sufficiently broad cross-racial coalition-building is to fall into an analysis that naturalizes existing hierarchies that are themselves the *product* of the racial order. As King wrote of the dominant reading of a "white backlash" to the civil rights movement (that would later give rise to the carceral state), "the white backlash is nothing new. It is the surfacing of old prejudices, hostilities and ambivalences" (King Jr. 1968, 72). In other words, to read antagonism as the problem is to lose sight of the ways in which the seeds of backlash already exist as part of a current racial order. In other words, if backlash is relatively predictable in a white supremacist society— as a response to most *any* form of Black resistance—then it becomes more important to foreground the evolving terms of racial order than to pick out forms of exceptional political action. Second, in this vein, the problem of *contemporary* neoliberal white supremacy is yet more complicated by the ascendance of what Keeanga Yamahtta-Taylor (2016) has called "Black faces in high places." Rather than the near-exclusively white power structure against which King fought, these very civil rights struggles led to the ascent of Blacks to political office in majority-Black districts and municipalities. For example, during the uprising over the murder of Freddie Gray in the West Side of Baltimore, a majority of the central officials seeking to contain the uprising were Black, including Mayor Stephanie Rawlings-Blake, Police Commissioner Anthony Batts, and eight of the fifteen members of the city council. If part of the problem is that politics within the bounds of Black descriptive representation have failed for working-class Black people, then surely, it is important to ask where political influence to transform such simultaneously class-inflected and racially ordered conditions of second-class citizenship might emerge otherwise (Yamahtta-Taylor 2016, 71–106). In this sense, the divisions about questions of tactics are already potentially implicated in the existing hierarchies the current racial order produces.

Such an insistence on the risks of reproducing these hierarchies points in two directions when it comes to examining activities like rioting, which serve as an example of an openly antagonistic, not agonistic, practice. First, as King recognized, the riot functions at least partly as a form of catharsis, an outlet through which otherwise de-legitimated anger can be expressed when representation—which today would include significant Black descriptive representation—fails to transform conditions of incarceration, unjust polic- ing, and systematic disinvestment from Black communities.[17] King refused the game of respectability politics, even as he played up at moments the differences between Black Power and his nonviolent philosophy. By ruling the riot implicitly out of bounds, the turn to mourning may too easily play into the now-ascendant respectability politics that slants the playing field in favor of elite-oriented expressions of political grievance aimed at generating sympathetic depictions of "good" Black vulnerability.

Respectability politics takes those actors who are deemed illegitimate— dismissed, for example, through the racialized language of "thug"—as ipso facto poorly disciplined political actors who need to transform their own self- presentation prior to entering politics (Harris 2012). Such a logic quickly slides into the mapping of expressions of political agency onto status in existing social and political hierarchies. At worst, this logic harkens back to earlier strains of American political thought that attribute white supremacist violence (in whole or in part) to Black criminality or Black "culture" (Gibran Muhammad 2011; Coates 2014). As Yamahtta-Taylor suggests, some Black elected officials have ironically benefited from their blackness because they can gain political capital by criticizing Black "culture" in the terms of respectability politics "in ways that white politicians could never get away with" (2016, 79). While the questions of strategy King posed to Black Power advocates are surely worth debating, the emphasis on mourning can skirt around these already existing hierarchies that often inform deep aspirational and strategic divides bequeathed through such material-institutional legacies. Of course, these material-institutional legacies of Black descriptive representation are themselves the traces of the half-successes of the past democratic struggles in which King was a central actor.

Further, to illustrate why respectability matters in a discussion of exceptional mourning, consider how traces of such a respectability politics appear often in representations of contemporary Black protest movements: Take the case in which rival gangs in Baltimore forged a truce during the protests in the wake of Freddie Gray's murder at the hands of police.[18] The police insisted that this truce must have been aimed at killing police, a false claim widely circulated in the media. From this perspective, the truce was not a "real" political action taken within a context lacking in other revolutionary party and durable organizational infrastructure.[19] Subtler examples abound as well, even in relation to actions that could not remotely be described as "riots." For example, the common refrain that Black Lives Matter draws on actions and methods such as blocking highways that the civil rights movement never used—however inaccurate on its face—is one example of the way that the focus on what is perceived to be the "good" militancy of mourning might pathologize the "bad" militancy of Black rage. That this critique has come in part from the civil rights old guard of the previous generation is indicative of how deeply these divides run and how the turn to mourning is likely to function at the point of reception to play into these potent, existing narratives (Reynolds 2015).[20]

Second, more than functioning as a crucial outlet for rage and disaffection at systematic disinvestment, abandonment, and state violence, as King often intoned, riots sometimes work. Juliet Hooker suggests that riots sometimes function as an instrument of democratic repair that force concessions from (typically liberal) elites. When the exemplary display of nonviolent action fails, riots are "inadequate, but necessary, forms of democratic repair for Black citizens in the face of racial terror" (Hooker 2016, 450). George Ciccariello-Maher (2015) points out that defining riots as violent and therefore illegitimate assumes inter alia that "so called 'peaceful' protests are effective in bringing attention to police murder, offering instead a moral imperative: the media *should* cover peaceful marches, the system *should* respond. But they don't and it doesn't."

Ciccariello-Maher's point is backed up as well by Frances Fox Piven and Richard Cloward's (1978) classic account of the rise and fall of poor people's movements. Building on Piven and Cloward's writings on the civil rights and welfare rights movements, a tradition within social movement theory suggests that disempowered and disenfranchised actors exert influence primarily through disruptive, mass *mobilization*. They contrast mobilization to *organization*, characterizing mobilization as a strategy of disruption that works by exercising one of the few levers the disenfranchised and dispossessed have: The capacity to disrupt institutions of state and capital through sheer numbers, and, as Piven re-emphasizes in recent writing, "to throw sand in the gears of the system" (2017). Of course, mobilization can (very crudely put) be violent, nonviolent, or both, but it is explicitly a form of antagonism that uses physical disruption as a way of creating leverage. It is much less geared toward the display of human finitude and vulnerability—even, in King's language, an "active" and "dramatized" form of this display—that is often part and parcel of a politics of mourning, which motivates change through contingent articulations of shared suffering.

I do not of course want to suggest that the turn to mourning necessarily take up the kinds of attitudes often bundled together with respectability politics as anything like a matter of logical or conceptual intension. And King's version of mourning is distinct from contemporary turns to mourning in important ways, not least of all the theological, elemental hope of redemption that infuses King's philosophy. These latter aspects are significantly tempered in nearly all of the quite different accounts of mourning I glossed at the beginning of this chapter. Still, with these caveats in mind, the question remains whether a politics whose appeal partly lies in maneuvering *around* militancy can avoid these questions of strategy, division, and responsibility, especially given the current composition of the U.S. racial order.

Thinking more re-constructively, then, I conclude on a final note: I ask whether it might be more illuminating to move from a focus on counter-memorial practices of mourning in themselves and more toward a focus on their conditions of circulation and reception.[21] By tracing these circuits, theorists might very well arrive at a different, more ambivalent picture of mourning. They might thus begin to acknowledge at the very least the presence of antagonistic politics, with its distinct claims about moral psychology and the politics of transformation—if not the stronger claim I have made more briefly here about its potential effectiveness.

Throughout this chapter, I have suggested that mourning depends on *reception* and thus on a capacity for response—thus, I would add now, on *responsibility*. Whereas the focus of mourning has to a large extent revolved around the practices of the marginalized, theorists might be better served in turning the lens of analysis around toward the conditions of mourning's reception. Consider, for example, the public discourse around the murder of

Michael Brown. In particular, as soon as the police released footage of Brown allegedly stealing cigars (or in some accounts dealing drugs) in a local convenience store, many took this as evidence that Brown was a "thug" (Eligon 2014). The point that none of this information was relevant to Brown being murdered in the street and his killer being subsequently set free was mostly muted. Implicit in my provocation here is the question of what it would look like to mourn *without exception*. As soon as some unsavory detail is discovered about the victim—from Brown, to Eric Garner, and even to Tamir Rice, a twelve-year-old boy—then many reject the need to mourn. My frame of reference here is not to Judith Butler's well-known claims about pre-ontological vulnerability, which seem to demand an abstract ethical commitment to mourning prior to entering into the field of political debate and contest.[22] Rather, I am asking what it would mean to draw ordinary people into webs of accountability in movements that refuse binaries of guilt and innocence, inside and outside, respectable and thug. In other words, how can the left build movements in which such internalized binaries can be worked out and acknowledged in order to create a responsibility to mourn without exception and in solidarity with rioters? Without giving a prescription here, my hope is that the turn to mourning can contribute to answering this question by supplementing its current considerations with a deeper engagement with these material conditions of race-class subjugation and the questions of power and responsibility they engender.

NOTES

1. I would like to acknowledge my gratitude to the following colleagues for helpful and generous feedback on this chapter: Nancy Luxon, Adam Dahl, Alex Hirsch, David McIvor, Elena Gambino, Alex Steele, María José Méndez Gutiérrez, Quỳnh Phạm, Bryan Nakayama, Charmaine Chua, Chase Hobbs-Morgan, Joe Soss, Sayres Rudy, and Eli Meyerhoff, as well as audiences from the Western Political Science Association Conference and Minnesota Political Theory Colloquium in 2017 and an anonymous reviewer.

2. For a productive engagement with the language of "state violence" and its analytic imprecision, see (Terry 2015). There is a much longer history of this analysis of war as an explicit critique of the hollow nature of liberal claims about the pacific character of civil society for Black people within the varied history of the Black freedom struggle. For one precursor that draws on the language of war and genocide, see (Civil Rights Congress 1951).

3. For example, #BlackLivesMatter organizers in the Twin Cities orchestrated an occupation of the fourth precinct police station in Northside Minneapolis in response to the murder of Northside resident Jamar Clark that lasted from just after Clark's murder on November 15, 2015 until police broke the encampment up on December 3, 2015; (Rietmulder 2015). For more critical takes on #BLM and the occupation, see (Kuti 2016; Mullen 2015).

4. Frederick C. Harris (2012) traces debates over respectability back to the famed divide between Booker T. Washington and W.E.B. Du Bois over the proper strategy for contesting the color line and fighting for Black "uplift." I follow Harris' useful gloss on respectability as a diffuse "public philosophy" that focuses on the "behaviors and habits" of the Black poor as an explanation of poverty with the political implication that Black movements can transform white supremacy by publicly communicating an image and comportment of respectability (2012, 103). As I argue below, I think the focus on mourning can shade into facilitating such a

respectability politics, if only by generating readings of Black politics that focus on vulnerability and finitude as opposed to aggressive (i.e. not "respectable") resistance.

5. Even these moments of "resistance" in psychoanalysis, Luxon points out, are confined to a play between analyst and patient in which there is room for creativity and reworking oriented toward reconciliation of self with self. Many organizers, by contrast, would argue that political action requires anger to be channeled and disciplined from an unruly subjective experience toward the pursuit of concrete, collective ends.

6. For Luxon, the turn to mourning, then, may "risk the pathologization of anger, by restricting it to certain subjects (either righteous or unreflective) and by occluding the very different kind of interpersonal resistances that are the grist of politics and not always of interpretation" (2016, 145).

7. In retrieving King as an unlikely ally in this critique, I am also influenced by the work of theorists who have increasingly seen anger and other so-called "negative emotions" as a durable—and even positive—political forces (Chakravarti 2014; Coulthard 2014; Dolgert 2016).

8. My use of the term "white moral psychology" is indebted to Charles Mills, whose widely discussed work postulates that the ideal contract of social contract theory is in fact a nonideal "racial contract" that hinges on a real-world hierarchy between racially defined full persons and unequally treated sub-persons. Mills conceptualizes racism's "major shaping effect on white cognizers" when it comes to affectively and cognitively registering who counts morally (and under what conditions). Whites (and to some degree often nonwhites) internalize the social and political hierarchies and "differential privilege" reproduced through the racial contract, which "requires in whites the cultivation of patterns of affect and empathy that are only weakly, if at all, influenced by nonwhite suffering" (Mills 1997, 95; 1998, 108). I invoke the term throughout this chapter neither to provide my own fully elaborated account of white moral psychology nor to champion the specifics of Mills's but rather to make the point that any account of transformative anti-racist politics will depend upon *some* assumptions about how white moral psychology functions; how malleable such functioning is (e.g., Mills's skeptical claims that whites are not "influenced by nonwhite suffering"); and thus what political actions are most likely to transform white supremacist relations of power and under what conditions.

9. In dialogue with Brandon Terry's work on the "romantic narrative" of the civil rights movement (2012), Hooker (2016) focuses primarily on the tendency of Ellison and Allen to romanticize Black suffering as redemptive. Hooker argues that they move too quickly from the normal reality of coping with political losses in democracy to the losses imposed on Blacks through the persistence of the U.S. racial order. Thus, for Hooker, Allen and Ellison downplay the perverse ways in which Blacks remain "perpetual losers" that bear the brunt of this suffering under U.S. white supremacy. My argument here is directed more at analyzing how the sensibilities of theorists of mourning in particular have risked collapsing the (human) situation of suffering, contingency, and finitude into the (structural and historically specific) situation of *imposed* sacrifice characteristic of white supremacy to which Hooker points.

10. On the "New South," see (King Jr. 1986b).

11. Previous scholars have already shown how New Right figures (and I would add, many on the liberal-left) have tried to sanitize King's radicalism. The later shift I am zooming in on is a core piece from King's legacy that is disavowed in that politically convenient revisionist history of the civil rights movement (Baldwin and Burrow Jr. 2013; Shelby and Terry 2018).

12. Other accounts also question the narrative focus on the nonviolent elements of the civil rights movement (Bermanzohn 2000; Cobb, Jr. 2015).

13. My aim here is not to provide a theory of the riot. For an interesting account through the lens of world-systems theory, see Clover 2016.

14. An important context for King's audience was the fact that the Black riot was a historically recent phenomenon that emerged as late as the 1943 Detroit uprising, when Blacks fought back against white mob violence on a wide scale for the first time since World War I. By the 1960s, the Black riot had displaced the white race riot as the preferred lens through which to see the American history of the riot despite the latter's more recent provenance (Abu-Lughod 2007).

15. "All this," King writes, "represents disappointment lifted to astronomical proportions" (1968, 36).

16. Naomi Murakawa documents how civil rights liberals pushed law and order ideology and race-neutral legal mechanisms that played into images of Black criminality, which led to the initial momentum toward contemporary mass incarceration (2014). While it would have been impossible to have predicted the explosion of mass incarceration, King refused the respectability politics that would have played into the very readings of Black personhood that enabled such a carceral politics.

17. Apropos of a moralism that would automatically condemn such violence, Isaac Deutscher wrote: "To preach non-violence to those always the object of violence may even be false" (Vazquez-Arroyo 2014, 66).

18. See ("Gang Members Deny Police Claims of Truce to 'Take Out' White Cops: 'They're Saying We're Animals'" 2015). The WBAL interview at the bottom of the page with unidentified members of the BGF, the Bloods, and the Crips features a spokesperson who talks directly to the question of respectability when the interviewer asks how looting and violence made the community look: "It's backing up what they're saying about us; they're saying we're animals and we're acting like savages out here. I don't agree with what's going on, but I understand what's going on. You know what I'm saying? I understand why people are mad, but we gotta handle things another way." See also (Johnson 2015; Curry 2015).

19. The police side of the argument was widely represented and circulated in the media (Mosendz 2017).

20. In her *Washington Post* editorial, Barbara Reynolds (2015) argues that "at protests today, it is difficult to distinguish legitimate activists from the mob actors who loot and burn." A special irony lies in this critique of blocking highways, since this disruptive practice is intended to problematize the long-term structural consequences of city and state officials directing the routes of highways built in major American cities in the 1950s and 1960s through Black neighborhoods. As James Baldwin pithily put it in an interview with famed psychologist Dr. Kenneth Clark, urban renewal "means moving the Negros out. It means Negro removal; that is what it means. And the federal government is an accomplice to this fact" (1963).

21. Heather Pool (2012, 2015) has done some of this deeply historical work on the limitations of mourning, and I cannot do better here than to cite her.

22. For a fuller explanation of this critique of Butler's conception of disavowal as reliant on a questionably pre-political conception of shared human vulnerability, see (Shulman 2011).

WORKS CITED

Abu-Lughod, Janet L. 2007. *Race, Space, and Riots in Chicago, New York, and Los Angeles.* New York: Oxford University Press.

Alexander, Michelle. 2010. *The New Jim Crow: Mass Incarceration in the Age of Colorblindness.* New York: The New Press.

Baldwin, Lewis V., and Rufus Burrow Jr., eds. 2013. *The Domestication of Martin Luther King Jr.: Clarence B. Jones, Right-Wing Conservatism, and the Manipulation of the King Legacy.* Eugene, Oregon: Cascade Books.

Bermanzohn, Sally Avery. 2000. "Violence, Nonviolence, and the Civil Rights Movement." *New Political Science* 22 (1): 31–48.

Butler, Judith. 2000. *Antigone's Claim: Kinship Between Life and Death.* New York: Columbia University Press.

———. 2003. "Violence, Mourning, Politics." *Studies in Gender and Sexuality* 4 (1): 9–37.

———. 2004. *Precarious Life: The Powers of Mourning and Violence.* Verso.

———. 2009. *Frames of War: When Is Life Grievable?* Verso.

Chakravarti, Sonali. 2014. *Sing the Rage: Listening to Anger After Mass Violence.* Chicago: University of Chicago Press.

Cicariello-Maher, George. 2015. "Riots Work: Wolf Blitzer and the *Washington Post* Completely Missed the Real Lesson from Baltimore." *Salon*, May 4, 2015. http://www.salon.com/2015/05/04/riots_work_wolf_blitzer_and_the_washington_post_completely_missed_the_real_lesson_from_baltimore/.

Civil Rights Congress. 1951. *We Charge Genocide: The Historic Petition to the United Nations for Relief from a Crime of the United States Government Against the Negro People*. New York: International Publishers.

Clover, Joshua. 2016. *Riot, Strike, Riot: The New Era of Uprisings*. New York: Verso.

Coates, Ta-Nehisi. 2014. "Charles Barkley and the Plague of 'Unintelligent' Blacks." *The Atlantic*, October 28, 2014. https://www.theatlantic.com/politics/archive/2014/10/charles-barkley-and-the-plague-of-unintelligent-blacks/382022/.

Cobb, Jr., Charles E. 2015. *This Nonviolent Stuff'll Get You Killed*. Durham: Duke University Press.

Cone, James H. 2001a. *Martin and Malcolm and America: A Dream or a Nightmare*. Maryknoll, NY: Orbis Books.

———. 2001b. "Martin and Malcolm on Nonviolence and Violence." *Phylon* 49 (3/4): 173–83.

Coulthard, Glen Sean. 2014. *Red Skins, White Masks: Rejecting the Colonial Politics of Recognition*. Minneapolis: University of Minnesota Press.

Curry, Colleen. 2015. "Baltimore Gang Members Say Police Allegation They Are Uniting to Kill Officers Is a Lie." *Vice News*, April 28, 2015. https://news.vice.com/article/baltimore-gang-members-say-police-allegation-they-are-uniting-to-kill-officers-is-a-lie.

Denzel Smith, Mychal. 2015. "A Q&A With Alicia Garza, Co-Founder of #BlackLivesMatter." *The Nation*, March 24, 2015. https://www.thenation.com/article/qa-alicia-garza-co-founder-blacklivesmatter/.

Dolgert, Stefan. 2016. "The Praise of Ressentiment: Or, How I Learned to Stop Worrying and Love Donald Trump." *New Political Science* 38 (3): 354–70.

Eligon, John. 2014. "Michael Brown Spent Last Weeks Grappling With Problems and Promise." *New York Times*, August 24, 2014. https://www.nytimes.com/2014/08/25/us/michael-brown-spent-last-weeks-grappling-with-lifes-mysteries.html.

"Gang Members Deny Police Claims of Truce to 'Take Out' White Cops: 'They're Saying We're Animals.'" 2015. Raw Story. http://www.rawstory.com/2015/04/gang-members-deny-police-claims-of-truce-to-take-out-white-cops-theyre-saying-were-animals/.

Gibran Muhammad, Khalil. 2011. *The Condemnation of Blackness: Race, Crime, and the Making of Modern Urban America*. Cambridge: Harvard University Press.

Harris, Frederick. 2012. *The Price of the Ticket: Barack Obama and the Rise and Decline of Black Politics*. New York: Oxford University Press.

Honig, Bonnie. 2013. *Antigone, Interrupted*. New York: Cambridge University Press.

Hooker, Juliet. 2009. *Race and the Politics of Solidarity*. New York: Oxford University Press.

———. 2016. "Black Lives Matter and the Paradoxes of U.S. Black Politics: From Democratic Sacrifice to Democratic Repair." *Political Theory* 44 (4): 448–69.

James Baldwin Interview with Kenneth Clark (Part 2). 1963. https://www.youtube.com/watch?v=bZ24OCXloKo.

Johnson, Adam. 2015. "Unverified 'Threats,' Uncritically Reported: A Tradition as Old as Protest." Fairness & Accuracy in Reporting. http://fair.org/home/unverified-threats-uncritically-reported-a-tradition-as-old-as-protest/;

King Jr., Martin Luther. 1968. *Where Do We Go From Here: Chaos or Community?* Boston: Beacon Press.

———. 1986a. "An Address Before the National Press Club (1962)." In *A Testament of Hope: The Essential Writings and Speeches*, edited by James M. Washington, 99–105. New York: HarperCollins.

———. 1986b. "Bold Design for a New South (1963)." In *A Testament of Hope: The Essential Writings and Speeches*, edited by James M. Washington, 112–16. New York: HarperCollins.

———. 1986c. "Eulogy for the Martyred Children (1963)." In *A Testament of Hope: The Essential Writings and Speeches*, edited by James M. Washington, 221–23. New York: HarperCollins.

———. 1986d. "Letter from Birmingham City Jail (1963)." In *A Testament of Hope: Essential Writings and Speeches*, 289–302. New York: HarperCollins.

———. 1986e. "Negroes Are Not Moving Too Fast (1964)." In *A Testament of Hope: The Essential Writings and Speeches*, edited by James M. Washington, 176–81. New York: HarperCollins.

———. 1986f. "Next Stop: The North (1965)." In *A Testament of Hope: The Essential Writings and Speeches*, edited by James M. Washington, 189–96. New York: HarperCollins.

———. 1986g. "Nonviolence and Racial Justice (1957)." In *A Testament of Hope: The Essential Writings and Speeches of Martin Luther King, Jr.*, edited by James M. Washington, 5–9. New York: HarperCollins.

———. 1986h. "Showdown for Nonviolence (1968)." In *A Testament of Hope: The Essential Writings and Speeches*, edited by James M. Washington, 64–74. New York: HarperCollins.

———. 1986i. "The Rising Tide of Racial Consciousness (1960)." In *A Testament of Hope: The Essential Writings and Speeches*, 145–51. New York: HarperCollins.

———. 1986j. "The Social Organization of Nonviolence (1959)." In *A Testament of Hope: The Essential Writings and Speeches*, edited by James M. Washington, 31–34. New York: HarperCollins.

———. 1986k. "Walk for Freedom (1956)." In *A Testament of Hope: The Essential Writings and Speeches*, edited by James M. Washington, 82–84. New York: HarperCollins.

———. 1967. "The Role of the Behavioral Scientist in the Civil Rights Movement." http://www.apa.org/monitor/features/king-challenge.aspx.

Kuti, Ikemba. 2016. "The 4th Precinct: A Black Anarchist's Perspective on Struggle in Minneapolis' Northside Streets." *M1AA* (blog). March 25, 2016. http://m1aa.org/?p=1169.

Lerman, Amy E., and Vesla M. Weaver. 2014. *Arresting Citizenship: The Democratic Consequences of American Crime Control*. Chicago: University of Chicago Press.

Luxon, Nancy. 2016. "Beyond Mourning and Melancholia: Nostalgia, Anger and the Challenges of Political Action." *Contemporary Political Theory* 15 (2): 139–59.

McIvor, David. 2012. "Bringing Ourselves to Grief: Judith Butler and the Politics of Mourning." *Political Theory* 40 (4): 409–36.

McIvor, David W. 2017. *Mourning in America: Race and the Politics of Loss*. Ithaca: Cornell University Press.

Mills, Charles. 1997. *The Racial Contract*. Ithaca: Cornell University Press.

———. 1998. *Blackness Visible: Essays on Philosophy and Race*. Ithaca: Cornell University Press.

Mosendz, Polly. 2017. "Gangs Unite to Kill Cops, Baltimore Police Department Warns," April 2017. http://www.newsweek.com/gangs-unite-kill-cops-baltimore-police-department-warns-325621.

Mullen, Mike. 2015. "Black Lives Matter Protesters Evicted from Fourth Precinct Occupation." *City Pages*, December 3, 2015. http://www.citypages.com/news/black-lives-matter-protesters-evicted-from-fourth-precinct-occupation-7876323.

Murakawa, Naomi. 2014. *The First Civil Right: How Liberals Built Prison America*. New York: Oxford University Press.

Nimtz, August. 2016. "Violence and/or Nonviolence in the Success of the Civil Rights Movement: The Malcolm X–Martin Luther King, Jr. Nexus." *New Political Science* 38 (1): 1–22.

Page, Joshua, and Joe Soss. 2018. "Criminal Justice Predation and Neoliberal Governance." In *Rethinking Neoliberalism: Resisting the Disciplinary Regime*, edited by Sanford F. Schram and Marianna Pavlovskaya, 141–61. New York: Routledge.

Piven, Frances Fox. 2017. "Throw Sands in the Gears of Everything." *The Nation*, January 18, 2017. https://www.thenation.com/article/throw-sand-in-the-gears-of-everything/.

Piven, Frances Fox, and Richard Cloward. 1978. *Poor People's Movements: Why They Succeed, How They Fail*. New York: Vintage.

Pool, Heather. 2012. "The Politics of Mourning: The Triangle Fire and Political Belonging." *Polity* 44 (2): 182–211.

———. 2015. "Mourning Emmett Till." *Law, Culture and the Humanities* 11 (3): 414–44.

Reynolds, Barbara. 2015. "I Was a Civil Rights Activist in the 1960s. But It's Hard for Me to Get behind Black Lives Matter." *The Washington Post*, August 24, 2015. https://www.washingtonpost.com/posteverything/wp/2015/08/24/i-was-a-civil-rights-activist-in-the-1960s-but-its-hard-for-me-to-get-behind-black-lives-matter/?postshare=5221440433

170944&utm_term=.a9b3de3011d4.

Rietmulder, Michael. 2015. "Meet the People of the Fourth Precinct Occupation." *City Pages*, November 20, 2015. http://www.citypages.com/news/meet-the-people-of-the-fourth-pre-cinct-occupation-7846325.

Shelby, Tommie, and Brandon M. Terry, eds. 2018. *To Shape a New World: Essays on the Political Philosophy of Martin Luther King, Jr.* Cambridge: Harvard University Press.

Shulman, George. 2008. *American Prophecy: Race and Redemption in American Political Culture*. Minneapolis: University of Minnesota Press.

———. 2011. "Acknowledgment and Disavowal as an Idiom for Theorizing Politics." *Theory & Event* 14 (1).

Soss, Joe, and Vesla M. Weaver. 2017. "Police Are Our Government: Politics, Political Science, and the Policing of Race-Class Subjugated Communities." *Annual Review of Political Science* 20 (May): 565–91.

Stow, Simon. 2010. "Agonistic Mourning: Frederick Douglass, Joseph Lowery, and the Democratic Value of African American Public Mourning." *The American Political Science Review* 104 (4): 681–97.

———. 2017. *American Mourning: Tragedy, Democracy, Resilience*. Cambridge University Press.

Terry, Brandon M. 2012. "Which Way to Memphis?: Political Theory, Narrative, and the Politics of Historical Imagination in the Civil Rights Movement." Yale University.

———. 2015. "After Ferguson." *The Point*, Summer 2015. https://thepointmag.com/2015/politics/after-ferguson.

United States Department of Justice Civil Rights Division. 2015. "Department of Justice Report on the Ferguson, Mo. Police Department."

Vazquez-Arroyo, Antonio. 2014. "At the Edges of Civic Freedom: Violence, Power, Enmity." In *Democracy and Freedom in an Imperial Context: Dialogues with James Tully*, 48–70. New York: Routledge.

Woltman, Nick. 2016. "Thousands Remember Philando Castile at Vigil." *Pioneer Press*, July 7, 2016. https://www.twincities.com/2016/07/07/thousands-remember-philando-castile-at-vigil/.

Yamahtta-Taylor, Keeanga. 2016. *From #BlackLivesMatter to Black Liberation*. New York: Haymarket.

Chapter Nine

Music, Mourning, and Democratic Resilience

Bruce Springsteen's The Rising[1]

Simon Stow

Neither mourning nor popular music have traditionally proved popular in political thought; either in and of themselves, or as resources for critical reflection. In the *Menexenus*, Plato famously mocks the Greek tradition of the funeral oration, asserting that "in many ways it's a fine thing to die in battle. A man gets a magnificent funeral, even if he dies poor, and people praise him even if he was worthless. Wise men lavish praise him . . . and the praise is so beautiful that although they speak things both true and untrue of each man, the extreme beauty and diversity of their words bewitches our souls" (1984, 234c). In the *Laws*, he combines mourning and the musical, forbidding dirges and public displays of grief, permitting only nighttime ceremonies for the dead lest public displays of emotion damage the city (2005, 959e–960b). In the *Republic*, the threat posed to the city by music and mourning are front and center. There Plato identifies the dangers to the polis of laments for the dead, suggesting that witnessing the grief of others corrupts the judgment of the good citizen (1992, 387e–388c). Likewise, he suggests that certain forms of music—specifically the complex music played on lutes, harps, and other stringed instruments—would be banned in the Ideal City lest they corrupt the reasonable citizen, even as he suggests that certain other forms of music—the rather more prosaic music of the lyre, the cither, and the shepherd's pan flute—would be encouraged for the harmony they might generate in the souls of their listeners (ibid., 399d).

Such claims about the stultifying power of music were later echoed by Theodor Adorno, who, in addition to arguing that popular music was a tool of class oppression—a cultural product that permitted a partial escape from the "boredom of mechanized labor"—also suggested that it was "wholly antagonistic to the ideal of individuality in a free society" (2002, 458, 442). Popular music, he argued, demanded and produced entirely predictable listening patterns and, as such, was not only itself homogenous, but also produced homogenous listeners. "The composition hears for the listener," he observed. "This is how popular music divests the listener of his spontaneity and promotes conditioned reflexes. Not only does it require his effort to follow its concrete stream; it actually gives him models under which anything concrete still remaining may be subsumed" (ibid., 442). While, in his 1987 work *The Closing of the American Mind*, Allan Bloom—Adorno's ideological opposite in every way except this—offered a similarly dismissive account of the dangers of popular music. "Never," he writes, "was there an art form directed so exclusively to children" (1987, 74). Indeed, his account of the impact of popular music on its listener echoes—unsurprisingly perhaps given his intellectual vocation—the Socrates of Plato's *Republic*, observing that for "[a] pubescent child whose body throbs with orgasmic rhythms; whose feelings are made articulate in hymns to the joys of onanism or the killing of parents; whose ambition is to win fame and wealth in imitating the drag-queen who makes music . . . life is made into a nonstop, commercially prepackaged masturbational fantasy" (ibid., 75).[2] As such, it is perhaps unsurprising—though no less disappointing because of it—that the library shelves set aside for works on music and political theory remain rather sparsely populated, with literature and film serving as the main focus of political theory's engagement with the cultural.[3] There is, nevertheless, now a considerable contemporary literature about the promise and problems of mourning, both public and private, for democratic politics; one that has generated a productive debate about its potential role, or otherwise, in a time of *iustitium*, exception, catastrophe, and/or emergency politics of the sort engendered by mass, or sometimes individual, death (Butler, 2004; Butler, 2010; Honig, 2013; McIvor, 2016; Stow, 2017). While some of these authors see the turn to the politics of mourning as an inevitable turn to the mourning of politics, others consider it a source of democratic renewal, resilience, or an opportunity for engaging with complex social and political issues.

This essay has two intersecting aims. First, it seeks to identify an example of a democratically productive, ethically generous, and capacious form of public mourning that might serve as a counter-example to the claim that the politics of mourning is inevitably antidemocratic. It is a form of mourning that might serve as resource for engendering democratic resilience: the doctrine that recognizes the always ongoing possibility of crisis or catastrophe, and seeks not prevention of such events, but rather preservation of important institutions—in this case, those of liberal democracy—in the face of them through the cultivation of values, practices, and other relevant resources in the face of loss. It is a mourning that would, in Josiah Ober's phrase, permit the polity to "go on together" in the face of loss (Ober, 2005). Second, it seeks to show the value of popular music as a resource for theorizing the political and, thereby, to offer a counter example to the strand of political thought that would dismiss its potential contribution to critical reflection. As these counter examples might suggest, the method here will not be to engage in a point-by-point refutation of the arguments made against mourning by various democratic theorists, nor those against music in political theorizing, but rather to "show by doing," demonstrating the ways in which what James Schmidt calls "musical memorials" (2010)—in this case, Bruce Springsteen's 2002 album, *The Rising*, his response to the 2001 terrorist attacks on the United States—can embody, and seek to cultivate in their audiences, a particular ethic in response to mass death, one that generates critical reflection, democratic engagement, and a rejection of revenge, and with it, a form of democratic resilience.

We Need You

Late in the afternoon on the day of the planes, the rock singer Bruce Springsteen was pulling out of parking lot in Sea Bright, New Jersey, when a passing fan rolled down his car window and yelled "Bruce, we need you!" (Springsteen, 2016, 440). The tradition of citizens turning to poets in times of crisis is a long one. Paul Woodruff and Peter Meineck observe of Ancient Athens, "At the city's moment of greatest need, after the disaster of 413 in Sicily, the Athenians turned to Sophocles as one of the ten advisers empowered to see them through the crisis" (2000, 96–97). While poets are now seldom, if ever, elected to high office[4]—Springsteen has resisted more than one attempt to draft him into senate or gubernatorial campaigns (MacAskill, 2011)—their cultural influence, that which led many to regard Sophocles as the man to save Athens, remains a powerful potential political force. Springsteen's response to the fan's cry was the release, in July 2002, of *The Rising*, his twelfth studio album and first with his reunited E Street Band in eighteen years.[5] Widely hailed as the first complex popular culture response to the 2001 attacks, the album precipitated a world tour in which Springsteen and his band situated the new music among his extensive back catalog, bringing the mixture of celebration and critique of America that had marked his music since at least 1978's *Darkness on the Edge of Town*, to a mass audience. Just as his 1982 record *Nebraska* had sought to puncture the myths of the Reagan presidency—even as his 1984 release, *Born in the U.S.A.* coasted, albeit uncomfortably, the wave of "Morning in America" jingoism that marked the former actor's second term—*The Rising* sought to celebrate the actions of individuals, and, typically for Springsteen, the communities of which they were a part, even as it complicated the narratives of victimhood that had inflamed the polity in the post-planes orgy of national grief. The album was, to be sure, not without its flaws.[6] Nevertheless, the record embraced a complex worldview, alternately tragic and nearly transcendent. At its heart were several songs of mourning and loss.

Suggesting the immediacy of the artist's response—and the way in which, as William Connolly suggests, poets and prophets seek to help the polity to navigate between the past and an always-emerging future (2013, 134)[7]—Springsteen had originally intended to debut a new song that he had written in response to the attacks on September 21, 2001, at a live telethon to benefit their victims (Springsteen, 2016, 440–441). Unable to finish it in time, he performed another track—the Curtis Mayfield–infused "My City of Ruins" about the possibilities of urban and spiritual renewal—that, while written prior to the planes, later closed *The Rising*. His performance at the telethon set the tone for much of what followed on the record. Opening the show clad in black shirt and jeans, with a black guitar, and a harmonica in a rack around his neck, Springsteen declared "This is a prayer for our fallen brothers and sisters." The song embodied a vulnerability and reflectiveness in the face of loss that, as its initially mournful tone built to a gospel crescendo, called upon its audience to respond productively to it. The song was, however, imbued with a recognition that such responses were far from easy; indeed, the singer's constant demand that the city, perhaps understood as both a physical entity and as a people, rise up in the face of loss—a demand repeated some nineteen times in this performance—implored the audience to act. The third verse captured not only the song's ethos, but also its appropriateness for the moment, recounting both loss and tears, but also asking how the singer might begin again in the face of both. In asking this question—one that would reappear in another form on the song "Mary's Place" from the full album—Springsteen offered a counterpoint to the certainty and single-mindedness offered by President George W. Bush at Ground Zero exactly one week earlier. Standing on a pile of rubble at Ground Zero, literally, in some cases, upon the graves of the dead, Bush declared: "I can hear you! I can hear you! The rest of the world can hear you! And the people, and the people who knocked these buildings down will hear from us soon!" (Bush, 2001). Where Springsteen embraced the complexity of the moment and the problems it posed to American pieties, Bush embodied the grief-wrath that the Greeks called *mênis*, that which, according to Nicole Loraux, erases all considerations of justice, reciprocity, and even self-interest in favor of its own singular perspective, and is the "worst enemy of [democratic] politics" (Loraux, 1998, 98). It was a viewpoint expressed most obviously on the telethon by Tom's Petty and the Heartbreakers' "I Won't Back Down," a musical counterpart to Bush's certitude, defiance, and bellicosity.

Just as Springsteen would later reconvene the E Street Band to record *The Rising*, drawing on the best of his past to move forward into an uncertain future, he was backed at the telethon by E Street Band members Clarence Clemons, Patti Scialfa (Springsteen's wife), and Steve Van Zandt, as well as adjunct band member Suzie Tyrell, and Lisa Lowell, a longtime friend and singer partner of Scialfa and Tyrell. Most interestingly, however, Springsteen delved even further into his past, calling upon Delores Holmes, a sometime member of the short-lived Bruce Springsteen Band, with whom he had last performed on Halloween night 1971, and Holmes's daughter Layonne, whom her mother had sometimes brought—as a baby—to band rehearsals.[8] In addition to providing a gospel sound that complemented the mournful tone of Springsteen's voice and guitar, infusing this performance of the song with a hopefulness that it might have otherwise lacked, the backing singers suggested both a diversity—of age, race, and gender—and of a family and/or community of the same that would be required if the singer-prophet's call was to be heeded by the nation to which it was addressed.[9] As the September 21, 2001, performance concluded, the backing singers raised their joined hands, gesturing toward the possibilities of a better America—in this case, a more diverse but more united one—that underpinned much of Springsteen's work prior to *The Rising*, and which would emerge again on that record. *The Rising* was, nevertheless, far from a simplistic paean to American idealism. It was marked by a complexity of perspective, embodied most obviously in several songs of mourning, the most powerful of which was the singer's meditation on heroism, loss, and hope in the album's second track, "Into the Fire."

Into the Fire

"Into the Fire" was the song that Springsteen had originally intended to premiere on the September 21, 2001, telethon.[10] Told from the perspective of a loved one, the song depicts a firefighter climbing the stairs in what is, perhaps, one of the Twin Towers, with the narrator recognizing that the love that he or she has for the firefighter will be trumped by the rescue worker's commitment to duty and love for those who might be saved from the inferno. In stark contrast to President Bush's revenge-driven bellicosity in the face of loss, the narrator declares of his or her lost loved one:

> May your strength give us strength
> May your faith give us faith
> May your hope give us hope
> May your love give us love

Making up the great majority of the song, the refrain is repeated nine times, closing with four repetitions, and a final "May your love give us love."

In a 2010 essay, philosopher James Schmidt identifies three works—John Foulds's 1923 *War Requiem*, Arnold Schoenberg's *A Survivor from Warsaw*, and John Adams's 2002 *On the Transmigration of Souls*—that he labels "musical memorials," "constructed not out of stone, but rather in sound" (2010, 454). The three compositions, Schmidt argues, approach questions of memory and mourning in different ways, seeking to produce quite different effects on their audiences. Foulds's *War Requiem*, he argues, sought comfort and consolation for its listeners, offering an account in which the suffering of the victims of the Great War was transcended by the peace achieved in death; Schoenberg, to recover the suffering of the Holocaust in order to probe the workings of cultural memory; and Adams, to create a space of both memory and forgetting in order that an imagined future might come into being. Although it draws on an entirely different set of musical traditions, "Into the Fire"—and *The Rising* more broadly—might nevertheless be thought to belong to the same genre. Opening with simple instrumentation, a single voice, and dirge-like tone, "Into the Fire" quickly transitions to a more complex soundscape, multiple voices, and a tone of both grief and resolve. Nevertheless, the song's status as a musical memorial to "our fallen brothers and sisters," is not what makes it into a potential model for mourning understood as a form of democratic resilience. Rather, it is the *type* of mourning that the song embodies: a complex, generous, and ultimately democratic response to loss that is imbued with the futurity of tragic hope.

John Adams, Schmidt notes, observed that the word "transmigration" from his title means: "'the movement from one place to another' or the 'transition from one state to another'" (ibid., 478). Adams, Schmidt observed, saw his work as being concerned with the movement of souls from "living to dead" and with "the change that takes place within the souls of those that stay behind" (ibid., 478). Adams's title might well have been Springsteen's. The narrator of the album's eponymous song is—like one of the characters in "Into the Fire"—a firefighter in the Twin Towers. The protagonist is confused, both about his physical location and his liminal position between life and death. The "rising" of the song's title captures both the narrator's climb up the tower—that which also structures "Into the Fire"—and his transition from life to death. Although the narrator at one point addresses a deity, there is little sense that the movement from life to death is to be embraced: repeatedly the narrator struggles to hold on to his life in the face of his transmigration. Likewise, he describes being bound by a chain, both the literal line he carries as a firefighter and his connection to his wife, the biblically named Mary (Springsteen grew up a reluctant Catholic), and to pictures of their children. It may even be that the entire song is the call of a dying man to his wife whose arms, and those of his children—made up, he notes, of his and Mary's mixed blood—he wishes to feel around him as he lets go of his life. Three times he declares that he wants the listener, and/or Mary and his children, to hold his hands. The song is about the movement from life to death. This is not, however, presented as a sacrifice for the nation, such as when Pericles declares, in his funeral oration to the Athenians concerning their Peloponnesian War fallen, "they thought it more honorable to stand their ground and suffer death than to give in and save their lives" (Thucydides, 1972, 149), a claim that found its contemporary echo in former New York City Mayor Rudolph Giuliani's assertion that an estimated 200 firefighters in the North Tower had willingly given their lives for others despite clear evidence that, due to communication problems including a lack of working interagency radios, most likely had not heard the evacuation order.[11] For although Springsteen's account of the protagonist's death is entirely bloodless, the narrator does not give up his life willingly, he struggles to hold on to it, acutely aware of everything that he will lose: it is an action of a human, not a national scale, that of an individual connected to his family and to some, but not all, of his fellow citizens. The song thus problematizes any attempt to offer a narrative of nationalistic sacrifice about, or to make a romantic hero—one whose death is aestheticized and imbued with a commitment to unity, even as it serves to suppress rather than resolve underpinning conflicts—out of the central protagonists of both it and its companion piece, "Into the Fire."

The narrative of "Into the Fire" is somewhat less clear-cut than that of "The Rising," capturing, perhaps, the confusion of the moment in a different way from the record's title song. The first verse begins with a narrator, a possible evacuee from the towers. He hears the firefighter's voice calling before the being passed by him as he climbs upward into the building.[12] Immediately, however, this narrator, or perhaps another, declares that he or she needs his kiss. Here the narrator could be the firefighter's loved one desiring his safe return, even as he or she recognizes that his love for his fellow citizens and commitment to duty will trump his or her desire. Alternatively, it could be the original narrator who, in a time of fear, seeks what Springsteen elsewhere calls a "human touch." The next verse is, however, far more ambiguous. The narrator seems to reference the fields of Shanksville, Pennsylvania, site of the crash of Flight 93. At the time that the song was written, it was widely believed that the passengers had overpowered the terrorists and deliberately crashed the plane so as to avoid further casualties on the ground, a story that later turned out to be untrue. In this context, it is perhaps a passenger on that flight who gave his or her love to the narrator as a fellow citizen, deliberately sacrificing his or her life so that others might live. The account of heroism offered here is much more romantic than the events of the day suggest: seeking to save others might have been part of the passengers' concern, but seeking to save themselves was probably a more immediate motive. Immediately, however, the narrative of Springsteen's song switches back to the person climbing the stairs, to the more prosaic actions of the firefighter, again called upon by (one of, perhaps) the narrator(s) to stay, even as that narrator recognizes that the firefighter is going upward, literally and/or figuratively. The final verse returns, more clearly, to the towers, to a—possibly the same—firefighter and another—possibly the same—evacuee. This time the narrator receives the "human touch," but only as a prelude to the central protagonist ascending the stairs once more.

I Ain't No Hero . . .

When Springsteen turned away from the epically romantic songs of his first three albums to focus on the social, cultural, and political themes for which his work has become much better known, he talked repeatedly of a certain everyday kind of heroism that he had seen in the people he knew growing up in working-class New Jersey. To the extent that there is heroism in the songs of *The Rising*—the puzzling interlude in the second verse of "Into the Fire" notwithstanding—it is generally of the same kind: quotidian actions of family, politics, and civil society, of people doing their jobs and trying to survive in difficult conditions. It is precisely these habits, Elaine Scarry argues, and their attendant thought processes that are necessary for the polity to go on together in the face of crisis or catastrophe. The danger in such circumstances is, she suggests, that a political community might abandon its established procedures, and with it the democratic responsibility of its citizens, in favor of a narrative of total change, unique conditions, and the inapplicability of the previous way of acting and being in the world: the rejection of what many on the political right called September 10th thinking. Such a worldview, Scarry argues, channels power to the state at the expense of the citizenry, making them even less capable of self-reliance and communal action in the face of disaster. She notes, furthermore, that emergency actions embraced by the citizenry can themselves be habits imbued with the critical thought that is lost when perceived crisis or catastrophe are seen as a reason for abandoning previous ways of being. CPR, she suggests, is an example of precisely that: a preplanned response to a potential crisis that emerges from training in habits imbued with thought that can then be employed to good effect in a time of crisis (2011, 5). Stephen Flynn, Director of the Global Resilience Institute at Northeastern University, argues, furthermore, that cultivating a self-reliant citizenry is one of the most important aspects of a non-prevention-based response to crisis. Such an approach, he suggests, can empower the citizenry through education, training, and the free flow of information: values that also, it should be noted, are of particular value to democratic thought and practice (2011, 130–40). Likewise, while Daniel Innerarity points to the necessity of a "postheroic" age in the cultivation of resilience (2012, 94). For resilience as a doctrine suggests that if there are to be heroes in a democratic society, they are of the sort identified by Springsteen: people who are heroic simply by virtue of doing their jobs and living their lives in the face of harsh conditions and tragic circumstances.

In the post-planes invocation of the greatness, such figures were largely absent from the pantheon of heroes. Flynn notes, for example, that in the wake of the planes, much attention was lavished on the firefighter, the police officer, and the EMT, even as, he observes, most first responders were, and always have been, members of the public (2008, 4-5). Springsteen, too, lauds rescue workers, but in a way that, in stark contrast to the nationalist narratives of patriotic sacrifice embraced by much of the nation following the attacks, points rather to the small moments of human struggle and sacrifice. Many of the songs on the record are written from positions of loss. "Nothing Man," the album's fourth song, deals with survivor's guilt and/or post-traumatic stress: the narrator who, having acted in a way that leads his community to laud him as a hero, keeps a gun by his bedside and suggests that his real courage resides in continuing to live in the face of his torment. Here, the heroism that Springsteen depicts exposes the vacuity of the nationalistic narratives embraced by so many in the days, weeks, and years following the planes, narratives that ignored the private trauma and health costs for those who were so publicly lauded. Likewise, hidden amid the erotically charged "The Fuse" are what Springsteen called "images of life at home during wartime following the Eleventh" funerals, hurried weddings, and the furtive desperate necessity for human/sexual contact by a possible military returnee damaged by war (Springsteen, 2016, 442).[13] The heroism that Springsteen depicts is a heroism with an afterlife, one that demands continued attention in its aftermath. Whereas Pericles declared of those who died in the first year of the Peloponnesian War, "in a small moment of time, the climax of their lives, a culmination of glory, not of fear, were swept away from us" (Thucydides, 1972, 149). Springsteen captures the fear and costs of such heroism, costs that continue for the families of the dead, and those traumatized and maimed by the 2001 attacks. The fallen, he suggests, were our brothers and sisters, not "my fellow Americans." It is this small-scale, more inclusive understanding of loss that underpins the whole record.

The Promised Land

One of the key arguments offered by critics of resilience such as Brad Evans and Julian Reid is, nevertheless, that it is both a manifestation of, and a cause of satisfaction with, the status quo; a status quo which, they suggest, is decidedly neoliberal in outlook and effect.[14] That Springsteen's rise was coterminous with the resurgence of neoliberalism in the 1970s and 1980s might suggest that their critique has teeth; nevertheless, even before Springsteen turned toward more social and political themes, his work dealt with the consequences of inequality for the lumpenproletariat of beach bums, drifters, dreamers, and hustlers who populated his earliest songs. Later, Springsteen would make clear that the everyday heroism he identified is predicated upon a profound dissatisfaction with the everyday world, with the ways in which it tears apart and destroys the dreams of ordinary people, leaving them shackled and drawn in the face of a system over which they have no control. It is in this context that Springsteen has repeatedly identified his job as being to measure the gap between the American dream and American reality. What separates Springsteen from mere nihilism here is the attempt to close that gap, even as he recognizes that it can never happen. His work is imbued with hope—a word that appears repeatedly in the Springsteen canon—and with it, the recognition of disappointment and of the tragic need to go on in the face of it.

Tragedy, argues Steven Johnston, "names not just a condition with recurring outcomes but also a dense web of convictions, dispositions, imaginings, moods, and possibilities. As an article of faith, tragedy presumes a world indifferent to human schemes, projects, and exertions. Tragedy conceives life to be animated by myriad forces engendering irreconcilable conflicts, terrible necessities, paradoxical demands, unavoidable dangers, and frustrating limits" (2007, 209). Such, perhaps, might be understood as tragedy as a condition. Although he does not employ this language, Johnston also identifies what might be called tragedy as a response to that tragic condition. "Tragedy at its best," he writes, "suggests an ethos in which resolve morphs into defiant creative energy. It counsels comportment toward being marked by modesty, good cheer, wonder, and generosity rather than, say, aggression, resignation, or ressentiment" (ibid., 209). Springsteen, Johnston argues, is not a tragedian, but there has, he says, been "a tragic ethos . . . present since the beginning of [his] recordings" (ibid., 209). His work, writes Johnston, serves to offer hope to those who have been denied and/or who have lost faith in their world and/or their existence. Nevertheless, despite being among the most astute—if not *the* most astute—of the handful of political theorists writing about politics and popular music, Johnston has little to say about what hope might mean in such circumstances. Unpacking the hope that Johnston identifies as being central to Springsteen's work suggests the ways in which the mourning at the heart of *The Rising* is generous, productive, democratic, and fundamentally tragic. Although there is a common tendency to see hope and optimism as synonyms, even the briefest reflection on what each one *feels* like suggests the opposite. While optimism frequently corresponds to certainty, hope encompasses both the desire for an outcome and the expectation that it may not happen, a quite different feeling from that associated with optimism. Hope, as Nietzsche observed, "is, in truth, the greatest of evils for it lengthens the ordeal of man" (1915, 102). His view is far from idiosyncratic. W.E.B. Du Bois and Frederick Douglass offer similar formulations, captured most poetically by Du Bois's account of "a hope not hopeless but unhopeful" (2017, 97). Likewise, Eddie Glaude, Jr., identifies a "hope against hope," that is captured "by the commonsensical understanding that a radical transformation of American society was implausible" (2000, 112). It is, he says, grounded "in a regulative ideal toward which we aspire but which ultimately defies historical fulfillment" (ibid., 112). Even though Springsteen's audience is almost overwhelmingly white, black music, and soul music in particular was an important part of his musical education, and has always been central to his self-understanding as a musician and performer.[15] As such, it is perhaps unsurprising that he should have borrowed, appropriated, or imbibed the tragic blues ethos by which much of it is underpinned, that which offers a coping strategy for going on together in the face of loss. Such is the theme of the longest song on *The Rising*, the six-minute-long (often over ten minutes when played live) soul-and-blues-infused "Mary's Place."

Let It Rain

Taking its refrain from a Sam Cooke song of a similar name, "Mary's Place" appears, superficially, perhaps, to be a good-time romp about a house party—certainly this was how Kelefa Sanneh of *The New York Times* understood the song in his review of the opening night of Springsteen's *Rising* tour—but just as Cooke's similarly upbeat song hid a dark secret (the "Mary's Place" of the title was a boardinghouse used by touring black gospel musicians excluded from whites-only motels), the party in Springsteen's song is a wake, either for Mary, or perhaps, at the home of the Mary who lost her partner in "The Rising." At its heart, the song asks questions about going on in the face of loss: how to live when one is brokenhearted and—echoing the similar question in "My City of Ruins"—how to begin again. In this, both the "we" and the party itself suggest the importance of communality in the face of death. This is further suggested by the song's self-referentiality: the song describes a party at which a record is playing. The record itself is of a live recording and depicts a singer demanding a response from an audience. The song depicts communality—hence, perhaps, the phrase "in concert"—between the music and the listener, one that imagines a wider audience in a shared experience. Springsteen—who has made repeated reference to how music gave him a sense of community and saved him from alienation, both as a teenager and as an adult—suggests the way in which the music on the record unites the mourning party guests, the singer, the band, and their audience: the grief and the celebration combined in one moment. In this, that which is depicted on the record—the uniting of the audience and the recorded performance—seeks an enactment of the same between the listener, the singer, and the band. Here, the writer/performer, the band, and their audience are united in a moment of communal grief, plugged into a larger community, even as, perhaps, they listen alone on their phones or car stereos. On the record, that community was further suggested by the addition of at least seven backing singers (including the Alliance Singers, consisting of two

African American men, three African American women [two of whom were sisters], and a white woman), a five-piece horn section, and a cellist, who together comprised a multiracial coalition with at least two sets of family relationships within it. In concert, of course, that community was enacted in the relationship between the audience and the band. Throughout his career, Springsteen has almost made a fetish of his connection with his audience, observing that "when the fans looked at those faces onstage, they saw themselves, their lives, their friends looking back at them" (Springsteen, 2016, 424). That Springsteen chose to record, and tour behind, the album with his long-standing musical partners—The E Street Band—suggests that the communality he sought to create in the face of loss was far from accidental. In concert, moreover, Springsteen sought to heighten both the sense of celebration and the sense of loss, repeatedly urging his audience to new heights of enthusiasm and then, at the peak of delirium, shushing the crowd and softly crooning "I've been missin' you," four times and then, as the rest of the band takes up the refrain, howling three times in an anguished falsetto, "all night long," before turning to the lyrics of loss at the center of the song, lyrics in which the narrator reveals that he or she wears a locket with a picture of his or her lost loved one. In this juxtaposition of celebration and mourning, "Mary's Place" might be thought to serve as a microcosm of the record as a whole, and, perhaps, for Springsteen's broader engagement with the nation, that which seeks to capture its promise and its problems even as it mourns for what it lost.

May Your Strength Bring Us Strength

This juxtaposition between celebration and mourning is, then, the broader context in which the song "Into the Fire" is situated. It is, like much of *The Rising*, a song of mourning, but it also embodies an approach to loss that seeks to enact a democratic resilience in its audience. The single voice that begins the song is quickly joined by several others. Indeed, while the narrator sings two choruses alone, there are, tellingly, seven more performed in unison with others. Similarly, and somewhat unusually, perhaps, the song is made up of three verses and nine choruses: the song performing the democratic communality in grief that it seeks to enact in its audience. The central protagonist of the song is heroic, but democratically so. He is not held up as a model for his audience to emulate in the manner suggested by Pericles in his funeral oration. Rather, the singer and the chorus offer an incantation in which they request of themselves that the best qualities embodied by the song's protagonist(s) become their own. There is no sense in which the loss is held up as something to be emulated, or avenged. Rather, the narrator and chorus seek the values that will enable them to go on in the face of such loss: strength, faith, love, and, most tellingly, hope. Indeed, the demand that the audience be able to take the values embodied by the song's protagonist(s) are themselves imbued with tragic hope: the "may your" refrain contains within it the recognition that the singer and the chorus who stand in for the audience, might not be able to achieve their goal. It, nevertheless, sets out a structuring aspiration for the same. The protagonist(s) of the song is/are not idealized in the way that Pericles idealizes the dead in his oration. The narrator of the song does not dwell on the faults of the fallen, but nor does he or she suggest, in the manner of Pericles, that the manner of their deaths blotted out such faults. Rather, the voices focus on what can be taken from the dead to help the living to go on even as they do so brokenheartedly. In this, "Into the Fire" answers the question raised in "Mary's Place": *this* is how *we* get things started in the face of such loss. The community comes together and tries to take the best values of the dead in order to move forward *as* a community. Those values are, however, far from romanticized, nostalgic, or idealized, they are the quotidian values of human relationships, values that could just as easily be shared—as in, for example, Aeschylus' *The Persians*—by the enemy in a way that would allow both to move forward in a potential politics of agonistic engagement (See Stow, 2017, 103–148).

In 2011, Bruce Jackson—Springsteen's former sound engineer—was killed when a plane he was piloting crashed near Death Valley. Springsteen did not attend Jackson's memorial service in Australia, but he sent a recorded message in which he reminisced about working with Jackson, noting his excitement about working with somebody who had previously worked with Elvis Presley. Addressing Jackson's four children, Springsteen closed his remarks by noting that Jackson loved flying, and that while many people held that view that it was nice when "people passed doing what they loved most," that he did not "really buy that 'cause I know what he really would have loved most was growing older with you" (http://vimeo.com/20820728). This anti-heroic, anti-romanticized understanding of death underpinned not only *The Rising*, but much of Springsteen's work since the mid-seventies.[16] It is an approach to mourning that promises the necessary complexity of perspective and fortitude for the polity to move forward in the face of death.

Norah Jones After Auschwitz

Theodor Adorno's famous comment about the supposed impossibility of poetry after Auschwitz, notes James Schmidt, is frequently mistranslated and misunderstood. What Adorno actually wrote, he notes, is that it would be barbaric to go on writing poetry that had ignored what had happened there; to be, perhaps, a poet who just stands back and lets it all be (2010, 472). In 2003, *The Rising* was nominated for "Album of the Year" at the Grammy Awards. It did not win. Rather the award went to Norah Jones for her record *Come Away with Me*, a retro-mélange of easy-listening jazz-tinged escapism—itself, perhaps, suggested by the name of title track—that closed with a cover of the Ned Jones and Hoagy Carmichael song "The Nearness of You." That this song was itself written for the—pre-Auschwitz—movie *Romance in the Dark* (1938) suggests sensibility of Jones's record. Indeed, the movie critic Leonard Maltin's review of *Romance in the Dark* might serve as a suitable assessment of 2003's "Album of the Year." The movie, wrote Maltin, offered a "stylish treatment of trite material." Although the National Academy of Recording Arts and Sciences, the body that awards the Grammies, has a long history of strange and/or conservative choices,[17] the 2003 decision might well be seen as a manifestation of romanticized nostalgia that infected the polity in the years following the planes.[18] Not only is such poetry "barbaric" by Adorno's standards—ignoring as it does the catastrophic events of its age—the polity's commitment to it might be thought to indicate its own barbarism in the face of that crisis and/or catastrophe. It is this barbarism that the mourning embodied by *The Rising*, and by *Into the Fire* in particular, seeks to address: drawing from loss the values that will permit the polity to move forward in the face of it. It is a generous, capacious form of mourning entirely mourning devoid of *mênis*. The American experience in the years since the 2001 attacks suggests that only such a complex response to loss imbued with tragic hope will permit the polity to continue in the face of this, and future, catastrophes.

Please Don't Let Me Be Misunderstood

The question—"have I been understood?"—with which Nietzsche concludes the intellectual autobiography, *Ecce Homo*, completed just a few weeks before his final breakdown, is, perhaps, the key question of the tragic condition. In 2002, for example, the Gettysburg Address—chosen as a eulogy for the New York City dead—was misconstrued as a simple paean to American greatness (Stow, 2007). This is, no doubt, a central issue faced by those— such as Bonnie Honig—who would address the problems posed by the "paradox of politics": that which suggests "you need good men to make good law, but you need good law to make good men" (2009, xvi). Citizens who do not wish to be educated will, it seems, take what they want from what they hear (Dobson, 2014). The transfiguring moment is a difficult one to achieve, depending as it does upon a fragile confluence of factors among which are the cultural traditions of the polity, the circumstances in which the poet works, the nature of the poetry, and the receptiveness of the audience. In "Empty Sky," one of the last songs written for *The Rising*, the grieving narrator declares:

> I want a kiss from your lips
> I want an eye for an eye

Performing in his native New Jersey in 2003, Springsteen took a moment after playing the song to address his audience directly:

> There's one thing that always bothers me a little bit, occasionally when I play that song, I hear some applause for, for a line, uh . . . "I want an eye for an eye" . . . and uh, as a songwriter, you always write to be understood . . . and I wrote that phrase as an expression of the . . . character's anger and, and confusion and grief and it was never written to be a . . . call for blind revenge or bloodlust (cheers) . . . so, I just thought given, given the times we live in, you can't be too clear about these kinds of things these days and uh . . . and I realize that it could've been a well-meaning few or perhaps borderline . . . some borderline psychotics out there who may have misunderstood . . . but uh . . . living in a time when there's real lives on the line and there's enough destructive posing going on out there as it is, I wanted to make sure that that line was clearly understood so, thanks for listening. (audience recording)

Such, perhaps, is the problem of tragic mourning in the contemporary polity, and yet, Springsteen himself offers a response to the difficulties that theorists and tragic poets face, one that is itself imbued with the *ethos* of hope that he seeks to generate in his audience.

Interviewed by Dave Hepworth of the BBC in 1985, Springsteen was asked about the attempted appropriation, by Ronald Reagan, of the artist's 1984 hit "Born in the U.S.A.," a complex indictment of America's treatment of its Vietnam veterans. Noting that there was "the song had an enormous amount of pride in it, pride in being American," Springsteen went on to observe that many listeners—such as Reagan's speechwriters and conservative pundit George Will—nevertheless missed what he called "the shameful part" ("Glory Days" Youtube video, 1/2/2015, https://www.youtube.com/watch?v=E68VKQ4S8Ro&feature=youtu.be). The song juxtaposes the titular, bombastic chorus with a tale of isolation and alienation of the military veteran. Calling the chorus, the "gospel" part of the song, and the verses "the blues," Springsteen enacted, in a musical moment, the tragic worldview of the Greek Dionysia. Faced with the recognition of the inevitable misunderstanding of his work, Springsteen offered a perspective imbued with hope that might itself serve as a model for those who would seek to inculcate a democratically productive tragic mourning in the American polity.

> What you do if somebody doesn't understand your song is keeping singing your song. And you'll sing it again down the road and somebody who didn't understand it before, they're gonna understand it then. (Ibid.)

We Learned More from a Three-Minute Record

Springsteen captures the value of music as democratic pedagogy, echoing Plato's similar remarks about the power of music to shape the polity. It is a lesson that he perhaps learned from the soul music that shaped his youth. As the late Dick Gregory once observed about the power of music on the radio over that of political rhetoric: "You'd hear Aretha three or four times an hour. You'd only hear [Martin Luther] King once" (Vincent, 2013, 201–204). It is a perspective with which, however, both Adorno and Allan Bloom could agree, arguing as they do, that this is part of its stultifying effect. Here, however, it has been argued, that Springsteen's work shows the power of music to embrace, and to seek to enact in its audience, a complex worldview. In this case, the worldview of political theory, and with it, that of a capacious and democratically productive form of mourning: one that seeks to draw from the post-crisis polity the very values that served it so well in the period before the loss, that which Scarry, among others, identify as being at the heart of the doctrine of resilience. As the singer observed in his autobiography: "The professionalism, the showmanship, the hours of hard work, are all very important, but I always believed that is was this dialogue [with his fans], this language, that was at the heart of our resiliency with our audience. *The Rising* was a renewal of that conversation and the ideas that forged our band" (2016, 443). Thus, in the face of crisis, Springsteen drew on the best values from his past to move forward into an uncertain future; that which *The Rising*, his response to that crisis, sought to engender in, and to demand from, its democratic audience.

NOTES

1. "Into The Fire" and "Empty Sky" by Bruce Springsteen. Copyright © 2002 Bruce Springsteen (Global Music Rights). Reprinted by permission. International copyright secured. All rights reserved.

2. As facile as Bloom's reading of popular music is, he is, perhaps, to be congratulated for the observation that "Mick Jagger tarting it up on the stage is all that we brought from the voyage to the underworld" (ibid., 79). For an account of the potential political consequences of the close connections between sex and grief, see Simon Stow, *"Portraits 9/11/01: The New York Times* and the Pornography of Grief" in eds. Jeanne Follansbee Quinn and Ann Keniston, *Literature After 9/11* (New York: Routledge, 2008), especially 231–233.

3. In terms of works by political scientists/political theorists, Nancy Love offers an excellent account of the ways in which music might be thought to engage in, and offer resources for, political theorizing; while Charles Hersch's work on jazz is also a notable exception. See, Nancy S. Love, *Musical Democracy* (Albany, NY: State University Press of New York, 2006); and Charles Hersch, *Subversive Sounds: The Birth of Jazz in New Orleans* (Chicago: Chicago University Press, 2009). Likewise, Steven Johnston's work offers an extensive and insightful engagement with the work of Bruce Springsteen, including *The Rising*. See, Steven Johnston, *The Truth About Patriotism* (Durham, NC: Duke University Press, 2007); and Steven Johnston, *American Dionysia. Violence, Tragedy, and Democratic Politics* (New York: Cambridge University Press, 2015). It should, of course, also be noted that there is a long tradition of combining mourning and music in African American political thought and praxis—see, for example, W.E.B. Du Bois's work on the sorrow songs, and the extensive engagement with the blues and jazz by, for example, James Baldwin, Amari Baraka, and Angela Davis—that is seldom considered by those who would dismiss the musical as a resource for, or as a way of, theorizing, about the political. Insofar as it re-creates this problem, this essay is concerned to show that other

musical forms and traditions beyond the blues and jazz might serve as similar resources. It seeks to borrow—or, perhaps, to appropriate—aspects of this black tradition and apply them in an alternative context. At the same time, it also seeks to borrow the methods of some of those who employ literature for critical political reflection. As Love notes, there are many of us for whom music, and popular music, have been just as important, if not more so, as books in helping us come to see, and think about, the world differently; indeed, this is a persistent trope in Bruce Springsteen's interviews and stage raps. See W.E.B. Du Bois, *The Souls of Black Folk* (Seattle, WA: Amazon Classics, 2017); James Baldwin, *The Cross of Redemption: The Uncollected Writings* (New York: Random House, 2010); LeRoi Jones (Amiri Baraka), *Blues People. Negro Music in White America* (New York: Harper Perennial, 2009); and Angela Y. Davis, *Black Legacies and Black Feminism: Gertrude 'Ma' Rainey, Bessie Smith, and Billie Holiday* (New York: Vintage Books, 1999). Springsteen's own relationship with African American music and politics is somewhat vexed. See, Simon Stow, "American Skin: Bruce Springsteen, Danielle Allen, and the Politics of Interracial Friendship," *American Political Thought*, 6, Spring 2017, 294–316.

4. Though, by Greek standards at least, former Senator Al Franken and the late Sonny Bono, a Congressman from California, might be considered as such.

5. Springsteen had disbanded the group on October 18, 1989.

6. The song "Worlds Apart," which sought to tell a love story of an American soldier and an Afghan woman by blending Appalachian fiddles with Islamic choral songs, was a particular clunker whose model of occupier-native interactions drawn from an entirely different type of war, was the least of its problems. While, in concert, the potentially poignant "Waiting on a Sunny Day" morphed into a cloying sing-a-long—including off-key caterwauling by a child plucked from the audience—that obscured the loss at the heart of its narrative.

7. "A world of becoming," writes William Connolly, capturing both the contingency of human existence and the resources available for responding to it, "is replete with multiple forces that sometimes intersect to throw something new into the world. So strategic events . . . periodically arrive when it is pertinent to dwell in an exploratory way in the gap between the disturbance of an emerging situation and those prior investments of habit, passion, faith, identity, progress, and political priority you bring to it. In the Greek tradition, those who specialized in similar activities were called seers; in religions of the Book they are often called mystics or prophets." William Connolly, *The Fragility of Things: Self-Organizing Processes, Neoliberal Fantasies, and Democratic Activism* (Durham, NC: Duke University Press, 2013), 134.

8. I am enormously grateful to Layonne Holmes for generously giving of her time to discuss both this performance and her mother's broader history with Bruce Springsteen.

9. "[P]rophecy," observes George Shulman, "is the office of singers who ask and answer the question, What is the meaning of our suffering? They help people endure catastrophe and exile by poetry that endows a painful history with meaning. From Jeremiah's lamentations to the sorrow songs and spirituals of slaves and their heirs, the office of prophecy is to voice traumatic loss and hopes of redemption." George Shulman, *American Prophecy: Race and Redemption in American Political Thought* (Minneapolis, MN: University of Minnesota Press, 2008), Kindle Location 226.

10. Layonne Holmes reports that Springsteen and the backing singers only rehearsed one song for the telethon, suggesting that the unfinished "Into the Fire" was never really seriously considered for the show. (Private correspondence with the author.)

11. "Rather than giving us a story of men, uniformed men fleeing while civilians were left behind," Giuliani observed. "Which would have been devastating to the morale of this country . . . they gave us an example of very, very brave men and women in uniform who stand their ground to protect civilians. . . . Instead of that we got a story of heroism and we got a story of pride and we got a story of support that helped get us through." Jim Dwyer and Kevin Flynn, *102 Minutes. The Untold Story of the Fight to Survive in the Twin Towers* (New York: Times Books, 2005), 251–252.

12. The pronouns here are male. Although three female rescue workers were killed at Ground Zero on the day of the planes, none were firefighters. It is not clear that there were female firefighters in either of the Towers. Eileen Reynolds, "On 9/11 Women were Heroes

Too," *nyu.edu*, September 9, 2016. https://www.nyu.edu/about/news-publications/news/2016/september/fdny-captain-brenda-berkman-on-9-11.html. Accessed 09/10/2017.

13. That the central character of the song is a military returnee is suggested by the repeated refrain "Shut out the lights," an echo of an earlier *Born in the U.S.A.* era returnee song, "Shut Out the Light."

14. Evans and Reid draw for their definition of the latter on the work of David Harvey. Neoliberalism is, he writes, a "theory of political economic practices proposing that human well-being can best be advanced by the maximization of entrepreneurial freedoms within an institutional framework characterized by private property rights, individual liberty, unencumbered markets, and free trade." Evans and Reid, *Resilient Life*, location 1689–1692. See David Harvey, "Neoliberalism as Creative Destruction," *Annals of the American Academy of Political and Social Science*, 610, 2007: 22–44.

15. In 1971, the Student Prince—the Jersey Shore club where Springsteen would later meet his saxophonist Clarence Clemons—billed him as "That Sensational Soul Man Bruce Springsteen." Dave Marsh, *Bruce Springsteen on Tour: 1968–2005* (New York: Bloomsbury, 2006), 51.

16. In 2007, for example, on his album *Magic*, largely a response to the post-planes wars in Afghanistan and Iraq, the song "Gypsy Biker" cut through the nationalistic narratives surrounding the return of the American dead with a tale of a family and a community destroyed by their loss.

17. Bob Dylan did not win his first Grammy until 1980, and then for "Best Rock Vocal," while Milli Vanilli, a duo later shown to have lip-synched to somebody else's vocals, won best new artist in 1990. Springsteen has never won album of the year.

18. Indeed, the winner of the 2002 award in the same category was the soundtrack—made up of pre-Auschwitz folk tunes—to the Coen brothers' movie *Oh Brother Where Art Thou?* itself an allusion to Preston Sturges's 1942 movie *Sullivan's Travels*, a film that lampooned efforts to create socially relevant artworks.

WORKS CITED

Adorno, Theodor (2002). "On Popular Music [With the assistance of George Simpson]," in Theodor Adorno, *Essays on Music* ed. Richard Leppert, translated by Susan H. Gillespie. Berkley, CA: University of California Press.

Baldwin, James (2010). *The Cross of Redemption: The Uncollected Writings*. New York: Random House.

Baraka, Amiri (2009) *Blues People. Negro Music in White America.* New York: Harper Perennial.

Bush, George W. (2001). "Bullhorn Address to Ground Zero Workers," *American Rhetoric.com*, http://www.americanrhetoric.com/speeches/gwbush911groundzerobullhorn.htm. Accessed 9/10/2017.

Butler, Judith (2010). *Frames of War. When is Life Grievable?* New York: Verso.

———. (2004). *Precarious Life. The Powers of Mourning and Violence.* New York: Verso.

Connolly, William (2013). *The Fragility of Things: Self-Organizing Processes, Neoliberal Fantasies, and Democratic Activism.* Durham, NC: Duke University Press.

Davis, Angela Y. (1999). *Black Legacies and Black Feminism: Gertrude 'Ma' Rainey, Bessie Smith, and Billie Holiday.*New York: Vintage Books.

Dobson, Andrew (2014). *Listening to Democracy. Recognition, Representation, Reconciliation.* New York: Oxford University Press.

Du Bois, W.E.B. (2017). *The Souls of Black Folk.* Seattle, WA: Amazon Classics.

Dwyer, Jim, and Kevin Flynn (2005). *102 Minutes. The Untold Story of the Fight to Survive in the Twin Towers.* New York: Times Books.

Evans, Brad, and Julian Reid (2014). *Resilient Life: The Art of Living Dangerously.* New York: Polity.

Flynn, Stephen P. (2008). "America the Resilient. Defying Terrorism and Mitigating Natural Disasters," *Foreign Affairs*, March/ April, 2; 4–5.

————. (2011). "Recalibrating Homeland Security. Mobilizing American Society to Prepare for Disaster," *Foreign Affairs*, May/June, 130–140.

Glaude, Jr., Eddie (2000). *Exodus! Religion, Race, and Nation in Early Nineteenth-Century Black America.* Chicago: Chicago University Press.

Harvey, David (2010). "Neoliberalism as Creative Destruction," *Annals of the American Academy of Political and Social Science*, 610.

Hersch, Charles, (2009). *Subversive Sounds: The Birth of Jazz in New Orleans.* Chicago: Chicago University Press.

Honig, Bonnie (2009). *Emergency Politics: Paradox, Law, Democracy* (Princeton: Princeton University Press.

————. (2013). *Antigone, Interrupted.* New York: Cambridge University Press.

Innerarity, Daniel (2012). *The Future and Its Enemies: In Defense of Political Hope*, translated by Sandra Kingery. Palo Alto, CA: Stanford University Press.

Johnston, Steven (2007). *The Truth About Patriotism.* Durham, NC: Duke University Press.

————. (2015). *American Dionysia. Violence, Tragedy, and Democratic Politics.* New York: Cambridge University Press.

Loraux, Nicole (1998). *Mothers in Mourning*, translated by Corinne Pache. Ithaca, NY: Cornell University Press.

Love, Nancy (2006). *Musical Democracy.* Albany, NY: State University Press of New York.

MacAskill, Ewan (2011). "Bruce Springsteen gets poll backing to run for New Jersey Governor," *The Guardian*, July 21. http://www.theguardian.com/music/2011/jul/21/bruce-springsteen-poll-governor. Accessed 9/3/2017.

Marsh, David (2006). *Bruce Springsteen on Tour: 1968–2005.* New York: Bloomsbury.

McIvor, David W. (2016). *Mourning in America. Race and the Politics of Loss.* Ithaca, NY: Cornell University Press.

Nietzsche, Friedrich (1915). *Human All Too Human: A Book for Free Spirits* translated by Alexander Harvey. Chicago: Charles H. Kerr & Company.

Ober, Josiah (2005). *Athenian Legacies: Essays on the Politics of Going on Together.* Princeton, NJ: Princeton University Press.

Plato (1984). "Menexenus," in *The Dialogues of Plato Volume One*, translated by R. E. Allen. New Haven: Yale University Press.

————. (1992). *The Republic*, translated by Allan Bloom. New York: Basic Books

————. (2005). *The Laws*, translated by Trevor J. Saunders. New York: Penguin Books.

Scarry, Elaine (2011). *Thinking in an Emergency.* New York: W.W. Norton & Company.

Schmidt, James (2010). "Cenotaphs in Sound: Catastrophe, Memory, and Musical Memorials," *Proceedings of the European Society for Aesthetics*, 2, 454–478.

Shulman, George (2008). *American Prophecy: Race and Redemption in American Political Thought.* Minneapolis, MN: University of Minnesota Press.

Sophocles (2005). *Oedipus Tyrannus* translated by Paul Woodruff and Peter Meineck. Indianapolis, IN: Hackett Publishing.

Springsteen, Bruce (2016). *Born to Run.* New York: Simon and Schuster.

Stow, Simon (2008). "*Portraits 9/11/01: The New York Times* and the Pornography of Grief" in eds. Jeanne Follansbee Quinn and Ann Keniston, *Literature After 9/11* (New York: Routledge, 2008), especially 231–233.

————. (2008). "Do You Know What it Means, To Miss New Orleans? George W. Bush, the Jazz Funeral, and the Politics of Memory," *Theory & Event*, 11:1.

————. (2017). "American Skin: Bruce Springsteen, Danielle Allen, and the Politics of Interracial Friendship," *American Political Thought*, 6, Spring, 294–316.

————. (2017). *American Mourning. Tragedy, Democracy, Resilience.* New York: Cambridge University Press.

Thucydides (1972). *History of the Peloponnesian War* translated by Rex Warner. London: Penguin Books.

Vincent, Rickey (2013). *Party Music: The Inside Story of the Black Panthers' Band and How Black Power Transformed Soul Music.* Chicago: Chicago Review Press.

Chapter Ten

Speaking Silence

Holding and the Democratic Arts of Mourning

Joel Alden Schlosser

In this essay I want to explore the democratic arts of mourning by identifying a tension between the developmental promise of "working through" and the enduring difficulty of holding the unspeakable. To do so, I turn to a genre of texts and performance that have often been interpreted as a cynosure for these arts of mourning: ancient Greek tragedy. Mourning does consistently appear as a theme in ancient Greek tragedy; it also aptly describes important elements of the work of tragedy in the context of ancient democratic Athens and the Greek *polis* more generally. Yet I note the absence of Euripides' dramas from these discussions and the concomitant occlusion of a powerful Euripidean theme. Writing significantly later than Aeschylus and perhaps more aware of the political fragility of his native Athens than Sophocles, Euripides' tragedies frequently dramatize not just losses needing the working through of mourning but instead catastrophic endgames beyond such work. Euripides faces his varied audiences with death itself: the end of language, of meaning, of relationships—and thus the end of the very possibility of mourning. He holds spectators and readers alike in a space and time without intelligibility, speaking silence that feels unintelligible.

Drawing on Euripides' *Trojan Women*, in this essay I suggest that one function of Greek tragedy lies in holding its audience in a space of unintelligible suffering. Moreover, this space exists in tension with the speech and intelligibility characteristic of the working through promised by mourning. The work of mourning privileges the intelligible over the unintelligible, the articulate over the inchoate. Euripides' *Trojan Women*, on my reading, illuminates and interrogates this hierarchy by insisting on what resists working through. Greek tragedy thus dramatizes what Jonathan Lear calls crises of intelligibility, moments when the world simply ends. Like the Crow elders Lear chronicles, the Trojan Women face the end of their existence. While the democratic arts of mourning emphasize the difficulty of coming to terms with loss and achieving the ambivalence of the depressive position, I suggest that the democratic arts of holding emerge from how Euripides educes the precariousness of our own structures of intelligibility and thus the limits of language for making sense of the human condition. *Trojan Women* confronts the democratic arts of mourning with the conditions of their possibility—and shows the destruction of these conditions.

Translating the challenge of *Trojan Women* to the psychoanalytic framework of mourning, I suggest that Greek tragedy introduces a tension between two moments involved in dealing with loss. Greek tragedy does not simply facilitate and model mourning; it does more than help its audience to come to terms with loss. Instead, Greek tragedy creates a holding environment with a distinct affective structure: the plays hold their audience in a space without comfort or explanation and in a time without the assurance of progress or development; the plays, in other words, force their audiences to experience the unintelligibility that permeates human experience. Their poetry evokes silence and their ambiguous forms refuse teleologies of health and development. Greek tragedy simply holds you tight.

Recasting Greek tragedy as holding and not just mourning changes the quality and implications of the political work it effects. On my argument, the forms of Greek tragedy can create structures of affect with their own politics. Metaphors, rhythms, and networks of relationships within tragedy suggest ways of speaking silence, of holding what is unintelligible; these forms also figure alternative modes of response available to the tragedy's audience. Silence is an end but can also be a beginning. While Greek tragedy does not always enact the work of mourning that many political theorists desire, it nonetheless holds the promise of transformation toward more resilient democratic subjects.

CRISES OF INTELLIGIBILITY

Euripides' *Trojan Women* depicts not merely a lamentable tragedy but the destruction of an entire world. The play begins with striking loneliness: a dark stage, the collapsed form of a woman in its center, and the silhouettes of two figures far behind her mass.[1] The stage will grow only emptier as women cross it, destined for doom. This emptying in the dramatic action combines with pervasive images of emptiness and the desiccation of language itself to make a stage that begins as barren nothingness lose absolutely everything. Troy, as Adrian Poole writes, "once full, rich, substantial, informed by presence . . . [is] now empty, hollow, drained, inhabited by absence."[2] As the

Chorus sings: "Troy is no more."[3] Images of evacuation, dispersal, demolition, and obliteration—of a city, a people, ideas, ideals, and values—dominate the play.[4] These images of emptiness climax in Hecuba's closing apostrophe to Hector's shield, which ends the series of final embraces and partings that take place under the shadow of a departure from Troy itself. To call this a farewell would be "grotesquely polite" for such a degree of "horrific actuality."[5] *Trojan Women* portrays the end of a world, a *Götterdammerung*, a "mind-shattering holocaust."[6]

With its devastating portrayal of the end of an entire way of life, *Trojan Women* anticipates what Jonathan Lear calls a crisis of intelligibility. In an essay that returns to his account of the Crow tribe and its "radical hope," Lear introduces this term to suggest that such hopes are not always possible. In situations of radical cultural collapse, the loss exceeds psychological understanding—it rather resides in the very being of those who lived within that culture. What they called "life" is no longer possible. They cannot exist. As Lear puts it:

> This issue is not primarily a psychological one; it is ontological. Because the culture has been devastated, I can no longer render myself intelligible (to myself or to others) in its terms. This form of unintelligibility does not imply that the past is incomprehensible to me as a matter of contemplation: it means that the concepts with which one had hitherto rendered oneself and others intelligible are no longer available to do that work.[7]

Trojan Women, on my reading, depicts this ontological condition in all of its annihilating horror. The play bears witness to the collapse of the weight-bearing pillars of the Trojan Women's structures of intelligibility: the justice of the gods proves empty; a mother's hope for the next generation is crushed; and the principles of fairness are trampled. Mourning cannot begin without any language of loss; the very possibility of these concepts has been vanquished. Examining the moments of hopelessness within the play shows how structures of intelligibility disappear and the helpless paralysis this engenders.[8]

No god can save these Trojans. The play opens with the gods aloof from the prostrate and torn body before them. Poseidon's entry from the "salty, Aegean depths," and his lyrical praise for Troy's lost glory detaches gods from mortals below. While Hecuba writhes and wails, Poseidon and Athena change their minds, deciding the Trojans have had their suffering and the Greeks shall face misery on the journey home. Yet this confab cannot ameliorate Hecuba's present condition; her body in the center of the stage insists on this. Leaving the Trojans derelict below, the gods seem to rob their plight of any sense. The gods disappear and Hecuba remains alone. Hecuba, once the queen of Troy, once the wife of Priam, King of Troy, once the mother to Hector, the great hero of Troy, is now nothing—without identity, a woman without a husband or a son, without a city, without posterity. Her clothes are in shreds, her skin scored, and her hair ripped out. Everything that defined Hecuba has been killed, raped, or burned, and the movement of *Trojan Women* only continues what was begun before it. As J. Peter Euben writes of Hecuba: "there is no relief for her suffering, nor words or song to provide solace, no ritual lamentation to ease her pain. Her agonies are beyond re-counting, beyond words, beyond sounds."[9] As the Chorus puts it with gut-wrenching understatement in Euripides' *Hecuba*: "Heaven's constraint / is hard."[10]

Hecuba cannot endure; she cannot wait for justice to return to the Trojans. What will be left of them, after all? Hecuba collapses. When the chorus tries to lift her, she refuses help, saying: "Let me lie here, fallen." "Fainting fits," she says, "what I suffer and have suffered and have still to suffer."[11] "The gods are poor allies."[12] Trying to console herself with a song of Troy's glories past, Hecuba lurches into painful lament. Hair cropped, flesh and clothing tattered, Hecuba weeps again for her father-in-law Priam, king of the Trojans; her husband, Hector, the greatest of the Trojan warriors; her daughter, Cassandra, the mystic herald of an unforgiving future; and her granddaughter Polyxena, a hope now murdered. This mother of kings will be a servant at the door, baking bread and sleeping on the ground.[13] Crying out, Hecuba wails: "I cast myself down, annihilated with tears; Call no man happy before he is dead."[14] Whatever cosmic justice may exist, the immediate pain of the present precludes any hope of working through toward understanding.[15]

As Hecuba and the Trojan Women continue to lament, Talthybius, the Greek messenger, enters to herald the awaiting enslavement of the Trojan Women. Hecuba and Cassandra's fate—to become slaves to Odysseus and to Agamemnon—terrifies and outrages them. Only Cassandra can grasp the meaning this might hold in the future, but her comfort is cold. She sings what her audience knows from the myth on which Euripides draws—that with her marriage to Agamemnon arises her chance for revenge, to kill the Achaean king and bring glory to the Trojans who died for their country. Yet this knowledge cannot diminish the pain onstage. Cassandra enters possessed in a frenzied wedding ritual to announce the great meaning of the unfolding events, but her crazed song goes unheard. Cassandra assumes that the meaning of Troy will outlive Troy, but what meaning? Troy is no longer. Its language, people, customs, and towers are silent, corpsed, forgotten, dust in the wind. What could it mean for a Greek to write Troy's history? Cassandra's wedding will prove more disastrous than Menelaus's to Helen,[16] but neither her dance nor her argument that follows can salve the Trojan Women's wounds. They are all destined to die. Hecuba collapses to the ground.[17]

The Trojan Women's enslavement by the Greek leaders figures a second collapsing element of their structures of intelligibility. Cosmic justice cannot provide a language of mourning; neither can the hopes lost with the destruction of the next generation. As the chorus tries to understand the death of Troy with a new song, Andromache enters. Pulled in a cart, her doomed child at her breast, Andromache offers a "new tower of pain" to Hecuba and the Women of Troy.[18] Her vision of the world is even more desolate than her surroundings. It would be better to be dead, she says, slaughtered like Polyxena at Priam's tomb, than to endure this suffering, empty of all meaning with Hector in the ground.[19] Hope was and is a delusion.[20] Any language that Andromache might have used to understand her misery is now vacant. For Andromache, everything is "hysterically irrelevant."[21] The hope of the heroic ethic cannot exist when heroes and poets are only corpses.[22]

This "maker of men," Andromache cannot mourn the next generation when she herself has an identity no longer.[23] Without Troy and the Trojans, she does not exist; the entirety of her world has been destroyed. The cart bringing Andromache onstage emphasizes her powerlessness; powerless without Troy to give her a place, she laments the loss of her husband Hector and the horrific fate ahead of her. Like Hecuba, she longs only for death:

A: Greek lords lead us away. . . H: Oh woe. . .
A: Lament like me . . . H: Ai-ai . . .
. . for grief like this . . . H: Oh Zeus!
A: . . .and misery.
H: Oh, children . . .
A: . . . as we once were . . .[24]

Andromache cannot leave the "once were," the thrall of loss that stands beyond repair. She cannot forget attachments because these form the substance of her self. The world destroyed was the world formed by Andromache's connections to her husband, now threatened by her enslavement by a new Greek husband; to her son who waits unknowingly in his mother's arms for death; to her identity as wife, mother, and daughter. In such a world, Andromache cannot continue to live. As if to reemphasize her brutal fall, Talthybius enters bearing the grimmest news. The Greeks have ordered the Trojan Women's final remaining hope—Astynax—thrown from the walls of Troy. The remaining hope just mentioned by Hecuba is extinguished. Andromache can endure no longer. She exclaims: "Aiai. Beyond measure is this grief!"[25] And echoing the order to throw Astynax from Troy's towers:

Cover my wretched body
Throw me into the ships.
A fine marriage I approach,
Having lost my very own child.[26]

The gods' love has vanished from Troy.[27] The "great, good place" that the Trojan Women describe in their first choral ode exists only in memory, hope,

or myth; the images within this fanciful chorus only make the barren emptiness of the play more intolerable.[28] The so-called "Telamon Ode" which
follows the dark climax of Andromache's plea for death with its decorative
epithets and highly stylized descriptions show all these stories, myths, songs,
and words as absolutely irrelevant. Poole writes: "The more beauty, hope and
idealism invested in the golden world of imagination, memory or myth, the
more brutal the subsequent bankruptcy."[29] Again and again unfathomable
suffering confronts Hecuba and the Trojan Women; again and again their
structures of intelligibility, the means of beginning the work of mourning, are
utterly vanquished.

The penultimate scene of *Trojan Women* destroys a third way of working
through this unbearable suffering—the juridical. The stilted *agon* that follows between Hecuba and Helen parodies the possibility of any judgment
about the future. You cannot hope for justice, cosmic or human. Just as the
gods' love reveals itself as capricious—as it both founded and destroyed
Troy—so too the human love which animates the world is without logic or
justice. The language rises to "the cold heights of Athenian judicial rhetoric,"[30] but the *agon*'s lack of conclusion as well as the scene's bloodless
treatment of this devastating human conflict fail to grant Hecuba any relief.
Despite her earnest engagement in the argument, Hecuba's repeated invocations of Aeschylean poetic justice go unheard; in this Euripidean world divine *dikē* is just another name for whim, as Helen's and Hecuba's arguments
reemphasize.[31] Again, spectators know the outcome of these arguments, but
this prescience is little help to Hecuba. Hope resides in her words, but not for
her. After the debate, Menelaus promises the proper end, but his humor
undermines any hope for just deserts: Helen is not heavy; the burden weighs
on Hecuba's shoulders.[32]

In the closing scenes of the play, the stage clears, leaving only Hecuba.
The towers of Troy fall; with them disappear any remaining ways of making
sense of these losses. The rituals of mourning are perverted to the point of
impossibility: no words will do; only the music of the women's lament
remains.[33] Talthybius has announced that the women must depart, and their
lamentation reaches new peaks. Having buried their last living hope, Hecuba
and the Trojan Women bear ritualistic farewell to the ruins of Troy. Darkness
surrounds them. The tragic lament reaches its climax, but so does the destruction around it. Everything is lost—they cannot see for the dust, they are
nameless, cityless, placeless, coerced by spear and flame.[34] Troy no longer
exists. Singing and wailing and striking the ground against and with the
rumble of collapsing towers, the hiss of smoke and flame, and the deep groan
of the unsettled, quaking earth—do these women rise with dignity to face
their fate or are their screams muffled with the coarse hands of their conquerors? Hecuba's final exhortation might seem hopeful: "Go to the slavish day

of life," she announces. But the play's last word confound such a reading: Achaeans. It bespeaks the final grim reality: Troy is no more. [35]

FORMS OF HOLDING

This reading of *Trojan Women* suggests an ambivalence within the structure of mourning. When a life has become impossible, the conditions of mourning no longer obtain. A crisis of intelligibility marks a limit condition of mourning because it involves the destruction of the very tools that make mourning possible: without a community, there is no shared language; without a shared language, there is nothing with which to work through trauma and loss. Tragedy doesn't only serve mourning. Indeed, tragedy may confront us with the very limits of mourning.

The tragedy of the Trojan Women comes to us, however, in the form of Euripides' play; the play itself does different work from what takes place within its form. That is, the structure of the play contains the catastrophe it depicts. This form, I want to suggest, *holds* what it depicts for the audience. In this sense it figures a holding environment for experiencing the limits of mourning, a time and a space that may lie adjacent to mourning but which does not yet (nor necessarily will it) offer the conditions on which the work of mourning depends. Examining three of these forms—of rhythms, networks, and song—limns how the holding environment accomplishes its work through structures of meaning that aren't fully intelligible or that operate at a different register from discursive intelligibility

Rhythms

Trojan Women holds its crisis of intelligibility in part through the rhythms of Hecuba's rise and fall. When Poseidon announces Troy's destruction he points the audience's gaze to Hecuba—"this miserable woman *here*"[36] —and thus challenges her to fill the vacancy left by the departing gods. Still unaware of the sorrows fated to Troy, Hecuba bears up beneath them. Poseidon describes the series of recognitions that will constitute Hecuba's burden: the death of Polyxena, the rape of Cassandra, the fall from prosperity later embodied by Astynax.[37] Shuddering from the weight of all of this, Hecuba rises. Having begun the play in miserable silence, her first words are of upward motion: "Rise up, miserable one," she tells herself.[38] Her rising and falling create a dramatic rhythm in the play, a rhythm that counters the relentless downbeat of destruction staccatoed by screams and the crashes of falling bodies.[39] Hecuba rises, refusing resignation, by asking how she might find words with which to begin: "Why keep silent? Why not? And why mourn?"[40] This question remains throughout the play. Each character challenges Hecuba's strength to rise, her courage to stand up against her suffering. But for as long as Hecuba remains onstage, she continues to rise.

Hecuba's rising creates a counterpoint to the crashing towers of Troy around her, the horrific downbeat of her grandson, Astynax, being hurled to his death. This contrapuntal rhythm echoes a great tragic trope of reversal. Even while the movement within the play tends entirely toward destruction, then, its form intimates a greater logic of rise and fall, how great become small and small great, in Herodotus' words.[41] The rhythms of Hecuba thus partake in a larger form of cosmic significance. This may offer no balm for the broken Trojan Women, but it holds their suffering in a space of possibility—and possible meaning—that the audience (but not Hecuba) can apprehend.

Networks

Within this rhythm of rise and fall, networks of images also hold the catastrophic action on stage. Cassandra initiates a series of images of that connect *Trojan Women* with the other plays in its tetralogy as well as broader structures of meaning beyond Euripides' plays. The stories of the *Alexandros* and the *Palamedes* offer clues to the importance of fire and light in the plays.[42] The *Alexandros* recounts the return of Paris to Troy after he has abducted Helen. But the background of the play, announced by the speaker of the prologue, is more important: Hecuba has had an ominous dream that she has given birth not to a child, but to a flaming torch, portending the burning and destruction of Troy. To avert this portent, Priam sends the child to the country to be exposed, but a herder pities the infant and brings him up as Paris. Disconsolate about the loss of their baby, Hecuba and Priam establish an annual funeral games in his honor. When he has reached adulthood, Paris competes in these games and vanquishes Hector and the other sons of Priam. Because of his arrogance to the other herders and because he is a slave, Paris is brought before Priam and denounced by Deiphobos, another son of Priam. Although Paris is acquitted, Hecuba and Deiphobos plot to murder him, and he is only saved when the herder who raised him confesses, and Paris is recognized as Alexander, the same Alexander destined to bring Helen and doom to Troy.

This description from *Alexandros* highlights how a dream of an ominous torch begins the trilogy which *Trojan Women* completes. Cassandra's entrance, maniacally waving a torch to celebrate her perverse marriage to Agamemnon, reemphasizes the imagery. Hecuba takes the torch from her, saying: "this torch you burn here is of painful misery, far from my great hopes."[43] Yet Cassandra's presence and words are ambiguous. In her madness, she prophesies revenge on Agamemnon and glory to Troy. Her torch recollects the beginning of Aeschylus' *Agamemnon*, and thus Agamemnon's death, Cassandra's revenge. Cassandra expands on the gods' promise at the play's beginning—the sufferings of Troy become a greater story. Cassandra's marriage will destroy those the Trojan Women hate most;[44] to Cassandra, her troubles and Troy's will seem "golden next to those fated for Odysseus and the Greeks."[45] The gods' absence will not prevent justice—Cassandra will fulfill their promise as justice incarnate. Do not weep, she tells her mother: "I shall come to the dead bearing victory."[46] With this speech, Euripides places Cassandra and the Trojan Women in a greater web of poetic and mythic meaning, holding their catastrophe while insisting on its essential unintelligibility.

Song

As Andromache leaves, Hecuba seems poised to cast herself down too, to similarly resign herself to fate, despite her words. Yet Hecuba rises in song. Beating her breast, she incites the chorus of bereaved and mourning women to sing a new story about their origins and the hope lost with Astynax.[47] Again Euripides offers stories and song as the only appropriate—perhaps the only *possible*—response to suffering. Cassandra's prophecy was not enough, nor were Hecuba's reasoned arguments for Andromache. The Telamon Ode resounds with images now smoldering in grimy ruins, depicting the gods' lost love for Troy: the city once blessed by Apollo now blazing in fire, a bird crying for its young, dewy bathing places and exercise courses destroyed. The gods' love has vanished from Troy.[48] Yet the song of the Trojan Women raises these laments in haunting beauty.

In the final scenes of the play the surroundings and ultimate doom of Hecuba and the Trojan Women leave unresolved whether or not they have found any words fitting to their suffering, yet they fill this godless and emptying space with songs of heartbreaking lamentation. After Helen leaves and the chorus begins to wail, Talthybius enters again. Announcing that one ship remains for Hecuba, Talthybius also bears the corpse of Astynax. Talthybius returns it for burial, allowing the Trojan Women and Hecuba a final sacred ritual. Talthybius has washed and cleaned the corpse's wounds, and now begins to help to dig its grave. Unasked and unneeded, Talthybius initiates the rites, perverted as they are by dust and blood, by the ignominious death and the ragged shroud. His generous action reveals itself momentarily and allows the Trojan women and Hecuba to perform the burial, a moment made more significant by its initiator—the envoy of the conquerors, a Greek and a man, the bringer of the worst of news.[49]

A moment of resilient clarity and beauty, the funeral of Astynax commemorates not just Hector's infant son, but the entire fallen Trojan civilization. Singing to her grandson's body, Hecuba interweaves the stories of the final three generations of Troy with poignant details of their quotidian lives:

Astynax's dark curls, his tiny hands and lips, his childish promises, the mark of sweat on Hector's shield. With her song Hecuba intones the story of the wonderful particulars that make a human life and human lives together even as these details disappear from all memory. At the brink of destruction, she has little; that which she has, she gives. For Hecuba, however, it comes too late.[50]

HOLDING THE UNINTELLIGIBLE

The working tension between mourning and holding that constitutes my reading of *Trojan Women* has implications for what Bonnie Honig has recently termed the "democratic need for public things." Honig posits that democracies need public things "over which to argue, around which to gather." Winnicott's concept of the "holding environment" provides a lens for Honig to reread Lear's *Radical Hope* and Lars von Trier's *Melancholia* to offer "new narrations of democratic maturation": seeing the need for public things not as infantile wishes but rather as the means of fostering resilience; calling attention to public things as sites for collaboration and empowerment much needed in an era of privatization and state withdrawal. The collaborative effort of securing a holding environment creates an "in between," neither fixated by loss nor past it.

For Honig, holding makes mourning possible, yet she does not dwell on what might make holding impossible. She describes von Trier's film as a "mourning song" and also writes that one of its characters, the boy Leo, "works through his fears" in his fantasy.[51] Yet Winnicott emphasizes in his writings on holding that such an environment must be secure prior to any development of object relations. When a baby is handled and held "satisfactorily" then it can be presented with an object that it can learn to use.[52] Satisfactory holding is "the basic ration" that Winnicott identifies as preliminary to maturation; its absence appears when people suffer "going to pieces."[53] In other words, holding environments differ from the work of mourning precisely because of their non-teleological character. Mourning works through whereas holding environments cradle, holding unintelligible material without the orientation toward integration that characterizes mourning. Holding is the condition of the possibility of mourning, but *Trojan Women* shows how holding and mourning are not synonymous.

Separating the moment of holding from the development account of maturity pursued by working through highlights an important difference between the situation of the Trojan Women and the representation of these women by Euripides. Von Trier's film depicts the imminent end of the world; the characters have nothing (or are soon to lose everything) but the audience has something—namely von Trier's film. The play itself creates a holding environment which holds the destruction of all structures of intelligibility depicted within it. Within the play a crisis of intelligibility unfolds; the audience, however, can witness this precisely because of the holding environment that allows them to understand what unfolds on stage. The Trojan Women themselves have no holding environment; their chorus can offer only perverted lamentation as the stage fills with corpses. Meaning, signs, and song cannot contend against the shattering experience of witnessing their world come to an end. "Troy is no more," they intone: there is no life without Troy and no survival either.

This dimension has broader significance within the political context of *Trojan Women*.[54] 415 BCE in Athens was a time of ostensible peace yet fraught with violence and war. The great leader of Athens, Pericles, had died barely over a decade earlier. Athens had just averted killing all of the inhabitants of Mytilene in revenge for their rebellion. And only a few months before the production of *Trojan Women*, the Athenians had not shown as much forbearance: upon meeting resistance to their demands of submission on the island of Melos, the Athenians had besieged them and then murdered all of the men while enslaving the women and children. The Athenians had been acting like the Greeks in Euripides' play. They were not simply subjecting others to their rule but annihilating all opposition to their hegemony.

Like the Trojan Women, the Melians had no holding environment; Euripides created something else. Rather than depicting the victims of the Athenians' conquests he mined the mythic past for resonant stories. The forms into which Euripides put the sufferings of the Trojan Women accomplished something different from what Honig suggests the Greek Chorus of tribal elders did: They allowed the Athenian audience to confront their own violence and fear; they held them in the painful and radically uncomfortable space of their own complicity. These forms afforded the experience of unintelligible suffering.

Yet what made this holding possible was the public thing of Greek tragedy. Greek Tragedy created a holding environment for experiencing and dramatizing the not yet integrated material of Athenian political life—exclusion, violence, and genocide. By confronting the audience with the crisis of intelligibility in *Trojan Women*, the play included a warning about the very conditions of mourning, the possibility of intelligibility and its collapse. Doing so, it confronted the audience with its own responsibility both for the forms of tragic holding as well as deeds analogous to those enacted on stage. When political theorists identify the form of holding with the work of mourning, however, they elide the difference between holding what cannot be made intelligible and the structures of intelligibility—the forms of rhythm, network, and song in the *Trojan Women*—that make this holding possible in the first place.

COLLECTIVIZED SUFFERING

Despite their differences, the work of holding and the work of mourning both require collective investment. Behind the work of holding stands a democratic culture sustaining Greek tragedy; the play itself, while ascribed to Euripides, would not have existed if not for the support of the *polis*. Securing the holding environment, as Honig puts it, requires collective action. In the political space of the Athenian polis, Euripides dramatized the unintelligible suffering of the Trojan Women; the play puts these sufferings into forms that afford different responses for the audience experiencing the drama, then and now. As I have suggested, within the drama, these forms fail to provide means of mourning. The utter domination of the Trojan Women means Hecuba will be dragged to the Greek ships, the fires of Troy will extinguish, and nobody will hear their songs. Yet Euripides presents this unintelligible suffering through forms of rhythm, networked metaphor, and song that hold the unintelligible for his audience while paradoxically also making it intelligible. In such a way *Trojan Women* speaks silence.

As Caroline Levine has suggested, form possesses different affordances.[55] Form allows for and facilitates different uses—it is portable, can hold different kinds of content, and can move between the cultural and political domains. Rhythm, networks, and song in Euripides' play prefigure sites of agency for responding to senseless suffering. In the context of democratic Athens, these forms resonate with spaces of woman's agency and gesture toward possibilities of truly popular power. More generally, forms *hold* suffering that cannot be worked through; they tarry with the unintelligible by ordering, patterning, or shaping it. These different forms hold different constraints but also contain the possibility of traveling in various ways. They afford working through but not any particular working through—nor only that.

Most relevant for considering the possibilities of the democratic arts of mourning, forms of holding entail a politics of form. As Victoria Wohl has argued in the context of Euripides, these politics are above all a politics of affect.[56] The tragic form structures the affective experience of its audience through the forms of rhythm, metaphor, and song, continuing how these forms functioned in the context of late fifth century BCE Athens. Borrowing a description from Raymond Williams's *Marxism and Literature*, Wohl highlights how the experience of Greek tragedy holds a "structure of feeling." Williams defines structures of feeling as "social experiences in solution . . . [experiences] at the very edge of semantic availability."[57] Wohl shows how Euripides' plays put into play "the barely articulated thoughts, feelings, experiences and beliefs that will precipitate out in real political action."[58] In other words, "structures of feeling" introduce affective spaces that function as holding environments, allowing for ambivalent emotional responses to the political situation. *Trojan Women* positions the audience between the desolation of the Trojan Women and the Athenians' own complicity in similar violent exterminations. The audience must choose sympathy against itself or refuse the piteous spectacle before them. Either way, the play "offers no hope of reconciliation." To borrow from Wohl's reading of Euripides' *Orestes*, *Trojan Women* "leads to an emotional and cognitive impasse that reproduces the tensions of Athens" in 415.[59]

Trojan Women also raises questions about the meaning of such suffering. The boundless suffering on display arouses fear and pity while also implicating spectators in the suffering depicted. While Elaine Scarry argues that beauty draws us toward the good,[60] Wohl reads these plays as calling into question the pity tragedy supposedly produces. You might pity the women of Troy but this brings no justice. Athenians experiencing this play in 415 may well have also witnessed their own sadistic investments in injustice: Political expedience trumps justice, as shown by Menelaus's lack of action on behalf of Hecuba; at the same time, Talthybius's pity demonstrates his implication. As Wohl puts it in her description of Euripides' *Hecuba*, the play's "ragged ending disrupts the beautiful balance of *dikê*."[61] Aesthetic contemplation is not enough and the affective responses of fear and pity elicited by the plays only put the burden of responsibility and action on the audience (including you).

Wohl's reading of the politics of form in Euripides emphasizes the affective experience and its disorienting complicity. While it may be tempting to ascribe a "pedagogy" to the plays, the forms hold deep ambivalence: the rise and fall of Hecuba entwines hope with despair; Cassandra's torch heralds the burning of Troy as well as her involvement in sanguine vengeance upon Agamemnon's return. The chorus of Trojan Women does not create a holding environment so much as heighten the affective dissonance experienced by the spectators: beautiful invocations of Troy jar against its smoldering ruins; the Trojan Women's song has baleful overtones given the macabre fate unfolding around them.[62] The violence and domination of Athenian collective life is articulated while remaining unintegrated, showing the fragmented state of the collective.

Fragmenting the fragile polis may seem destructive, but this takes place within the broader holding environment of the institution of Greek tragedy. Greek tragedy holds and handles the infant polis, reassuring it of its wholeness even as it intimates its imperfections. Many interpretations of Greek tragedy have emphasized how tragic forms afford a political confrontation with finitude. Employing psychoanalytic terms, however, Fred Alford argues that Greek tragedy's fundamental contribution comes from its throwing into deepest doubt what is good and what is bad.[63] Rather than holding these basic categories apart in what Melanie Klein calls the "paranoid-schizoid position," Greek tragedy reveals their deep imbrication—and the unspeakable suffering that comes from maintaining their rigidity. Yet by collectivizing suffering, in Peter Euben's phrase, Greek tragedy not only shows that human beings suffer their characters but creates a collective experience of this suffering for its audience as well. Alford calls this a "humane antihumanism" because Greek tragedy holds human beings in the antihuman world, a world—the actual world—where human projects run aground, where forces beyond the human militate against human fantasies of control and agency, where human desires are wrecked against the ephemerality of life. Poets like Euripides can humanize death with ritual and glimpses of reciprocity, yet its fundamental otherness persists. The *catharsis* of Greek tragedy clarifies the human condition, one of subjection to impossible desire and painful loss of connections to others.[64] It also holds the fragile collective psyche in this space, cradling even while intoning a shattering song.

THE DEMOCRATIC WORK OF HOLDING

Holding an unintelligible content in a manner that refuses resolution, tragic forms undertake the paradoxical work of "speaking silence." *Trojan Women* speaks and sings the suffering of its women yet it remains silent about the meaning and the intelligibility of this suffering. This silence appears in the disturbing openness of the play's stark fiction, the way it holds but also does not lead to any place of reconciliation.

The democratic work of holding opens two moments that are often collapsed into the democratic work of mourning: holding tarries with silence, non-meaning, and unintelligibility; holding precedes the developmental process of working through. Holding can encompass the lack of concepts, language, and structures of meaning that the Trojan Women experience—the desolation characteristic of Lear's "crisis of intelligibility" also suffered by the Crow people. *Trojan Women* shows how the holding environment can contain a "potential space" that also resists its potential with unintegrated content pulling against its actualization. Within the play itself, *Trojan Women* confronts us with a space and time utterly lacking in potential. Hecuba has nowhere to go from there. Seen within the broader context of democratic Athens, *Trojan Women* indicates the persistent unintelligibility haunting every project of democratic mourning.

By creating and sustaining the institution of Greek tragedy, the Athenian people made this work of holding democratic. The texts of Euripides were performed as part of a political institution sponsored by leading citizens and each performance was preceded by dramatic displays of the democratic *polis*: the ten most important generals of Athens sacrificed piglets and poured out wine to the gods; men were recognized for their service; bars of silver were paraded across the stage to represent what enemies were now compelled to pay Athens; and war orphans whose fathers had died were honored. Such a spectacle of self-affirmation may well have created the conditions for Athenian citizens to confront the stark fictions displayed in plays like *Trojan Women*, performing a kind of democratic narcissism that the subsequent tragedies cut down to size. At a deeper level, the democratic creative effort embodied by Greek tragedy insisted on the continuing existence of the Athenians over and against the ontological crises they then experienced in the dramas. The festival as a whole sustained an existential ambivalence characteristic of holding.

By distinguishing the moment of holding from the larger project of working through, I do not mean to deny the place of mourning in democratic culture. Yet separating these two kinds of democratic practices calls attention to the conditions of democratic development and their obstacles. *Trojan Women* not only depicts the absence of such conditions but dramatizes this experience for the Athenians. This holding environment may well incite mourning simply through the poignancy of its display of bereavement. Yet the practice of holding does not always happen satisfactorily, as Winnicott observes. Insisting on these holding environments as "potential spaces" denies the reality indicated by crises of intelligibility, a reality upon which the Trojan Women insist. Some suffering cannot simply be metabolized; some experiences refuse integration. [65]

Bearing the unintelligible, the democratic work of holding nonetheless furnishes forms that can travel beyond the shattering experience of Greek tragedy. The forms of *Trojan Women* afford potential uses not available within the play; indeed they reveal how solidarity, hope, and connection might come under conditions of unspeakable loss. As Levine writes, forms offer some place of agency—the audience can hold the unintelligible in various ways, some with forms that empower and some with forms that constrain. The politics of form in Greek tragedy suggest a democratic means of doing this. The forms of tragedy construct structures of feeling that bring audiences to confront the contingency and fragility of their being while doing so in forms the audience itself has collectively created and sustained. These forms facilitate affective dissonance within a broader institution of collective affirmation.

The burial of Astynax at the end of *Trojan Women* offers one powerful image of how a form can speak the unspeakable while affording alternate uses. This intimates a form of connection made impossible within the play yet possible beyond it: the tenderness of Talthybius as he washes his enemy's corpse; how Hecuba transforms Hector's shield from an instrument of war to a tiny coffin; the lugubrious lament for Astynax's nameless future and annihilated past. This shattering scene anticipates Alford's remark: "If cradling is the first act of holding, funeral rites are the last."[66] Cradling and burial take place in tragic simultaneity.

Astynax's burial does not redeem the suffering of the Trojan Women nor can its perverted rituals count as structures of intelligibility. Astynax has no proper burial, no grave, no mourners; he will be forgotten more quickly than his tiny body disintegrates. Yet the form of this desperate collective effort limns a dimension of holding perhaps most striking in Greek tragedy: the poignant need and possibility for connection, a need always shadowed by terrible exposure to distrust, pain, fear, and death. Under the conditions of its own impossibility, this burial becomes somehow possible through the cooperation of Talthybius, Hecuba, and the Trojan Women. Bearing the body of the lost future of Troy, these disparate people assemble to hold the unintelligible, speaking silence through their tragic forms.[67]

NOTES

1. See Eric Havelock, "Watching the Trojan Women."
2. Poole, "Total Disaster," p. 265.
3. 1292. All citations refer to the Oxford text (Diggle, 1981); all translations of *Trojan Women* are my own unless otherwise noted. For other plays, I have relied on the Oxford Greek Tragedy in New Translation edited by Peter Burian and Alan Shapiro.
4. This idea of emptiness, anticipating the beautiful way Charles Taylor talks about "fullness," appears with incisive poignancy in Euripides' *Children of Herakles* when Makaria laments that it is "Better , far better, to die / than live so empty a life" (543–4).
5. Poole, p. 262.
6. Poole, p. 259.
7. Lear, p. 55.
8. *Trojan Women* stands alone as one of the most popular plays by Euripides, but its brutal interrogation of the heroic conventions of its time associates it with other plays of distressed women, in particular *Alcestis, Medea, Hippolytus*, and *Andromache*. All of these plays depict the failure of the conventions by which the women lived; they show lives ruined by the shattering of structures of intelligibility.
9. Euben, "War Words and Words of Silence," p. 17.
10. *Hecuba*, 1395–6.
11. 466–7.
12. 468.
13. 491.
14. 509–510.
15. Euripides' *Iphigenia at Aulis* provides a fascinating counterpoint on the question of hope in Euripides. There each character appears complicit in the scheme to sacrifice Iphigenia; no one is free from moral tarnish. The "happy ending" of the play is risible; not a single character seems deserving of even a promise of happiness.
16. 358.
17. By showing how hopes for future revenge and cosmic justice fail to provide a language for mourning the present catastrophe, *Trojan Women* thus rejects Lear's concept of radical hope. When structures of intelligibility collapse entirely, nothing can suffice.
18. 607.
19. 634 and following.
20. I should add: an *attractive* delusion. It's too easy for readers to distance themselves from the pain of having hopes crushed—of even having to describe what were once givens as "hopes." Euripides' *Phoenician Women* gives a sense of how hope has a sweetness made even more bitter by its disappointment. Polyneikes says to Jokasta: "Hope's lovely to look at, but

lives in the future." Jokasta answers: "And doesn't time say plainly hopes are vain?" (*Phoenician Women*, 436–7).

21. Poole, p. 275.

22. The portrait of Andromache in *Trojan Women* also appears in Euripides' *Andromache*. There Andromache voices very similar sentiments: "Why should I value life? What should I think of?/ Shall I look to the past or to the present? / The last eye of my life is this one child / and those who have power are going to kill him" (*Andromache*, 409–412).

23. Elizabeth Markovits' *Future Freedoms* helped me to begin to see the stakes of intergenerational freedom—or unfreedom—in Euripides' plays. Euripides focalizes these questions again and again through *women*, whose identities depended so much on future generations. This in turn opened women to what Markovits calls "intergenerational vulnerability": women like the Trojan Women are vulnerable by virtue of subsequent generations' vulnerability. As Phaidra puts it in Euripides' *Hippolytus*: "All women, all of us, / are violated by destiny" (*Hippolytus*, 1001–2).

24. 573–588.

25. 723.

26. 777.

27. 858.

28. Poole, p. 268.

29. Poole, p. 268.

30. Clay, p. 79.

31. Helen argues that the goddess should be chastised, not her (948). Hecuba argues that Aphrodite is a euphemism for the madness of love (989). Both could be true: the gods possess us with divine madness that is also our own—assigning blame becomes impossible.

32. 1050.

33. Euripides glories in this scenes of rituals gone awry—how the very practices created to work through suffering fail or become perverted. *Herakles* offers one example, as Christian Wolff writes: "supplication doesn't work, sacrifice goes very wrong, Bakkhic celebration turns murderous" ("Introduction," p. 21). Consider also (of course) Euripides' *Bacchae*.

34. 1310–20.

35. When Hecuba is dragged—or walks, depending on a dramaturg's intuition—to the Greek ships, she completes the sense of inevitability hanging in the air since the play's beginning. Like *Trojan Women*, Euripides' *Electra* works this theme of necessity, fulfilling what Castor at the end of the play calls "necessity's binding demand" (1349).

36. 36.

37. 39–44.

38. 98.

39. This contrapuntal rhythm also highlights a similar rhythm within the tragic genre itself—that of *reversal*. How much of the effect of tragedy depends on an audience's expecting reversal, even after the action ends? How much does Euripides rely on this? I cannot be sure.

40. 110.

41. Herodotus, *Histories*, 1.5.

42. I rely on Diskin Clay's rendition of the *Alexandros* and *Palamedes* in this section, as treated in the introduction to his translation of *Trojan Women*.

43. 344–345.

44. 403–4.

45. 433–4.

46. 460.

47. 855.

48. 858.

49. Yet such work, as Adrastos says in Euripides' *Suppliants*, is a "terrible burden and a shame" (730). The heroic ethic is not merely besmirched but completely undone by the perversion of the ritual, the participation of a Greek and a commoner like Talthybius in the burial rites of the heroic Hector's son.

50. This sense of knowledge or succor that comes to late is a classic trope of Greek tragedy. Among Euripides' plays, *Rhesos* exemplifies this with brilliant epistemological melodrama. If

any redemption comes, it can come only through a god (which it does in tragicomic plays such as *Alcestis, Ion, Iphigenia at Tauris*, and *Helen*).

51. Honig, *Public Things: Democracy in Disrepair*, p. 79 and p. 76.

52. D. W. Winnicott, *Playing and Reality*, p. 150.

53. D. W. Winnicott, *The Family and Individual Development*, p. 26.

54. Here I draw on the helpful historical introduction by Peter Burian in the Oxford translation of *Trojan Women*.

55. Levine, *Form: Whole, Rhythm, Hierarchy, Network*.

56. In this and the following paragraph, I draw on my review of Wohl's book.

57. Raymond Williams, *Marxism and Literature*, pp. 133–4.

58. Wohl, *Euripides and the Politics of Form*, p. 138.

59. Wohl, *Euripides and the Politics of Form*, p. 127. This quotation describes Euripides' *Orestes*; I mean to suggest it is equally applicable to *Trojan Women*.

60. Scarry, *On Beauty and Being Just*.

61. Wohl, *Euripides and the Politics of Form*, p. 60.

62. In one production I saw of *Trojan Women*, Athena and Poseidon dressed as ringleaders in a perverted, zombie-like circus. The Trojan Women's songs were delivered in this style, as hurdy-gurdy tunes both achingly beautiful for their poetry and horrifying for their melodic anticipation of the Women's destiny.

63. Alford, *The Psychoanalytic Theory of Greek Tragedy*, p. 7.

64. These last few sentences may sound awfully Lacanian and I intend this resonance. Alford's move to relationality in his reading of Greek tragedy suffers, I think, from a kind of mania for closure—the same kind of which he accuses Melanie Klein in her reading of the *Oresteia*.

65. Here I would affirm but also resist David McIvor's reading of the tragic poet who "provides a holding environment in which those anxieties can be engaged and worked through" (McIvor, *Mourning in America*, p. 122). Alford's reading of these cultural rituals is more consonant with mine: "It is Winnicott's insight that far more mature, symbolically mediated interactions also constitute a form of holding, for example, an insightful, well-timed analytic interpretation that recognizes the analysand's deepest anxieties and responds to them. . . . Similarly, a cultural ritual may be a form of holding, containing the members' anxieties by translating them into a shared language and so allowing shared defenses to be constructed against them" (Alford, *The Psychoanalytic Theory of Greek Tragedy*, p. 106). Much depends on what counts as "shared language" here. On my argument, the language of Greek tragedy can speak the unspeakable precisely because of its ability to hold the unintelligible through forms of metaphor, movement, and song.

66. Alford, *The Psychoanalytic Theory of Greek Tragedy*, p. 106.

67. Here I am inspired by Alford's general comments on mourning and holding: "What do we owe death? . . . Psychoanalysts have generally interpreted this question in terms of mourning. . . . In viewing the relation between life and death exclusively in terms of mourning, psychoanalysis is once again in danger of reducing a fundamental issue to a less crucial one. Mourning is important. But the relation between life and death concerns not simply how to come to terms with loss. For the tragic poets, coming to terms with death involves more than coping with the subjective experience of loss, the pain of which they hardly ignore. They care more, however, about how one acts responsibly to acknowledge and preserve, albeit in a new form, a real relationship when one of the partners is gone. In the poets' concern with death there is a devotion to the objective reality of relationships missing in most contemporary psychoanalytic accounts." Alford, *The Psychoanalytic Theory of Greek Tragedy*, pp. 90–1.

WORKS CITED

Alford, C. Fred. *The Psychoanalytic Theory of Greek Tragedy*. New Haven: Yale University Press, 1992.

Burian, Peter and Alan Shapiro, eds. *The Complete Euripides*. Five Volumes. Greek Tragedy in New Translations. Oxford: Oxford University Press, 2009–2011.

Clay, Diskin. "Introduction," in *Euripides: Trojan Women*. Newbury, MA: Focus Publishing, 2000.

Diggle, James. *Euripides: Fabulae*. Three Volumes. Oxford Classical Text. Oxford: Oxford University Press, 1984.

Euben, J. Peter. "War Words and Words of Silence." Unpublished Manuscript. 2008.

Havelock, Eric. "Watching the Trojan Women," in *Euripides: A Collection of Critical Essays*, ed. E. Segal. Englewood Cliffs, N.J.: Prentice Hall, 1968.

Honig, Bonnie. *Public Things: Democracy in Disrepair*. New York: Fordham University Press, 2017.

Lear, Jonathan. *Wisdom Won From Illness*. Cambridge, MA: Harvard University Press, 2017.

Levine, Caroline. *Form: Whole, Rhythm, Hierarchy, Network*. Princeton: Princeton University Press, 2016.

Markovits, Elizabeth. *Future Freedoms: Intergenerational Justice, Democratic Theory, and Ancient Greek Tragedy and Comedy*. London: Routledge, 2017.

McIvor, David W. *Mourning in America: Race and the Politics of Loss*. Ithaca: Cornell University Press, 2016.

Poole, Adrian. "Total Disaster," *Arion*. New Series Vol. 3 (1976): 257–87.

Scarry, Elaine. *On Beauty and Being Just*. Princeton: Princeton University Press, 1999.

Schlosser, Joel Alden. Review of Victoria Wohl, "Euripides and the Politics of Form" (Princeton, 2015). *Polis: The Journal for Ancient Greek Political Thought*. Vol. 33, no. 1 (2016): 213–217.

Williams, Raymond. *Marxism and Literature*. Oxford: Oxford University Press, 1978.

Winnicott, D. W. *The Family and Individual Development*. London: Routledge, 2006.

Winnicott, D. W. *Playing and Reality*. London: Routledge, 2005.

Wohl, Victoria. *Euripides and the Politics of Form*. Princeton: Princeton University Press, 2015.

Wolf, Christian. "Introduction" to "Euripides' Herakles," in *The Complete Euripides*. Volume IV. Burian, Peter and Alan Shapiro, eds. Greek Tragedy in New Translations. Oxford: Oxford University Press, 2009.

Chapter Eleven

Rituals of Re-Entry

An Interview with Bonnie Honig

David W. McIvor and Alexander Keller Hirsch

David W. McIvor: We'd like to start by asking you about a shift in your writings on the theme of mourning. For instance in *Democracy and the Foreigner* (2001)—a text that feels as timely as ever in an age of immigrant scapegoating—you argued that the *Book of Ruth* shows how "there are institutional and cultural conditions for the proper work of mourning" and that this work of mourning was linked to forms of "meaningful and empowered agency" in the always transitional politics of migration. Yet in *Antigone, Interrupted* (2013) you asserted that a "politics of lamentation" risks sliding "into something more like a lamentation of politics." Do you see this as a shift, or are these two approaches to a politics of mourning compatible on some level?

Bonnie Honig: You are right that, in *Democracy and the Foreigner,* I talk about mourning, even mentioning briefly some comparisons between the Biblical *Book of Ruth* and Sophocles' *Antigone.* The *focus* there, however, is less on lamentation, as such, than on transitions, specifically migrant and immigrant transitions and the material and cultural circumstances that shape them. I argue that receiving countries have certain investments in the symbolic politics of citizenship, which may allow for multicultural diversity or may insist on assimilation as a sign of loyal membership and gratitude to the receiving country. The larger symbolic politics of citizenship, then, sets the terms for new immigrant arrivals.

Where the assumption of that larger symbolic politics is—as in the case of U.S. exceptionalism—that the home left behind is inferior to the one newly claimed by immigrants, mourning the loss is treated as a kind of ingratitude to the host. Like all forbidden mourning, however, such as when people are told to "get over it," or when they are told, as Antigone was, that the person they mourn was a traitor, here too the prohibition creates obstacles to the very thing demanded. The demand is that people move on or let go. But the rituals and practices by way of which people find their way through loss are here disallowed, themselves cast as betrayals. What can we learn from this? One lesson might be about the incontrovertibility of the need to mourn loss. I grant that. But the other lesson has to do with the symbolic politics of immigration and how we lean on it to solve certain problems of citizenship for democracies that are not taking up the challenge of solving those problems for themselves. We can loosen the demands on immigrants and others if we confront the issues of citizenship that we project onto them.

Historically, democracies have turned to newcomers to verify the objectivity of law, re-perform their choiceworthiness, or embrace the demands of citizenship with the enthusiasm of the new convert, thus—the hope is—inspiring the more jaded residents of longstanding. When at the Democratic Party convention of 2016, Khizr Khan, an immigrant to the United States from Pakistan whose son died fighting as a member of the American military in Iraq, pulled a copy of the U.S. constitution from his pocket and asked the Republican nominee if he had even read it, Khan was performing the timeless scene of new U.S. citizenship for all to see. That said, his doing so was underwritten by his family's ultimate sacrifice, the loss of their son, whom they clearly still mourn. I cannot say much about it, it is too intrusive, but that small constitution in the father's breast pocket is fundamentally connected to the terrible wound of his loss of his son. If this synecdoche, or substitution, of constitution for son, of a genetic future for a political future, was not discussed by us all at the time, it was surely partly because—again—the loss was too much and because it was assumed, even by Khan himself, to be remediated by the worthiness of the cause for which the son paid with his short life.

DWM: As I take it, then, on your reading there is both an insistence and a refusal of mourning placed on new arrivals—an insistence because the former way of life (including one's language) should be given up, but a refusal because any attempt to draw this out in a way we might name as "mourning" is stigmatized. Mourning is both forced and forbidden. But with the Khan example it seems that mourning is permitted to re-enter. However, this is only because of the substitution of, in your words, the "constitution for son," of "genetic future for a political future." The Khans' mourning is legible not as immigrants from Pakistan but as a so-called "Gold Star Family." Even the language of sacrifice—the book Khan wrote after the convention is entitled *An American Family: A Memoir of Hope and Sacrifice*—seems to betray an elevation that is all too common to public mourning discourse. Isn't this an instance of mortalist humanism, to borrow one of your terms, or at least of mortalist patriotism?

BH: It is sort of similar but it may belong to a somewhat different political economy. When I wrote about "mortalist humanism" in *Antigone, Interrupted*, I was thinking of how, in some recent theoretical work, political clash is avoided by way of a turn toward shared ethical vulnerability, which has its powers but also its risks. It tends to seek out the common ground of vulnerability and not the power of shared action in concert, I worried; or, perhaps better, it treats the former as a condition of the latter. Once mourning or mortality is an ethical ground, however, we may find that the divisions of political conflict are themselves lamented as offenses against a universal humanism. But such conflicts are inescapable and those who want to work for greater equality need to be ready for them. Thus, the point was to consider the *risks* of the politics of mourning, which, as I said in the book, all too often slides into a mourning of politics. This is what I call the "Antigone effect," not because it happened to Sophocles' heroine, but because it happens, often, to scholars who tarry with her.

DWM: I want to talk about Antigone but first there is a theme in your work of persistent skepticism toward what you refer to, in *Emergency Politics*, as a "harbor" that could protect us from the uncertainties of political life. So the risks of mortalist humanism are not only a form of sentimentalism that reifies gender roles but, perhaps more importantly, a kind of complacency about ongoing dynamics of political contestation and action. In this respect humanism betrays a desire for secure narratives of belonging that it can never really obtain. Nationalism and universalism also betray this desire, albeit in slightly different ways. If this seems correct, then I have two questions. First, are there exemplars for what you might see as a more agonistic style of public mourning? And second, does agonism completely overcome the desire for harbor?

BH: I don't know that I would use the word "complacency." But you are right that my view is that humanism might itself be a longing for secure narratives of belonging. However—or therefore!—it also may serve as a common basis on which to stage or empower action or resistance, against inhuman forces, such as the technologization of work, alienation, or indifference to the suffering of others. My critique of mortalist humanism, in particular, involves the claim that even though it is powerful as an agent of mobilization in some contexts, as in the case of the Madres of Argentina, it is not a natural but a performed identity, and it boomerangs, often, against those who deploy it. Thus, the Madres dressed as traditional grandmothers and performed the commonality of mortality in a specifically ethnically and gendered way that brought into being what they claimed as their ground: the identity of the authentic—not urban, but traditional—mourning mother. The power of the Madres was to bring down a government. But, as I argue in *Antigone, Interrupted*, drawing on Diana Taylor's work, the Madres' gendered performance also left them vulnerable to a gendered re-privatization: once the Generals were toppled, the women were told to go home.

In short, mortalist humanism communalizes the human by privileging mortality over other traits, but it may *dis*empower rather than empower us for political action. And also it may forgo other commonalities that are more politically productive. Thus, mortalist humanism finds in our shared condition of mortality—the fact of finitude—the ethical basis for a possible politics. But why privilege mortality as our common "human" trait, and not, as Hannah Arendt does, natality? Might it be because the mother is at the scene of birth, but not normally at the scene of death? There's a thought! Arendt, in any case, manages also to avoid the problem of the birth-mother by focusing on the *second* birth, that of political action, which gives expression to the ontological (but not the biological) fact of natality. This is *not* to agree with her and others that mother-avoidance (if that is what it is) is a good idea. Merely to say that if such avoidance is one's aim, we need not give up on natality after all.

In any case, all of this this is just one way of circling around the key theoretical question: why privilege one trait—like mortality—over others we share? Why privilege mourning and not, say, singing? Why finitude and not beginning? And how might our conception of political life be deepened were we to think of politics in relation to *both* mortality and natality without letting either become the essential core or figure of political life?

Alexander Keller Hirsch: In *Public Things* you turn to Lars von Trier's *Melancholia*. The film features Justine, who constructs a "magic cave," a "doorway to brightness," in response to the world-ending planetary catastrophe promised by the ominous collision of Earth with a rogue planet. You suggest that Justine's magic cave is not like the dark cave of melancholia—by definition anti-mediating, a stickiness to the past that is precisely a recursive loop of painful attachment. Rather, the cave promises a future, in the sense that it generates what D. W. Winnicott describes as a "holding environment," a shared space in which to endure the "most unthinkable of all abandonments." You contrast this holding environment with what Jonathan Lear describes as the "radical hope" of Plenty Coups, a leader of the Crow who responded to the impending ruination of his people, faced as a result of the "passing of the buffalo," by espousing a hope that anticipated a good for which those who had the hope as yet lacked the appropriate concepts with which to understand it. In part, your argument stresses the idea that where the magic cave carves out a trans-formative space for meaning-making in collaboration with others, radical hope focuses the individual in an imaginative exercise that ultimately throws them back on themselves, thus denying a political birthright that compounds the catastrophe such hope is meant to shore up. If rituals that clear the ground for new beginnings are key to understanding the produc-tive (if tensional) political relationship between mourning and resilience, what form ought these rituals to take, and why? As you so clearly demon-strate above, forbidden mourning may obfuscate what is demanded by way of ritualization, but what about unforbidden mourning? We take it that all forms of unforbidden mourning may not be alike.

BH: When mourning is forbidden, as it is by Creon in Sophocles' *Anti-gone*, and by Claire and her husband, in von Trier's film, it acquires a kind of clarity and simplicity. Under a ban, the emphasis is on the need to mourn, and not on its precise choreography or purpose. So moving to unforbidden mourning, as you suggest we do here, helps to open up some questions: what are we doing, or hoping to do, when we mourn? How are mourning practices part of a politics? How might they provide a tether to an imagined collective past and a bridge to an imagined future? Different practices will bring different realities into being. I am not in a position to provide a taxonomy of the practices on offer. Such a project would be quite interesting! What I have done is to suggest that where others see mourning as a kind of raw or naturalized pain, we may see performance and conspiracy, as in Antigone's dirge for herself, carefully crafted to defeat Creon's world, and not just his ban. Where others see universal commonality in the face of death, we may (also) see the divisions of political conflict. And where others see mourning as a fidelity to the dead, or connection to loss, we should also see it as a fidelity to a future.

Your question presses me to say something I may have stopped short of in my reading of Lear in *Public Things*. Much of the loss he records, the catastrophe he traces, is a result of colonialism's pervasive and forced practices of individuation and privatization, which destroy indigenous ways of life and rituals that are collective. If the focus in response is on one person's heroic capacity to exercise radical hope in the face of all this, then we surely mime that which we want to combat. My reading of the materials Lear has so importantly put before us emphasizes not the power of Plenty Coups to hope (though there is no denying that) but his wisdom in trying to refurnish the world of his people with shared objects and public things so that they have something to hold on to and to be held by—shared points of orientation. The risk of emphasizing the radical hope of an exceptional individual is that it participates in the very individualization that indigenous peoples want to oppose.

We can also see this dynamic in a story Lear later tells, in an essay that he wrote after his *Radical Hope* book came out. The essay is focused on the story of another exceptional individual, a soldier and a member of the Crow tribe, who fought for the U.S. army in World War II and returns home shaken, ripe for PTSD. The tribal elders welcome him back. Sensing his trouble, they offer him a holding environment: they call him a warrior and ask him to share his stories in the old way and they knit his wartime experiences into the tribe's. They hold him together as they hold the tribe together. The elders' collective act does not necessarily mourn those he killed but they do mourn what he did. Their collection of his actions and his suffering into a tribal story is healing because it takes what is ruptural and offers repair. Not all such efforts are equally admirable, of course. There are stories of white disempowerment and loss that offer succor to those who feel uncertain of their place in changing social formations. The mourning work done in such contexts, by those who worry about "white genocide," is anticipatory, and it is not a work of democratic repair. One way to think about the politics of mourning is to look at whether the mourning is part of a larger array of practices and rituals and whether or not it is aimed at bringing into being a world of greater equality.

DWM: In other words, mourning is not merely about mortality but also about survival—in terms of the *sur-vivance,* or "more life" as you described in your work *Emergency Politics*? I was struck by your reading of Bernard Williams in that book, and specifically the idea that acting for the best in tragic situations "includes remaining around for the cleanup." Many of the chapters above talk about mourning in precisely these terms—attending to the (contested) aftermath of action, loss, or catastrophe. In this respect we might see mourning as being animated not just by a sense of loss but also a commitment to that which might endure or survive loss, such as democratic norms or ideals.

A: Yes, I think that is right. Mourning is about loss and so it involves withdrawal from the world. But it is also a ritual of re-entry; it charts a path from worldlessness (the isolating effects of loss) to world (among others, both living and dead). It is in Winnicott's sense that mourning rituals are *holding environments*. And, indeed, most of them involve a community holding together a person who is said to be coming apart (at the seams), torn apart by loss. Mourning is often about being held, held by others, held by ritual, until one gets through the rupture. The rituals support those who, in their loss, need to hold themselves together: "get yourself together," we say, acknowledging the dispersion of self that may be an effect of loss or trauma. The person who suffers and mourns may say: "I need to collect myself in order to give this eulogy." The idea of the self as needing *collecting* is a very Winnicottian idea, as I argued in an early reading of the *Bacchae* alongside *Melancholia* (that essay "Out Like a Lion" appears in the von Trier volume I co-edited with Lori Marso). The *Bacchae* is the Greek tragedy in which the sovereign, Pentheus, is dismembered and then re-collected, put back together, by his mother in mourning. (This is a reading I am now revisiting for a new book on refusal.) I suggested there that Pentheus, like Leo, the boy in von Trier's film, suffered from inauthenticity or conformism—Pentheus is a *young* king!—and thus the dismemberment might be seen in psychological terms, as wished-for. In Winnicott, the desire of the adolescent is to be dis-membered, in order to be able to reassemble him/herself in a truer way.

It is notable that ancient mourning rituals of many kinds enact the rift of death by literally, as it were, scoring or tearing their skin; the Hebrew bible specifically forbids this and proposes a symbolized substitute— tearing one's garment—rending it, to show that one's reality is rent. You mention the idea of survivance. Sur-vivance in a Greek context also might refer to the idea of an over-life or overliving, in which one lives past the time when one ought to have died. We now call this living on borrowed time. Perhaps it is time that is rented not owned, as they say in the Broadway musical *Rent*.

AKH: On the subject of forbidden mourning, there is also often a corre-sponding yet perhaps subtle emphasis that certain forms of life are them-selves illegible or illegitimate. As Judith Butler has often pointed out, it is not just denied grief but the denial of certain forms of life that determines "grievability."

BH: Yes, for Butler grievability indexes the value of a life, the value it is acknowledged to have. This is part of what I call mortalist humanism, however. I would say that grievability is *one* indicator, an absolutely important one, and Butler has given us tremendous, inspiring writing to think with on this topic. But if grievability is the only or privileged indicator of membership in the human, then we are privileging grief, even if inadvertently, as the essential common experience that defines or makes us human. As I said earlier, there are others, too, we might consider, including natality, spontaneity, and so on. These are also under assault, targeted now in the United States, especially in workers, people of color, and marginalized groups whose movements are more policed and more tracked than others', and whose spontaneity and creativity, arouse suspicion rather than admiration, and are cast as irritations to an otherwise (supposedly) smooth functioning system rather than as sources of an admirable individuality.

I think here of another of my sources in the Refusal project, Charlie Chaplin, who in the great film *Modern Times* starts out a willing enough worker but his body twitches on the assembly line and he—inadvertently, at first—"routs the line" (as Creon says of Antigone). What begins as inadvertence becomes willful, though, as Chaplin's character learns, as it were, from his body, and its obstinacy, to *refuse* and not just to twitch in response to the demands of the assembly line, whose repetitions and choreographic demands drive him a bit mad and so he is hospitalized. Notably, he moves from the factory's assembly line to a protesters' assembly when he, later in the film, stumbles into a march of communists. The two assemblies—the factory line and the protest march—position him as unindividuated worker and as flag-bearing leader, respectively. The consequences in both cases are isolation from the public world inside a disciplinary institution: first a hospital and then a prison. In both, notably, Chaplin's little man receives more "care" than on the outside. This is a comment on the outside, more than it is a comment on any utopian quality of the institutions in question.

AKH: I wonder if thinking about groups who engage in anticipatory mourning in order to shore up a perceived loss can be applied to the present moment in gender and sexual politics in the United States. Similar anti-democratic modes of repair seem to be emerging in reaction to the #metoo movement. Roy Moore supporters, for instance, may be engaged in anticipatory mourning for a world they fear will come into existence— one where women are believed when they voice sexual assault allegations. If we are at the precipice, as some now claim, of flipping into such a world, can *Stranger Things* teach us something about it, given its profound meditation on the upside down, as is indicated by your *Contemporary Condition* essay on the subject, "Trump's Upside Down"?

BH: Anticipatory mourning is problematic since often the thing being "mourned" is quite powerful. Whiteness in this country is quite powerful. The claim that its power structures are endangered is part of its power. Its narrative of victimization at the hands of the Other, the foreign, the independent female, people of color, is what mobilizes many whites, in fear, in defensiveness, to support candidates like Moore in Alabama, though of course many others, *more* others, did not do so; not this time, not in December 2017. As for the #metoo movement, it is still too early and too complicated to know what to say about it. It has certainly allowed women to go public with their experiences of loss and violence. Men who were allowed for years—enabled, even!—to target, groom, and betray women in their businesses, to crush their creative ambitions, demean and destroy some, wounding others, have been rightly exposed, though of course the president remains for the moment unscathed by it all.

In my post about *Stranger Things,* Season 1, I noted the series' nostalgic quality and how that nostalgia for the 1980s had a worm in it, a kind of anti-government Reaganism that was indulged, transferred quietly to the series' audience, but never thematized: specifically, I noted the series' antagonism toward federal agencies as technocratic, intrusive, and alien, while the local sheriff, flawed but heroic, is depicted as a man with an excellent moral compass informed by local sensitivities. The humanism of the show, that is to say, is shot through with a political anti-federalism that has operated since the 1950s as a defense *against* integration, equality, and justice for minorities and indigenous peoples. In this sense, the local sheriff of *Stranger Things* both is and is not Bull Connor. So far this 1980s worm of Reagansim has gone mostly unremarked. Like the worm inside the little boy who returns from the Upside Down, it will out though.

DWM: I want to come back to Antigone to ask about the relationship between rupture and repair. Antigone's conspiracy against Creon is an attempt, you argue, not simply to bury her brother's body but to interrupt the political order in ways that anticipate something radically different. Antigone's dirge is not just mortalist but natalist—angry, provocative, and creative. Yet an emphasis on rupture seems to paint a picture of *irreparability.* Once a relationship—say between Creon and Antigone—is deemed irreparable, then political action seems to require conspiracy. Instead of trying to repair or build working relationships with our antagonists, we act or speak around them. Certainly this seems to describe the dominant modes of political communication in our polarized democracy. Do you see this as unproblematic, inevitable, worrisome, or something else? And what does it say about the possibility for a resurgence of public things?

BH: Thanks, that is an interesting formulation, but with some associations or assumptions I also want to resist. I do not think that rupture means beyond repair. I think rupture is precisely what calls for repair. Whether or not something is irreparable is something we will find out as we engage in the effort of repair. Surely, what calls for repair is precisely the irreparable. Anything *else* can be fixed or mended. Thus, no relationship is irreparable, as such, at least not in the sense of being beyond repair. This does not mean, though, that repair is always the right practice for every breach. Although nothing is irreparable, not everything is *best* approached through practices of repair, either. Some people cannot be persuaded or softened no matter what and, sometimes, in democratic organizing, we need to work around them, isolate them, marginalize them, so that we can do what we can together to democratize our arrangements further. Our opponents can join us later if they come around. Politics is not essentially about division—I am no Schmittian—but, when it *is* about division, it is no good using persuasion with those who want to kill or exile you. And talk of repair is surely then misplaced. Antigone saw that Creon was beyond the reach of persuasion. Haemon saw it too but it took him longer to process the point. Patriarchy may well be the reason both for the quickness of Antigone's apprehension and for Haemon's slowness to reach the same conclusion. Different people are differently blinded—or not—by their structuring assumptions, symbols, structures.

That we are often divided is not a problem for public things. It is their occasion. After all, as I argue in the book, public things are precisely *not* things on whose importance or meaning everyone agrees. Rather, they are sites of material engagement that interpellate us into citizenship, sometimes in diverse ways. The bridge at Oka, that was closed and occupied by the Mohawks in Québec in the 1990s, works as a public thing precisely—and paradoxically—*because* it means different things to different people. As I argue in *Public Things*, the bridge represents a distinguished history of Mohawk labor and craftsmanship, a source of pride to the tribe's members now. That same bridge stands—in French Québec—as testimony to the ingenuity of Francophone engineering at a time when Québec elites were Anglo and their prejudices against French speaking Québecois were deep-rooted, and structurally secured.

If we are committed to democratic life and self-governance, then we must also build and cherish and maintain public things because these materialize and inspire democratic pathways and organization. We cannot always gain agreement first and then build a monument to our unity. On the contrary, many public things are now visible reminders of fault lines or fractures by which we are divided. But we may also think of how we are united by these divisions, as Nicole Loraux said of the Ancient Athenians. Division can also be a bond. When we think of mourning we think of loss and fragmentation. But division unites us in loss; and the work of repair, borrowed from mourning politics and rituals, may model ways for people to do the work of moving forward together, as natal and not just mortal creatures.

Index

About the Authors

David W. McIvor is Assistant Professor of Political Science at Colorado State University. Dr. McIvor received his BA in Political Science at Western Washington University and his MA and Ph.D. in Political Science from Duke University. His work has appeared recently in *Political Theory, Constellations, Contemporary Political Theory*, and *The James Baldwin Review*. His first book—*Mourning in America: Race and the Politics of Loss*—was published by Cornell University Press in 2016.

Alexander Keller Hirsch is Associate Professor of Political Science at the University of Alaska Fairbanks. Dr. Hirsch received his BA in Social Thought and Political Economy at the University of Massachusetts, Amherst, and his MA and Ph.D. in Politics with a parenthetical emphasis in History of Consciousness. He is the editor of *Theorizing Post-Conflict Reconciliation* (Routledge 2011, now translated into Indonesian), and his work has appeared in *New Political Science, Postmodern Culture, Theory and Event, Contemporary Political Theory*, and *Law, Culture and the Humanities*.

C. Fred Alford is Professor of Government Emeritus at the University of Maryland, College Park. He is author of over fifteen books on moral psychology, including *Trauma and Forgiveness: Consequences and Communities* (2013), and *Trauma, Culture, and PTSD* (2016). He co-edits the Psychoanalysis and Society Book Series with Cornell University Press, and served as Executive Director of the Association for Psychoanalysis, Culture and Society for over ten years. He curates the blog www.traumatheory.com .

Steven Johnston is Neal A. Maxwell Presidential Chair in Political Theory, Public Policy, and Public Service in the Department of Political Science at the University of Utah. He is the author of *Wonder and Cruelty: On 'It's a Wonderful Life' in Cinema and Experience* (Lexington Books, Politics, Literature and Film series, 2019), *Lincoln: The Ambiguous Icon*(Rowman and Littlefield, Modernity and Political Thought series, 2018), *American Dionysia: Violence, Tragedy, and Democratic Politics*, Cambridge, 2015), *The Truth about Patriotism* (Duke, 2007), and *Encountering Tragedy: Rousseau and the Project of Democratic Order* (Cornell, 1999). He has published articles in Theory and Event, Political Theory, Political Research Quarterly, Polity, Contemporary Political Theory, and Strategies. He has been a longtime contributor to The Contemporary Condition.

Heather Pool teaches political theory at Denison University. Her scholarship focuses on racial formation and violence in the United States, as well as occasional work on feminism and pedagogy. She is in the process of completing her first book: *Political Mourning* (forthcoming, Temple University Press).

Claudia Leeb is an Assistant Professor in political theory at Washington State University. She is the author of *The Politics of Repressed Guilt* (Edinburgh University Press, 2018), *Power and Feminist Agency in Capitalism* (Oxford University Press, 2017), *Working-Class Women in Elite Academia* (Peter Lang Publisher, 2004), and *Die Zerstörung des Mythos von der friedfertigen Frau* (Peter Lang Publisher, 1998). She has articles published in Political Theory, Contemporary Political Theory, Theory and Event, Perspectives on Politics, Constellations, Social Philosophy Today, The Good Society, Philosophy and Social Criticism, Open Cultural Studies, The Berlin Journal of Critical Theory, and Radical Philosophy Review. She has also contributed several book chapters to anthologies on early Frankfurt school critical theory.

Osman Balkan is a Visiting Assistant Professor of Political Science at Swarthmore College. His research and teaching interests include political identity, migration and citizenship, religion and politics, race and ethnicity, political ethnography, and necropolitics. His work has been published in journals such as *Studies in Ethnicity and Nationalism, Journal of Intercultural Studies*, and *Contemporary French Civilization* as well as in edited volumes, including *Muslims in the UK and Europe* and *Turkey's Necropolitics*.

Vicki Hsueh is Director of the Women, Gender, and Sexuality Studies program and an Professor in the Department of Political Science at Western Washington University. Her teaching and research interests include the history and historiography of political theory, protest movements and civic action, indigenous politics, and post-colonial theory. She is the author of Hybrid

Constitutions: Making and Unmaking Power and Privilege in Colonial America (Duke University Press, 2010) and articles in The Review of Politics, Contemporary Political Theory, Journal of the History of Ideas, and History of Political Thought.

Shirin S. Deylami is Associate Professor of Political Science and affiliated faculty in the Program for Women, Gender, and Sexuality Studies at Western Washington University. Her research interests are in the intersections of feminist theory, sexuality, popular culture and Islam. Her work has been published in a variety of journals including *Polity*, *International Feminist Journal of Politics*, and *Religions*. She is currently finishing a book on the concept of *westoxification* in contemporary Islamic political thought with specific attention to the ways in which Islamism is vitalized by rejections of Western conceptions of gender and sexuality. Her new project is on the uses of anger for a democratic politics that centers the marginalized.

David Myer Temin is an Assistant Professor of Political Science at the University of Michigan. His research in political theory focuses on the politics of settler colonialism in North America (19th–20th c.), Native American and Indigenous political thought, and the politics of race and empire. He is currently finishing a book manuscript entitled *Remapping Sovereignty: Indigenous Political Thought and the Politics of Decolonization*, which traces how key Indigenous theorists such as Vine Deloria Jr. reshaped ideas about sovereignty, land, and citizenship in North America. David's work has been published in *Political Theory* and *Political Research Quarterly.*"

Simon Stow is a Professor of Government and American Studies at the College of William and Mary. His most recent book is *American Mourning. Tragedy, Democracy, Resilience* (Cambridge, 2017).

Joel Alden Schlosser teaches political theory at Bryn Mawr College, and previously held the Julian Steward Chair in the Social Sciences at Deep Springs College. He has published numerous articles on ancient political theory as well as politics and literature. His first book, *What Would Socrates Do?* was published by Cambridge University Press in 2014. He is currently finishing a book on politics and ecology, *Herodotus in the Anthropocene*.

Bonnie Honig is Nancy Duke Lewis Professor in the depts. of Modern Culture and Media (MCM) and Political Science at Brown University. She is author of *Political Theory and the Displacement of Politics* (Cornell, 1993), *Democracy and the Foreigner* (Princeton, 2001), *Emergency Politics: Paradox, Law, Democracy* (Princeton, 2009), *Antigone, Interrupted* (Cambridge University Press, 2013), and *Public Things: Democracy in Disrepair*,

(Fordham University Press, 2017). She has edited or co-edited: *Feminist Interpretations of Hannah Arendt* (Penn State, 1995), *Skepticism, Individuality and Freedom: The Reluctant Liberalism of Richard Flathman* (Minnesota, 2002), the *Oxford Handbook of Political Thought* (Oxford, 2006), and, most recently, *Politics, Theory, and Film: Critical Encounters with Lars von Trier* (Oxford, 2016). She is currently at work on a new project called *Theaters of Refusal*, to be delivered as the Flexner lectures at Bryn Mawr College in the fall of 2017 and to be published by Harvard University Press. In 2018, she is serving as the Inaugural Cranor Phi Beta Kappa Scholar.

www.ingramcontent.com/pod-product-compliance
Lightning Source LLC
Chambersburg PA
CBHW022307280326
41932CB00010B/1015